FAMILY FILE

Edited by Linda Sonntag

Contributors: Peter Brooke-Ball, Deborah Evans,
Philippa Farrant, Clive Gregory, Mike Lawrence, Roz Morris,
Linda Sonntag, Brian Ward

WHSMITH

EXCLUSIVE
· BOOKS ·

General editor   Linda Sonntag
Editor   Kate Phelps

Contributors
Peter Brooke-Ball *(Inside the Home)*
Deborah Evans (*Setting Up Home*)
Philippa Farrant *(Education)*
Clive Gregory *(Family Finances, You & Your Car,* part of *Later Life,* part of *Getting Married)*
Mike Lawrence (*Home Improvements*)
Roz Morris (*You & Your Job*)
Linda Sonntag (*Getting Married, Family Problems*)
Brian Ward (*Starting a Family, Family Health, Later Life*)

Designed, illustrated and typeset by Talkback International Limited

First published in 1992 by Grisewood & Dempsey Ltd,
Elsley House
24-30 Great Titchfield Street
London W1P 7AD

10 9 8 7 6 5 4 3 2 1

© Grisewood & Dempsey Ltd 1992

Printed in Spain

ISBN 1 85696 012 9

While every effort has been made to ensure that the information contained in *Family File* is clear and accurate, some simplification of the subjects covered has been necessary due to the introductory nature of the book. The Publishers can accept no liability for the accuracy and completeness of any of the material contained in *Family File* and recommend that the reader seeks legal advice wherever possible.

FAMILY
FILE

CONTENTS

INTRODUCTION

Running a household and bringing up a family are great responsibilities. There will be times when you need to be doctor, teacher, psychologist, economist, mechanic, builder, plumber and electrician, as well as bringing in enough money to pay the bills. Of course, you can't be expert in all these fields, and this is where *Family File* can help.

On the practical side, *Family File* explains the basics about two of the biggest investments you'll ever make: your home and your car. It will help you maintain your car in good running order, keeping service bills low. The three chapters on the home cover everything from buying and selling, through home improvements and interior design to understanding the structure and services and maintaining the fabric of your property.

Family File will give you the background knowledge you need to make vital decisions, so that you know when to tackle a job yourself and when to call in the experts. And it will provide you with enough backup to be able to ask the experts the right questions, and to understand their answers. This way you can remain in control over what's done on your behalf, which means that jobs will be well done and not overpriced.

On the financial side, there's a chapter all about family finance that covers such topics as budgeting, saving, tax, making a will, how to control debt and claiming benefit. There's advice on pensions in the chapter on careers, plus tips for succeeding at an interview and useful information on your rights at work.

If you are just starting out on life together, you will be particularly interested in the chapters on getting married and starting a family, two times in your life when it really pays to plan ahead. Many couples today prefer not to marry – you should know the legal implications of living together married or single, especially if you intend to have children.

One of the main concerns in any family is health. The chapter on family health deals with common ailments and frequently prescribed drugs (useful at a time when people tend to consult their pharmacist as often as they do their doctor), as well as first aid and coping with emergencies. It tells you what sort of treatment you should expect from your GP and hospital and gives sound advice on preventative medicine, in the form of a healthy diet and exercise.

Many parents feel left behind when it comes to their children's education because the choice of subjects has widened so much since they themselves were at school, and teaching methods have changed with the advance of technology. The chapter on education helps you choose the best school to suit your child's needs and get the best out of the school for your child.

No family is without its problems, and the chapter of family relations aims to give courage and confidence to see through the difficult times. Finally there's a chapter on how to make the most out of your retirement, with advice for the rest of the family on caring for the elderly.

GETTING MARRIED

Today in the '90s, marriage is still as popular as ever, and this despite the rising divorce rate and the increasing number of single-parent families. The fact that men and women are still prepared to swear to be faithful to each other for half a century or more until parted by death expresses a faith in the permanence of love and a desire for perfection which are an intrinsic part of our make-up as human beings. The truth is that most people are still idealists, especially when they are in love. However, many couples choose to commit themselves without the public ceremonial of marriage and simply move in together. Living together is much more acceptable in the eyes of the world today than it was 20 years ago. The sexual revolution that started with the advent of the Pill in the '60s has brought men and women nearer to equality and meant that we can express our sexuality with more openness and ease.

Whether living together or married, equality of rights also means equality of responsiblity and initiative, and no longer are male and female roles in a relationship strictly defined. Instead of fulfilling set roles, we are free to fulfil ourselves as people.

There is no longer any social or economic need to have a large family, and with men sharing child care and increased awareness of the need for creches at work, women can enjoy a new freedom to pursue their own training and careers. Inside the relationship, surveys show that expectations have changed a great deal since the '50s. Forty years ago what people most wanted from their partners was moral respectability and financial security, whereas today the most important criterion is active enjoyment of each other's company. Marriage, whether formalized or not, is a partnership on which all aspects of a couple's life are centred, and from which all its activities flow. For some couples, the decision to marry or not may be based on financial or legal considerations.

The legal and financial aspects of married life and cohabitation

While in many social circles it now makes little difference to your status whether you are married to your partner, there are financial and legal implications tied in to the decision to marry or live together without the blessing of the Church and recognition by the State. Ignoring these implications may well make little apparent difference to your lives together for a number of years. If you are not particularly aware of what your tax allowances are for example, you will neither know nor possibly care that you could be better off married. There comes a time in most people's lives however, when the full impact of the manner in which they live with each other hits home. And in many cases, it would have made their lives simpler had they realized what lay ahead some time before.

Legal responsibilities of marriage

Whether you marry in church or in a civil ceremony at a register office, the law views your life together in a new light as soon as you have taken the vows. There are three broad areas of legal responsibility acquired by the newlywed couple:
• to look after one another
• to live with each other
• to consent to sex. This has come under increasing question in recent years.

Stable relationships, married and unmarried, take on board all three

of the above as a matter of course. As with many legal matters it is when things go wrong that the law's divisions come into play. People in an unmarried relationship can part, find a new partner and marry entirely at their will. Where a marriage collapses, the legal side of the relationship has to be untangled before there is freedom to remarry. This need not be difficult but can be so if one party objects.

One of the most contentious areas of the law has been the traditional and upheld legal view that a husband could not rape his wife in circumstances where in all other respects the marriage was a normal one. This view has come under increased pressure and it has now been held that where the wife does not consent to sex, the husband can be found guilty of rape.

Contrary to many people's expectations, there is no need for a new wife to adopt her husband's surname – it is purely to follow custom that people do this. As far as the law is concerned, people can call themselves what they like as long as there is no fraudulent purpose involved.

Where the law will step in with a married couple however is in court itself. Because of the nature of a marital relationship it is expected that couples will confide in each other to a degree far beyond any other relationship. So, if the husband commits or is accused of committing a crime, the prosecution cannot call his wife to give evidence against him. The same immunity from giving evidence applies to the husband if it is the wife being prosecuted. The sharing of confidences obviously takes place in non-marital relationships but the immunity does not apply.

Who owns what?

Where property is concerned, it always pays to be quite clear as to who owns what. It is particularly important to secure your rights to property if you are unmarried and going to lose independence in the relationship – by staying at home to look after any children for example.

When a married couple split up, the law may share the value of the home between husband and wife and grant the wife maintenance even where there are no children involved. Even if the home is solely in the husband's name, the above still applies.

While an unmarried couple may be just as much of an institution with as many assets, the law works on the basis that they are two individuals and any property should go to the true owner. Unmarried couples each wishing to protect their interests should always ensure that both parties' names are on the title deeds to their home for example. Only in exceptional circumstances would a court decide that although one party's name was on the deeds, the other could claim part ownership.

The most obvious examples of this would be where the partner not named on the deeds did in fact earn the money used to pay the mortgage or had put up a large part of the purchase price. It is also

possible to stake a claim to part of the property by virtue of having made a substantial contribution to it. Doing most of the housework or even all of the decorating would not be sufficient to warrant a claim. Rebuilding a shell with one's own hands could well be.

Even if it was decided that the partner not on the deeds did have a claim to a share in the value of the property, a long time would have elapsed, and probably a lot of money would have been spent, in proving it. The golden rule when buying a home therefore is to make sure your name is on the title deeds however optimistic your view of the years ahead.

Where there are children

The law has one major guiding principle when it comes to disputes over children and that is that the welfare of the children must come first. So whatever your relationship, if you split up your wishes will only be taken into account once the court is satisfied that the children's needs have been met. That said, there are differences in parental rights between married and non-married parents.

Where parents are not married, it is the mother only who has automatic legal rights over questions such as religion, schooling and medical welfare. The father will not even automatically be registered as the child's father when the birth is registered although it is not usually difficult to arrange this.

Should an unmarried couple split up, the father has no automatic rights of access or parental control over the children. These may, of course, be granted amicably but if not the father will have to get a court order. A court order may also be necessary for maintenance of any children if the parents cannot come to an agreement.

Maintenance is not payable for an unmarried partner however.

Sorting out your finances

In recent years many of the differences between the financial affairs of married and unmarried couples have disappeared. Fine distinctions do remain which in the main are of benefit to those who are married.

Income tax: unmarried couples are treated as two single people for tax purposes. Married couples are now taxed as two individuals too but in addition to their personal tax allowance of £3,445 each, they also have the benefit of the £1,720 married couple's allowance. The value of this is gradually being eroded as it has not been increased in two successive budgets.

Married couples may also gain some advantage where transfers of gifts or large amounts of money are concerned because of certain exemptions. Both Capital Gains Tax and Inheritance Tax may become payable if unmarried couples transfer assets to each other.

At the other end of the financial scale, when drawing social security benefits, the only relevant factor is whether you live independently or with someone else. Rates of benefit are lower for couples, married or not, than for people living on their own.

Responsibility for debts

In simple terms we are all responsible for our own debts and are not responsible for paying off other people's, whether we are married or not. In practice the situation can be rather different since a deserted partner may find themselves paying the telephone bill even if their name is not on it, simply to avoid the unpleasantness of being disconnected. You should also note that if a partner runs up a debt on a joint account, of a credit card for example, you will be liable to pay it if they do not.

If one partner dies

We all hope that death is many years away but it can strike when least expected. Some of the differences between being married and unmarried at such a time are:
• Unmarried partners do not have an automatic right to the estate of the deceased. Relatives of the deceased will have prior claims. This can prove very awkward if the deceased was still married but living in a new relationship.
• Unmarried partners do not receive a widow's pension or widowed mother's allowance.
• A deceased husband's national insurance contributions can be taken into account when assessing a woman's entitlement to state retirement pension if she has not paid enough contributions herself. This does not apply if unmarried.
• Unmarried partners may not have a right to their deceased partner's pension payments.

Protecting your interests

Married or unmarried, there are several ways of making sure your intentions are carried through either if there is a dispute with your partner or if one of you dies.

Writing an agreement: setting out who owns what on paper is a good way of getting your thoughts in order and avoiding arguments if there are any disputes in the future. Each of you must take part in the process and it is well worth while your both signing the document and having a copy each. You will need to review this document from time to time to establish the ownership of gifts received since the original agreement. Getting the advice of a solicitor when drawing up this agreement will ensure that the courts view it favourably should the need arise.

Also see a solicitor if your name is not on the title deeds of your home, and you feel you are entitled to a share in it. Have the solicitor draw up a deed of trust. This details the share in the property of each partner.

Writing a will: if you die without having written a will your estate will be divided according to the intestacy rules. These probably do not match your own wishes and can cause much heartache, particularly for the surviving partner of an unmarried relationship. You can write your own will or engage a solicitor to do it for you.

Some couples choose to announce their engagement in a newspaper.

Getting engaged

An engagement is not a legal requirement, but once you have made the decision to marry, you may decide to get engaged as a convenient way of letting the world know your plans. It is worth remembering that a formal wedding cannot be arranged in less than six weeks, so probably the minimum practical length of time for an engagement should be three months.

The first people to be told should be your parents. This courtesy is especially due to the parents of the

---

Mr J. M. Lemon and Miss F. A. Godfrey

The engagement is

announced between

Jeremy Lemon, eldest son of

Mr and Mrs Alfred Lemon

of Bexleyheath, Kent, and

Fanny Anne, younger

daughter of Mr and

Mrs Harry Godfrey of

Styvechale, Coventry.

bride-to-be, as they may be involved in a great deal of work and expense at the wedding. When other relations and close friends have been told, you may decide in addition to place a simple newspaper announcement.

Giving an engagement ring is a custom that dates from Victorian times. A diamond is the usual choice of stone because it is so hardwearing, but another option is to choose the bride's birthstone.

Calling it off

It always takes courage to admit to a mistake, but if the mistake is an engagement that has been publically celebrated, it takes more courage than usual. Nevertheless, a broken engagement is much less painful than a broken marriage. Friends and relatives can be told quietly and without any fuss – no explanation is due and none should be asked for, though a confidante may help you over a difficult time. Presents of any value, including the ring, should be returned.

Marriage, a legal contract

As marriage is a contract recognized under law, certain conditions must be fulfilled by those entering into it, and this involves more paperwork and organization than you might think. Firstly, you must be over 16 before you can marry, and until the age of 18 you need your parents' consent. You will need two witnesses to the ceremony. The hours between which weddings may take place are 8.00am and 6.00pm, unless you have a Jewish or Quaker wedding.

Church of England

An Anglican wedding usually takes place in the parish church of either bride or groom, and one or both of the parties should have been baptized. However, some clergymen stick less rigidly to the rules than others. If you want to marry in a different parish, you may be required to take up 'residence' there for 15 days, perhaps staying with a friend, though you can get round this requirement if you marry by special licence rather than by banns (see below).

The most common and cheapest way of getting married within the Church of England is by calling the banns. On three consecutive Sundays, the parish priest asks the congregation if anyone knows why the two parties should not be joined together in marriage.

To get the banns read, you need to furnish the priest with written details and pay a small fee. If no one objects, you have three months in which to marry after the final banns have been called, but the banns must be called again if you do not marry within this time.

If you do not wish the banns to be called for whatever reason – perhaps you want to get married quickly, or without alerting the whole community – you can apply for a common licence. Your vicar will tell you where to get it. You will need to provide names and addresses and proof of baptism (if possible) and of marital status (i.e. certificate of divorce or death certificate of spouse if you were married before). There will be a fee. It usually takes less than a week to get a common licence.

A special licence, which is more expensive, will allow you to be married at any time and in any place, such as a different parish church, or in hospital or prison. You should ask your vicar about the procedure for getting a special licence, but be ready for a delay of up to three weeks, as it has to be authorized by the Archbishop of Canterbury. If one of the parties is ill, it may be possible to speed things up.

Civil permission to marry

Strange though it may seem, all marriages not conducted by an Anglican minister (above), need civil permission, whether they take place in a register office or in another religious establishment. If you are marrying in another religious establishment you will need to take the document(s) to the priest so that the marriage can take place.

Confusingly, there are two types of document granting civil permission to marry. Each of you needs a document unless you both live in the same locality. The more expensive document allows you to marry almost immediately.

The cheaper document is called a certificate without licence. To obtain this, you should each go to your local registrar not less than three weeks before you wish to marry, taking with you proof of name (birth certificate if possible), address within the area (you must

have lived there for seven days), marital status (if married before), the place where you wish to marry, and the fee. If you both live in the same place, only one of you need give notice and sign the form declaring that there is no reason why you should not marry. The registrar will issue a certificate 21 days later and you may marry within three months of that date.

For people in a hurry, there is a certificate with licence, which costs more than twice as much as the certificate without licence. You must both be in England or Wales, but only one of you need give notice (see above). One of you must have lived in the district for 15 days, and the wedding must take place in that district. The registrar will issue the certificate within one clear day of application (Sunday, Christmas Day and Good Friday do not count as clear days), and you may marry within three months of that date.

Other denominations

If you belong to a religious denomination other than the Church of England, you will need civil permission to marry (see above). You should also check that your chosen minister is an 'authorized person' and that the building has been registered for the purpose of conducting the marriage ceremony. If the clergyman you have chosen is not an 'authorized person', a registrar must be present to record the marriage. One way of getting round this often adopted by Sikhs and Hindus is to arrange for a civil ceremony to take place on the day before, or in the morning of, the religious ceremony.

If you are Roman Catholic and want to marry a non-Catholic, you must get special dispensation from your priest, and you will need special dispensation from a bishop if you wish to marry in a non-Catholic church. For marriage in a Catholic church, you may need to give the priest as much as six months' advance notice, and both of you may be expected to attend a course of instruction on marriage and its responsibilities. You will be required to promise to bring up any children of the marriage in the Roman Catholic faith.

The religious ceremony for Jewish couples usually takes place in a synagogue, but it may also be held in a private house, or even out-of-doors. Both parties must be Jews whose parents were married according to Jewish rites. If one party is non-Jewish, then he or she must have been proselytized into the Jewish faith.

The religious ceremony for Quakers may take place in the Quaker meeting house.

A simpler marriage

English people who wanted to elope and avoid the red tape that surrounds marriage south of the border used to flee to Gretna Green, just a few miles into Scotland. There they made a declaration in front of two witnesses over the anvil in the famous blacksmith's forge and immediately became man and wife. Since 1977 the marriage laws in Scotland have been tightened, but tying the knot there is still a simpler process.

You should notify the registrar of the place in which you wish to marry 14 days in advance. You do not need to live there, or even in Scotland. The marriage can take place either at the office where you applied, or in a church in the vicinity, in which case you should collect the certificate just before the wedding, and return it, signed and witnessed, within three days after your marriage.

Even simpler, and perfectly legal, is to get married in Las Vegas. All you need is a licence from the County Clerk and a ten-minute ceremony in a wedding chapel. Note: if you plan to marry in another country, or one of you is a foreign national, you should check carefully with the relevant consulate to make sure that the marriage will be legal in both countries and that you have all the necessary documentation before the ceremony.

Second marriages

There is no limit to the number of times you may marry as long as you are free to do so. But there may be problems with second and subsequent marriages if you want a church wedding. You may only be remarried in the Roman Catholic faith if a previous marriage has been annulled, which can be a lengthy and complicated business. In the Church of England some ministers will perform the ceremony with the permission of their bishop, but generally not unless the former partner has died. If the full ceremony is refused, the minister may bless the marriage after the civil ceremony.

Planning for your wedding

Your wedding will surely be the most spectacular celebration of your life. The organization of such a big, expensive and emotional day is no mean task. Whatever the type of wedding and the degree of formality you choose, it will need to be planned like a grand stage performance or a military campaign. The bride and her mother, by tradition the masterminds behind the operation, should be prepared to delegate as much as possible.

Who picks up the bill?

This thorny question needs to be settled right at the beginning. Until fairly recently in this country, the bride's father paid all the wedding expenses, but with the increasing equality of the sexes, this custom, a direct descendant of the dowry system, is disappearing. It is quite likely today that the bride and groom will want to pay for much of the wedding themselves.

Choosing your attendants

The idea of having attendants at a wedding – bridesmaids, a best man and ushers – originated with the belief that evil spirits, envious of the couple's happiness, would be out to harm them, but would be confused by the presence of so many similarly dressed people.

The bride will probably want to choose her closest friend as chief bridesmaid; she will be required to offer moral support, to help dress the bride, to hold the bouquet while the bride signs the register,

and to look after the younger attendants and the older guests at the reception. A bride can have any number of bridesmaids, though most have fewer than five, and usually at least one small child from either family is chosen to be a bridesmaid or page. A married friend who is chosen is called a matron of honour.

The ushers are upwards of three male friends of the groom, chosen for their friendliness and unflappability. As their name suggests, they usher people to their pews in the church, lay out the order of service sheets and hand out the hymn books.

The best man is a key figure at any wedding. The bride's mother is planner-in-chief, but on the wedding day itself the best man takes over as prime organizer. His first duty is to be 'minder' to the groom, to see that he gets to the right place at the right time, to hand the ring or rings to the minister on cue, to take charge of the groom's transport and the guests' parking, and to deliver a good speech at the reception. In addition, he may organize a stag night beforehand and play master of ceremonies and introduce the speakers at the reception if there is no toastmaster. All this requires a cool head and reliability.

Dressing for the wedding

Allow as much time as possible to organize your outfit, whether it's hired, bought or made, and remember that you may need several fitting sessions.

White wedding dresses have

been in the forefront of bridal fashion since Queen Victoria broke with the royal tradition of a silver dress and opted for white for her wedding to Prince Albert. But if the fairytale look is not for you, then you may choose an elegant outfit of any colour, perhaps a suit, or a stunning dress and jacket. If the wedding is in a Free Church, then simplicity will be your keynote. The important thing is that you look and feel your best.

Obviously your choice of headgear will complement your dress and to some extent dictate your hairstyle, but beware of torturing your hair into an elaborate and unnatural style on this of all days. Generally speaking, if you choose your headgear to suit your normal hairstyle and not the other way round, you won't go far wrong.

Make-up is another area potentially full of pitfalls for the bride. The less of it you can get away with, the better. Remember that you will be in the public eye for a good number of hours, and that you will probably get quite hot with excitement. Put on your make up with a light hand, and avoid greasy foundations and eyeshadows that will 'crease'.

The bridesmaids and pages usually wear clothes which they or their parents pay for, so unless their outfits are hired, it is sensible to choose dresses and suits that can be worn again. The chief requirement is, of course, that they look good when grouped around the bride.

The groom and best man, as well as the other chief male guests,

normally wear morning dress at a formal wedding, though for a more modest church or civil ceremony, dark suits are appropriate.

The mothers of the bride and groom will want to look their best, though they must take care not to try and upstage the bride. It is useful for the two mothers to compare notes so that their outfits are neither identical nor absurdly different in style or degree of formality.

The flowers

Flowers have always played a central role in weddings. Your choice of flowers may be elaborate, as is the modern trend, or simple. They should reflect the mood of the occasion, the style of your dress and, most important of all, your own personality. There is a special pleasure in using seasonal flowers, and it often costs less too. Always consult the vicar before planning to decorate the church. Yours may not be the only wedding on the chosen day, and you may be able to share the cost of church flowers with the other brides. There may also be regular volunteer flower arrangers who would help if you wished.

The bride's flowers need to be chosen with great care. You will want to feel comfortable holding them, and of course they will need to complement your dress. If possible, take a sample of your dress material and a sketch of the dress along to your florist when you make your choice. If it's a long dress with a sweeping train, you will need a fairly large bouquet to balance the effect; a short dress

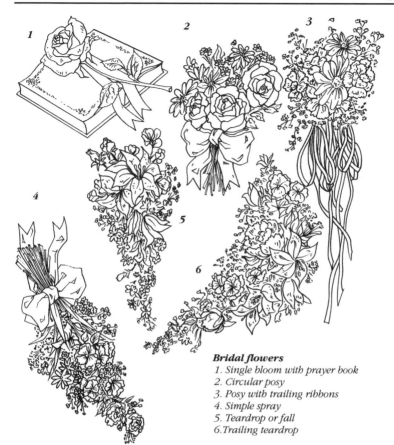

Bridal flowers
1. Single bloom with prayer book
2. Circular posy
3. Posy with trailing ribbons
4. Simple spray
5. Teardrop or fall
6. Trailing teardrop

will look better with a neat posy. A single flower attached to a prayer book is both simple, and a lot cheaper.

The photographs

Your wedding photographs will hopefully be something you will always look back on with pleasure, so it's important to choose a professional to take them, unless you know someone who is especially talented with a camera.

The photographer needs to be booked well in advance, particularly if you are getting married on a Saturday. Prices vary substantially, so it's worth shopping around. Some studios offer package deals, with a flat fee for the day and a separate charge for the number of prints ordered; others itemize each operation; others still may offer 'special effects': misty finishes, photographs printed on champagne glasses, etc. Check with the vicar whether he will allow photographs inside the church. Some will, as long as there's no flash; many forbid photography during the actual ceremony as it can be too distracting for the bride and groom.

Videos

Videos are increasingly popular wedding souvenirs. Visit several firms and see examples of their work before you make a decision. Pay particular attention to the quality of sound, the continuity, and the naturalness or otherwise of the wedding party: no one wants a cameraman who makes them feel self-conscious.

Some firms offer a make-up service for the bride in with the price. Consider whether you want this: you may feel less like an actress and more like yourself if you put on your own make-up as usual.

Consult the vicar to see if he will allow the service to be filmed. If he will, visit the church with the technician to finalize the position of lights, microphones and wires: they will need to be as unobtrusive as possible.

Music

Bells, organist and choir should be paid for by arrangement with the vicar. The organist will charge his own fee, but he and the choir will be entitled to professional rates if you intend to record the music, so check first. If there is no choir in residence, a local school may be able to provide one.

The music in a typical Anglican ceremony has five phases, and ideally should build up to a resounding climax. The first phase takes place as people are finding their seats, and the music needs to be robust enough to drown out settling-down noises. The next stage is the entrance of the bride: the moment everyone has been waiting for needs a stirring and exciting accompaniment.

Third come the hymns. You will have most success if you choose a couple of the best loved ones that most of the congregation will be able to sing without too much difficulty. Then there is more music while the register is signed. For the congregation this represents a lull in the proceedings.

Finally, and most rousing of all, is the recessional, the triumphant progress of bride and groom down the aisle.

Transport

If you want to hire a traditional wedding car, look in the Yellow Pages to find a list of firms. Some brides like the novelty of a vintage car or a pony and trap, which are likely to come even more expensive than a Bentley or Daimler. The alternative is to use the cars of family or friends.

You will need two or three bridal cars: one for the bride and her father, one for the bridesmaids, and possibly one for the bride's mother and a companion. The best man traditionally drives the groom to the church in his own car.

After the ceremony, the bride and groom are driven to the reception in the first car, followed by the bridesmaids. It is the best man's duty to secure enough parking for the guests, and sometimes this may involve consultation with the police. The bride and groom will also need transport to their honeymoon destination, or to station or airport. No one who is likely to drink too much should be allowed to drive.

The invitations

Ideally, your guests should receive their invitations at least six weeks before the wedding, to avoid disappointment.

Specially printed invitations will take roughly three weeks to order, or you can buy ready-printed ones and fill in the details yourself, which is of course cheaper. If you opt for customized invitations, the stationer will show you a selection, but generally the wording is illustrated below.

The name of the guest is handwritten in the top lefthand corner.

If it is a register office wedding, most of the invitations will be to the reception only. If it is a big wedding with a midday reception and a party in the evening, you may be inviting two entirely different sets of guests.

Wedding presents

Every guest invited to the wedding normally gives a present. Some of your close friends and family will have very definite ideas about what they want to give you, but the majority will just want to please, and the best way to help them, and avoid ending up with a houseful of

You are cordially invited to the wedding of

Chris Jones and Anne Blunt

Date: **7th February** Time: **2.30 pm**

Place: **All Saints Church Nr. Croxted Road Barnhurst**

And afterwards to the reception at **the Church Hall**

R.S.V.P.

electric irons and no toaster, is to make a present list and keep it at a large department store in your locality.

Specify the make and pattern of items that you would like. Then large expensive items, such as dinner sets, can be broken down into several individual gifts. Guests who ask to see the list can go and choose a present at the shop, and the present can be duly ticked off the list. Or, even easier, they can consult the list and order by telephone, and pay by card.

It is also customary for the key people in the wedding party to exchange lasting mementoes. Bride and groom exchange gifts, the groom's parents give something to the bride, the bride's parents give something to the groom, and the groom also gives presents to his best man, possibly to the ushers, and always to the bridesmaids, usually jewellery.

Stag and hen parties

After the planning is over and before the action begins, some couples like to celebrate separately with friends of their own sex. The usual purpose of stag and hen parties, which are traditionally arranged by the best man and the chief bridesmaid, is to get the principals drunk, and for this reason it is never wise to hold them on the night before the wedding. In primitive terms, this evening represents a shaking out of the evil spirits that could yet get in the way of the couple's marriage: once both have survived it (which inevitably they do), it should be plain sailing to the wedding day.

Planning the reception

A large formal wedding will usually be followed by a lavish reception, but there is no reason why a small simple wedding should not also lead into a grand party: it is a matter of taste, and, of course, of expense.

At one end of the scale is the full wedding breakfast, which could take place in a hotel, on a river boat or in a marquee in the garden; then there is the buffet lunch, which could be held in a club or hall; and, cheapest and most intimate, canapés and champagne at home. The entertainment may also be in two stages, with a lunchtime spread for the family followed by an evening party for friends.

If money is no object, there are firms that will take care of every detail to do with the reception, including cake, flowers, music and champagne; they will also arrange booking of your venue, whether it be in a hotel, a museum or a stately home.

In the medium price range, the most important decision you will have to make is whether to do the catering yourselves or hire a company to do it for you.

It goes without saying that even catering for 30 people is a mammoth task that few would relish, particularly on top of all the other complex responsibilities of the wedding day. To employ a good caterer, even for a buffet at home, will surely be money well spent, and give the bride's family time to enjoy the occasion.

The seating plan

Wherever the reception is held, certain seating requirements will need to be fulfilled. Traditionally, tables are arranged so that as many people as possible can see the bride, groom and speakers without craning their necks. If you are having a stand-up buffet, seats should be provided for old or infirm relations; and you may also need to set aside an area for young children, with high chairs, and maybe a room where babies can be breast-fed and changed.

For a formal reception, the bridal party usually sits along one side only of the top table, where they can see and be seen. The table may be on a stage or dais if the room has one. The bride and groom sit in the centre, hopefully not obscured behind a towering cake, with the other key figures ranged to their left and right.

The trouble with having a 'top table', apart from the possible friction between divorced parties and irritation on the part of those who feel they should be sitting at it but aren't, is that it is cut off from the rest of the gathering. The solution can be to have a roomful of round tables, and this, combined with short speeches which occasion minimum neck-craning and interruption of conversation, can make for a much more successful party than the traditional arrangement.

As for the seating on the other tables, this should not prove problematical, as long as you put guests in groups of friends, and single people, and older relations who have not seen each other for a long time, and make a good mix of men and women. Remember that a wedding is not always a happy event for single people, who may feel that all the world is married but themselves, and if possible, try to seat them next to other single people they might like.

It is a good idea to pin a copy of the seating plan on a board inside the room where everyone can see it, but not at the doorway, where it will cause a bottleneck.

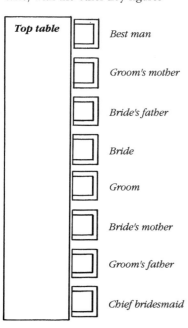

Top table

Best man

Groom's mother

Bride's father

Bride

Groom

Bride's mother

Groom's father

Chief bridesmaid

Food to serve at a wedding

The food should be both delicious and practical. If you choose a chicken salad, make sure your caterer does not understand by this a withered looking chicken leg and two brown-edged lettuce leaves. Canapés should be designed so that they do not fall to pieces en route to the guest's mouth. Inevitably, some guests will have travelled a long way to see you, so make sure if you're providing finger food that there's also something a little more substantial, such as a good selection of cheeses and crusty bread.

Remember to consider everyone's tastes. Some of your guests may be vegetarian or vegan, and others may be prevented from eating certain foods because of an allergy or religious beliefs.

The cake will be the focal point of your reception. Whether you choose a many-tiered iced cake or a frosted sponge, the tradition is for the bride and groom to cut it together, with his hand over hers, as the last part of the formal ceremony. If the icing is particularly hard, make the cut beforehand and disguise it under some decoration. After the first cut has been made, the cake is usually taken behind the scenes to be cut up into slices, which are then handed round to the guests. You may like to send absent friends a small piece of cake in a little box. (If so, remember to order the cake boxes along with all the other stationery.)

Single people are supposed to put a slice of cake under their pillow, to make them dream of the person they will marry.

Cutting the cake

Wedding cake is traditionally served in 2.5 cm/1 inch square pieces, or 5 x 1 cm/2 x 1/2 inch slices. The information in this table will help you calculate what size cake you need, based on the number of guests you have invited. Don't forget extra pieces to send to absent friends and relatives.

Size of cake	No. of slices (fruit cake)	No. of slices (sponge cake)
13cm/5 inch round	14	7
13cm/5 inch square	16	8
15cm/6 inch round	22	11
15cm/6 inch square	27	14
18cm/7 inch round	30	15
18cm/7 inch square	40	20
20cm/8 inch round	40	20
20cm/8 inch square	54	27
23cm/9 inch round	54	27
23cm/9 inch square	70	35
25cm/10 inch round	68	34
25cm/10 inch square	90	45
27.5cm/11 inch round	86	43
27.5cm/11 inch square	112	56
30cm/12 inch round	100	50
30cm/12 inch square	134	67

There is much less wastage if a cake is cut in slices as illustrated, rather than in wedges, and as you can see, a square cake is better value than a round one.

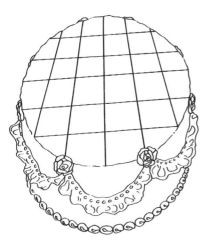

Drink to serve at a wedding

Choose the drink according to your taste and pocket. If you can't afford champagne, méthode champénoise wines make a good substitute at less than half the price. Make sure there are plenty of soft alternatives and mineral water for drivers, teetotallers and children.

If you are ordering in bulk from a wine merchant, you can do so on a sale or return basis. As a rough idea, allow about half a bottle of wine per head, slightly more if the guests are sitting down. If the caterers are pouring at a stand-up do, you can agree in advance on how quickly you want them to refill glasses. If you are having a buffet reception in a hall or a club, you could stand the first couple of rounds of drinks, and the bubbly for the toast, but have a well staffed cash bar where guests could also buy their own refills.

Countdown to the wedding day

Whatever type of wedding you choose, it could turn into an organizational nightmare unless each part of your plan dovetails with the next. So tick off the boxes as you complete each operation, or strike them out if they don't apply, and you will be able to see at a glance what remains to be done.

As early as possible

❏ Draw up a budget of the costs, deciding on the size and type of wedding, and the number of guests you would like to invite.

❏ Set the date, booking the church

and minister, or register office, and the venue for the reception.

❒ Choose your attendants – best man, bridesmaids etc. – and get their acceptance.

❒ Draw up the guest list.

❒ Book your wedding day transport.

❒ Book the photographer and video company (if you want one).

❒ Book your honeymoon.

❒ Order a passport, if necessary, and arrange to have your name changed on your passport if you want.

❒ Order your cake.

❒ Decide on and buy or arrange to hire your wedding dress and headdress, or place your order with a dressmaker.

❒ Decide on and buy or arrange to hire the bridesmaids' and pages' outfits, or place an order with the dressmaker.

❒ Buy or arrange to hire the groom's clothes.

❒ Visit the minister and arrange for the banns to be called, if and when required.

❒ Book the organist, choir and bellringers.

❒ Choose the hymns and wedding music.

❒ Book music or entertainment for the reception, if required.

❒ Book the caterer and wine merchant for the reception, if required.

❒ Secure the services of a master of ceremonies or toastmaster, if required.

❒ Order the wedding invitations.

❒ Order the service sheets, cake boxes, seating cards and any other stationery.

❒ Book the florist.

Well in advance

❒ Draw up your wedding present list and place it with a suitable shop or shops.

❒ Buy the wedding ring or rings.

❒ Decide on the food and drink for the reception.

❒ Decide on your going-away clothes, your honeymoon clothes, and your wedding accessories, such as shoes and underwear.

❒ Arrange a rehearsal in the church. This will certainly be necessary for a big wedding.

❒ Plan your pre-wedding parties.

❒ Book a hotel for the wedding night.

❒ Speak to both mothers about their outfits, to make sure they will look compatible.

❒ Send out your invitations at least six weeks ahead.

❒ Choose gifts for the key members of the wedding party.

❒ If you need to be immunized before your honeymoon, get this done early, as you may feel rotten afterwards.

❒ If you need it, get family planning advice.

Six weeks before

❒ Check that all your invitations have been answered: if any are outstanding, check that they have been received.

❒ Confirm arrangements with photographer, florist, car hire, dress hire and catering firms.

❒ Check that the wedding dress and headgear are perfect in all their details.

❒ Wear your wedding shoes round the house to get them adapted to your feet. Ill-fitting shoes on the day would be excruciating.

❏ Practise walking in your dress and veil or train.

❏ Practise getting out of a car, kneeling, and getting up from kneeling in your veil and train. (If you don't want anyone to see you and your garage is too small to manoeuvre in, get someone to hold a tray over your head to represent the roof of the car while you're sitting down, and practise indoors.

❏ Try out hairstyles, and book a hairdresser if necessary.

❏ Make a seating plan for the reception if necessary.

❏ Give final numbers to caterers as soon as possible.

❏ Double check your honeymoon arrangements.

❏ Announce your wedding in the paper, if you wish.

❏ Make arrangements for guests to stay overnight if they are travelling some distance.

❏ Make a record of the gifts you receive and write thank you letters as they arrive.

❏ The bride should arrange for her change of name to take place after the wedding day on official documents (bank account etc.), if she wants.

The week before

❏ Confirm any arrangements left outstanding as early as possible.

❏ Arrange times to take delivery of the wedding dress and bouquet, the groom's and bridesmaids' outfits, buttonholes, posies, corsages etc.

❏ Attend the rehearsal.

❏ Make sure everyone knows what their duties will be on the day, and that the groom and best man have prepared speeches.

❏ Make sure the cake has been delivered.

❏ Make sure the best man has organized your going-away car.

❏ Confirm the exact time with the transport firm, once you have timed the journey yourself in similar traffic conditions.

The day before

❏ Pack for your honeymoon.

❏ Make sure your mother or the chief bridesmaid has an emergency kit (tissues, needle and thread, make-up) to hand.

❏ Make sure your dress is ready to put on, and not creased.

❏ Transfer your engagement ring to your right hand.

❏ Make sure the best man has the ring(s) in a safe place.

The wedding day checklist for key persons

The bride

❏ Give presents to bridesmaids.

❏ Arrange for honeymoon luggage and going-away clothes to be taken to the reception venue.

❏ Get to the church on time!

❏ Walk up the aisle on father's right arm.

❏ On reaching the bridegroom, hand bouquet and gloves (if wearing) to chief bridesmaid.

❏ Lift veil with aid of chief bridesmaid.

❏ Exchange vows and rings (or receive ring).

❏ Sign register in vestry.

❏ Process down the aisle.

❏ Leave church for reception.

❏ Greet guests at reception.

❑ Enjoy the wedding breakfast and speeches.
❑ Cut cake with groom.
❑ Change into going-away outfit.
❑ Toss bouquet to chief bridesmaid and leave for honeymoon.

The groom

❑ Give best man his present.
❑ Arrange for going-away clothes and luggage to be at reception.
❑ Arrive at the church with best man 20 minutes before wedding.
❑ Stand in front right-hand pew with best man.
❑ Step into aisle as bride approaches.
❑ Exchange vows and rings (or give ring).
❑ Sign register in vestry.
❑ Process down the aisle.
❑ Leave church for reception.
❑ Greet guests at reception.
❑ Enjoy wedding breakfast.
❑ Propose toast to bridesmaids.
❑ Cut cake with bride.
❑ Change into going-away outfit.
❑ Leave for honeymoon.

The best man

❑ Check bridegroom has luggage and going-away clothes at reception
❑ Check going-away car is at reception venue.
❑ Have fees ready in sealed envelope.
❑ Have ring(s) ready to hand to vicar.
❑ Have wedding documentation ready.
❑ Collect buttonhole and wedding telegrams from bride's mother.
❑ Get groom to church 20 minutes before wedding.

❑ Stand in front right-hand pew.
❑ When bride joins groom stand at groom's right-hand side (or just behind) at the altar.
❑ Place ring(s) on prayerbook when minister requests.
❑ Sign register in vestry.
❑ Hand over fee to vicar.
❑ Leave church for reception with chief bridesmaid.
❑ At reception may act as toastmaster.
❑ Give speech.
❑ Read telegrams.
❑ Make sure couple have honeymoon documentation and see them off.

Chief bridesmaid

❑ Help dress the bride.
❑ Have an 'emergency kit' (tissues etc.) ready for bride.
❑ Arrive at church five minutes before bride and wait inside the door.
❑ Look after younger bridesmaids and pages.
❑ When bride arrives, check she looks her best and arrange her train for procession up aisle.
❑ Follow bride up aisle.
❑ Take her bouquet (and gloves) when she joins the groom.
❑ Help her with her veil.
❑ Follow her into vestry to sign register.
❑ Return her bouquet to her for procession down aisle.
❑ Follow her down aisle.
❑ Leave church with best man for reception.
❑ Greet guests at reception.
❑ Help bride change into going-away outfit.
❑ Catch her bouquet when she tosses it.

SETTING UP HOME

A place to call home is a basic need for all of us. This section of the book deals with buying and renting, explains surveys and mortgages and the duties of your solicitor, and sees you through the stressful job of moving in. It also gives suggestions for room planning and decorating in your new home. It is important to note that the legislation regarding renting and buying property is quite different in Scotland to the rest of Great Britain. The arrangements described in the first half of this chapter apply to England and Wales.

Rent or buy?

For many young people, setting up home means moving into college digs, student rooms or other rented accommodation near work or place of study. When you come to set up home with a view to family life, however, priorities change. Security of tenure and location take on new significance. For many, renting is the only option when they first set up home: for others, it may actually be preferable.

Advantages of rented accommodation

- Convenient if you only want to live in a place for a short time, while studying or training, for example.
- No lump sum needed for a deposit.
- No extra costs: surveyor's fees, mortgage arrangement fees, solicitor's fees.
- You are unlikely to have major costs (due to repair work, home improvement or furnishing a home).
- A useful option if the property market does not favour buyers (if there is not enough property on the market, or if prices are expected to fall, or rise more slowly, in the near future).
- It may be the only option if you would like to wait and buy when you get married, if you are expecting an inheritance that will give you a good deposit, or if you have only just started a career and would find it difficult to get a mortgage.

Disadvantages of rented accommodation

- Many types of rented accommodation are only short-term and do not offer any security.
- All the money you pay out goes to the landlord, rather than being an investment in a piece of property that you will eventually own.
- You may not have a free hand in decorating or adapting a property to suit your needs.
- You may have to share facilities, such as bathroom and kitchen.
- You may face restrictions over whether you can keep pets or have children living in the accommodation.
- You may have to put up with furniture and fittings that are not to your taste.
- Some people find that rented accommodation never really feels like home.

Types of rented property

There are various arrangements for renting property, and the type you go for will depend on your budget, the degree of security you want, and what is available in the area where you want to live.

Most rented property is available on a lease, which states the terms on which the property is let, such as whether it is furnished, how often the lease has to be renewed, what restrictions there are on the tenants in terms of maintaining the interior, and so on. Unfurnished properties usually offer better security, but are hard to find.

The local authority lets many unfurnished properties, but they are not readily available to everyone. Factors such as where you live or work, whether you are homeless, and how long you have been on their waiting list all affect how easy it would be for you to get a council house or flat.

Holiday lets are properties let for short periods of time, intended only as temporary accommodation.

Company lets are becoming more common. A company is the tenant of the flat, and the occupiers pay rent to the company. The occupiers do not have so many rights, but the arrangement is often used by companies who want to provide accommodation for staff who have to move around the country or to provide temporary accommodation for relocated staff.

Flat-sharing arrangements may be an option for some, either moving in with friends, or finding a flat through newspaper advertisements. If you are a student, your college will have special arrangements for accommodation.

Finding rented accommodation

Properties to rent are advertised through accommodation agencies, estate agents and in the local and national press. It is a good idea to start by getting the local paper for the area in which you wish to live. This should give you some details of likely estate agents and accommodation agencies. Check the Yellow Pages for agencies as well. In some parts of the country, evening papers carry the best selection of properties available, but you may well find that there is a lot of competition and you need to buy the paper as soon as it is published to be in with a chance of even viewing the right type of accommodation.

You can put your name on the housing list of the local council, but many people do not have the special needs that will push them up the waiting list. Students should seek advice from their college accommodation office.

Questions to ask when you go to view rented accommodation

- **What is the monthly/weekly rent, and when is it payable?**
- **What does the rent include: power, heating, water rates?**
- **Who is the landlord?**
- **What are the running costs, over and above the rent?**
- **What arrangements are there for shared facilities: cleaning of communal areas, use of garden, rota or other organization for use of shared kitchen.**
- **What are the other tenants like?**
- **What is the area like: is it safe at night, attractive, convenient, etc.**

So you're going to buy

Until the late 1980s, most people felt that houses were a good investment. There was a feeling that prices would always rise, or at

least keep up with inflation. But even before then, property prices had to be looked at in terms of the value of all properties. Most people want to buy another property when they sell, and the prices of other properties may have been rising faster than that of yours, so a rise in the value of your property does not necessarily mean you are better off in real terms.

Many people have had their fingers burned in the rush to get on the housing ladder. It is vital not to set your sights too high. When you are looking at the capital outlay and monthly outgoings, don't forget the other expenses: you may have to furnish the place, you may need extra finance for home improvements such as central heating or a new kitchen, and your circumstances may change unexpectedly. If you're setting up home with a view to starting a family, remember that children will mean extra expenditure and possibly the loss of, or a drop in, one income.

Having said that, don't be overcautious. You must enter the market confident that you can meet your needs – and be prepared for a few knocks on the way.

How much can you afford?

Most of the finance for the property you buy will probably come from a mortgage – a loan against the value of the property. Mortgages are available from building societies, banks and through brokers. Sometimes, local authorities have funds for mortgages.

The first thing a lender will look at is your income. The general pattern is that building societies will lend the value of two-and-a-half times a single income, or three times the first income plus the second income.

If the loan is to be based on one income of, say £15,000, the amount is likely to be up to £37,500. In the case of a couple, one earning £15,000 and the other earning £12,000, the amount is likely to be up to £51,000. Different societies and banks have different attitudes as to which income counts as the major income, what type of properties they will lend on, and whether they will lend to two men or two women buying a home together.

Some lenders will favour borrowers who have saved or banked with them for a few years. It is a good idea to open an account with a major building society even before you start seriously considering buying a house.

If you are basing a mortgage on two incomes, but are planning to start a family, it is advisable to base the mortgage on the main breadwinner's income.

Brokers have different criteria for assessing how much to lend, and

are often prepared to lend to people who have not had a steady income over the last few years. They are generally more expensive than banks or building societies. Some people are able to get mortgages through their employer at particularly good rates.

A lump sum

Besides the mortgage, you will need to have saved a certain amount of cash before you can consider buying. Most lenders expect you to pay a certain percentage of the price in cash – probably at least 10 per cent of the price of the house. You will also need cash for the solicitor's fees and expenses, and moving costs. And remember you may need cash for decorating, furnishing, a new car, perhaps.

If you are buying a new property, with special mortgage arrangements with the builder, a deposit may not be necessary.

Your lump sum will also have to cover the costs involved in buying and moving home: the solicitor's fees, surveyor's fees, fees for arranging the mortgage, removal costs, redecoration or rebuilding work, any major structural repairs, woodworm, damp-proofing, rewiring, replumbing and so on.

Starting out

If you think you can put together a suitable deposit, and are likely to be able to take out a large enough mortgage, setting up home begins with a two-pronged attack. You need to familiarize yourself with the housing market, and familiarize your building society or bank with your plans, to get some idea of how forthcoming a mortgage would be.

Browsing in the windows of estate agents, skimming through the local papers and picking up some national magazines such as *Dalton's Weekly*, *The Lady* or some of the country home magazines should become an almost full-time hobby.

Don't be put off if all the prices in the area where you thought you'd like to live are way above your head. There are plenty of other options. You will find that you are constantly having to revise your plans and preferences. Take time to explore the possibilities, and the areas where you feel you could settle.

Drive around: perhaps there are modern mews flats tucked away in an area where all the other homes are more like mansions: or perhaps there is an old terrace of delightful cottages in an area where you thought there were only uniform '30s semis.

And what about the '30s semi you thought you couldn't bear to live in? The rooms are usually a convenient size, and conveniently arranged, and many developments have convenient shops and schools.

Similarly, a Victorian artisan's cottage might remind you of your grandparents' first home, but with up-to-the minute decor and plenty of improvements it could be a compact and comfortable home for a first-time buyer.

New homes are often an attractive option: many builders and developers have special

schemes for helping buyers, with perhaps 100 per cent mortgages (you don't need a deposit) and new carpets and curtains included (something you would never get in an older property).

Make an appointment to see someone at your building society or bank if you are planning to get a mortgage. Familiarize yourself with all their literature about different types of mortgage, different interest rates, special arrangements for first time buyers, and so on.

Viewing houses

Once you have a better idea of what you want, and how much you can afford, start to contact the estate agents in the area. You could drop in, phone, or write. Ask for details of a particular property you have seen advertised, or ask to be put on their mailing list. Most agents will want to have some idea of the type of property you are after, the size, how much you think you can afford, and they will probably ask whether you have a property to sell at the same time, whether you have made any mortgage arrangements, and whether you have any particular needs.

When you've found details of a property that meets your criteria, you can ask to view it. If possible, check out the road first, to make sure it is as you expected. This can save everyone a lot of time. After a few months (and it often takes that long) you will be experienced enough to know which properties on the lists are likely to be suitable. If you found the property through

What do you want?

Decide what your overall needs (and tastes) are, and how this will affect the type of house you choose.
- Are you looking for a small place, which you can 'trade up' in a few years' time, or can you afford a house that will be the family home for decades to come?
- Do you want a house or a flat?
- Would you prefer a larger home out of town, or something smaller towards the centre?
- How many bedrooms do you need?
- Do you have any special requirements, such as a room for a study, a second bathroom or a utility room?

- What general condition are you prepared to accept? Do you have the time/money/energy for rebuilding or redecorating?
- Do you want a garden?
- Is the location important? Do you need to be near work/a station/a bus route?
- Do you need any particular facilities nearby, within walking distance: schools, shops, sports facilities?
- Do you have any preferences as to which way the house faces?
- Is the age or style of the house important: are you looking for period features or built-in furniture, for example?

an agent, he will make the appointment for you. If the vendor is selling privately you will have to make the arrangements.

When you come to view

It is all too easy to walk round a house and be swayed by one or two particular features, such as the state of the front garden, the colour of the front door, or the pattern of the living room carpet. Try to be objective about the property. Here are some points to look out for. They may not mean that the property is a hopeless case, but

Points to look for outside

- Check what you can see of the roof, gutters, drainpipes and waste pipes. Look for tell-tale signs like missing tiles, damage, and stains on the walls where pipes or gutters have leaked, which may indicate damp permeating into the interior.
- Look around the bottom of the house for rising damp, which may show as dark patches on the walls.
- Look out for uneven brickwork, particularly around the windows

and doors, which may indicate movement. Look out for cracks running up across the brickwork.
- Look at the condition of the pointing (the mortar between the bricks).
- Look vertically up the walls to check for bulges.
- Look out for chimneys in bad condition and (especially if the house is built on a hill) a general slope in the building.

SETTING UP HOME

they may help you spot some of the points the surveyor will be looking for. Often, the lender will hold back some of the mortgage until the repairs have been done.

Once you've found your home

When you've seen a house that suits your needs and pocket, you can make an offer. If you viewed the property through an estate agent, write to him, or discuss the possibilities with him – he may know, for example, whether the vendors will be prepared to accept less than the asking price, whether they are in a hurry to move, and so on. Remember that it is the vendor who pays the estate agent's fees. If you are buying the property privately, without an estate agent, you will have to deal with the owner direct.

Put your offer in writing. The letter should not commit you in any way, but you must make it plain that you are serious about buying the property. If anyone else is after the same property, the vendor is likely to choose the prospective buyer who seems to be the most efficient and most likely to follow the purchase through. A sample letter is shown overleaf.

At this stage, apart from your personal investigations, you will have no detailed knowledge of the structural condition of the building, or whether it has any serious faults such as rising damp, wet or dry rot or an infestation of woodworm. If these show up in a survey later (see over), you may be able to ask for a reduction in the price.

Points to look for inside

• Sniff the air: mustiness may indicate damp or rot.
• Look at the corners of the room. Wrinkles in the wallpaper may indicate that the walls have moved slightly (or they may indicate bad wallpapering).
• Look out for signs of rotten woodwork, particularly around the windows.
• Feel for draughts – around the outer and inner frames of doors and windows.
• Listen for creaking floorboards and stairs, which may indicate structural problems, rot or woodworm.
• Look out for white powdery patches on walls, or dark patches where decorations are damp. Stains on the ceilings in the top floor may indicate a leaking roof.
• Ask about the heating and hot water systems. Make sure they work if you don't want to replace them straight away.
• Check cellars, lofts and attics for signs of woodworm and rot. In many older properties, a little dampness in a cellar is not usually a problem, as long as the floor above is sound and dry.
• Don't be swayed by the decor. Smart new decorations may have been used to disguise problem areas; while the ugliest of colour schemes can be prettied up with changed wallpaper and paint.

If your offer is accepted, the next stage is to alert your solicitor (find one if you do not already have one) and apply for a mortgage.

Letter making an offer

```
A & B ESTATE AGENTS                    YOUR ADDRESS
THE HIGH STREET
ABTON

                                       DATE
```

Dear sirs,

RE: 18 ABBEY AVENUE.

I have recently viewed the above property, and would like to put in an offer.

I understand that the vendor is asking £65,950 for it. In view of the leaking roof/somewhat out-of-date kitchen/state of the property market/other obvious problems I wonder if the vendor would consider accepting £63,000?

I am getting in touch with my solicitor [insert name and address if you have it] and would be grateful if you could let me have the name of the vendor and details of his solicitor.

I am applying for a mortgage with the Abbey building society who have indicated that they would be prepared to lend me up to £50,000 and I have sufficient savings for the remainder.

I look forward to hearing from you.

Yours sincerely

L. McBain.

Both the mortgage company and the solicitor will want to know various facts: the name of the owner, the address of the property, whether it is freehold or leasehold, and the agreed price.

You may be asked to pay a deposit at this stage. In some cases, you may want to offer a deposit, to show you mean business. The size of such a deposit should not be more than a couple of hundred pounds. You should only pay a deposit 'subject to contract'. If you decide that you do not want to buy the property, because of problems that are revealed by surveyors or solicitors, and do not enter into a contract with the vendor, the money is returnable in full. It is safest to pay the deposit to the vendor's estate agent, to hold 'as stakeholders': with this condition, the estate agent holds the money until completion of the sale, so it will be easier to get back if things go wrong.

Getting a survey done

Whoever you go to for a mortgage, they will want to know more about the property they (and you) are investing in. The normal procedure is for the lender to do a survey. This is particularly important in assessing the condition of older houses.

The survey may be a valuation report, which simply checks the value of the property concerned, but most banks and building societies now offer surveys known as home-buyers reports, which use a standard form to check certain points. The lender will organize the survey, but you will have to pay for it. These surveys may save you having to have your own private survey done on the property.

You might want to have your own full structural survey done to try to establish that your investment is sound – particularly if you are putting a lot of your own money into the property. The survey for mortgage purposes is only concerned that the loan is secure. You might also want your own surveyor to report on the feasibility of any structural alterations you feel would be necessary: knocking down walls between rooms, converting a loft and so on. It may also be necessary to get specialist reports and estimates from builders, damp-proofing firms and infestation specialists, as the survey does not usually advise you on costs of any necessary work.

Types of mortgage

At this stage, you will also have to decide on the type of mortgage you want. If you've done your homework, you will have already shopped around a bit for a good deal: low start mortgages, special offers for first-time buyers and so on. Two terms you will come across are repayment mortgage and endowment mortgage.

With a repayment mortgage, you borrow the sum, the lender works out the interest, and the total is divided up to be paid off in equal instalments over a fixed term –

usually 25 years. You will almost always have to take out a life insurance policy to cover the value of the loan (in case you die next week).

With an endowment mortgage, you borrow the sum, the lender works out the interest, and just the interest is paid off in equal instalments. At the same time, you pay an insurance premium, which matures at the end of the agreed term (again, often 25 years). When the policy matures, it gives a lump sum that is used to pay off the mortgage, and there is usually a certain amount of cash left over for the mortgagee. The value of the insurance policy is not absolutely guaranteed to be sufficient to pay off the loan, but it is very unlikely that it will not be enough. Endowment mortgages usually cost a little more than repayment mortgages, but give you extra cash at the end.

With either repayment or endowment mortgages, the payments will go up or down according to the current interest rate. There are more and more special mortgages available, sometimes on fixed terms, or with interest rates set for a certain number of years, which is attractive if interest rates are likely to rise, but not if they are going to fall. There are also low-start mortgages for first time buyers (a good option if you do not plan to start a family soon) and pension mortgages (which work in a similar way to endowment mortgages) intended mainly for the over 30s. Do try to discuss all the options with one or two possible mortgage lenders.

The solicitor's work

At the same time, your solicitor should be starting his part of the operation. If you do not have a solicitor, one of the best ways to find one is to ask friends if they can recommend one. Your estate agent or mortgage lender may be able to help, or you can get the names of suitable practitioners in your area from the Law Society. It is often advisable to go to a solicitor in the area where the house is, as he will have a good knowledge of the local authority and the property market in general in that area.

Give your solicitor all the details you can, as soon as possible, particularly if other parties are interested in the property.

The solicitor's job is to do your conveyancing: he has to ensure that the property is rightfully yours once the money is handed over. He has to investigate the deeds of the property, to see that the vendor is indeed the owner; he has to ensure that the boundaries of the property are clearly defined; and he also checks that there are no factors that might devalue the property in the near future – a road widening scheme, a new factory estate next door. He will also handle the handing over of the money at the right time, so he will liaise with whoever is lending you the money, and check that any conditions they demand are met.

Search and enquiries

In order to find out more about the property, the solicitor will do what is known as a search. This involves making certain enquiries with the local authority, at the town hall or appropriate office. Most solicitors use a standard form, which lists the questions that have to be asked in most cases. The information comes from various different departments: the borough surveyor, the planning department, the public health department and so on; it may take some time for the form to be returned. In some areas the whole operation is computerized. There is a small charge made by the local authority.

The solicitor will also be in touch with the vendor, through his solicitor, to make various enquiries. These include matters like the details of the lease (in leasehold properties); maintenance and service charges, if applicable; guarantees on any rot, woodworm and damp-proofing work that has been done on the property; any special conditions imposed by the planning authority on buying a new property, and so on.

The solicitor will also check that the property is on the Land Register. This is a register of most of the properties in England and Wales. If any details have changed since the property last changed hands (for example, if the vendor is keeping part of the garden in a large property) or if the property has not yet been registered, your solicitor has to ensure the authorities make a record of the details of the property. If the property is not on the Land Register your solicitor will have to see the title deeds, which record the exchanges of ownership of the property, and are held by the owner (or the mortgage company).

A note on leasehold properties

When you buy a leasehold property, you buy a lease on that property for a set number of years. In the past, most properties were sold on a 100-year lease. This means that after that time, the property reverts to the ownership of the landlord or freeholder. For example, a flat converted and sold with a 100-year lease 30 years ago would now have only a 70-year lease. The shorter the lease, the less worthwhile the investment. It is difficult to sell a property if the lease is less than about 60 years: this may not affect you now, but if you bought a flat with a 70-year lease, it might not be easy to sell it in five years' time: remember, whoever bought it from you might be thinking about selling it in five years' time, and they might have to reduce the price considerably.

However, it may be possible to extend the lease, or even buy the freehold yourself. Under new legislation, leaseholders may have the right to buy the freehold of their property. This will not apply if the current freeholder is the landlord of the property, or the property is owned by a charitable trust or the Crown. In houses that have been converted into leasehold flats, it may be possible to buy a commonhold: each flat-owner would have the freehold of their own flat, plus a commonhold of the shared areas, such as hallways, front gardens and so on.

When buying leasehold property, particularly if a service charge is involved, it is important to find out exactly what the terms are: who is responsible for leaking roofs, rising damp, the decoration of the outside of the building, and so on. Your solicitor should be able to advise you on all aspects of the leasehold of a property.

The contract

The date on which the house becomes yours, plus all the other details of legal ownership, are set out in the contract. The process of house buying involves enabling both parties to exchange contracts. The date on which the property becomes yours (completion, when the money is handed over) is usually set at a month from the date on which the contracts are exchanged.

The vendor's solicitor will send out a draft contract, which your solicitor will amend as necessary, in light of the conditions imposed and anything he discovers through his search and enquiries. This may involve a certain amount of bargaining. The whole process usually takes a minimum of a month.

When everyone is happy with all the details, and the solicitor is sure that you can come up with all the money, contracts can be signed and exchanged. Normally, 10 per cent of the price of the house is paid at this stage. (The amount of any original deposit may be deducted from this.) Once you have exchanged contracts, the deposit cannot be returned.

If the money you need for the deposit is coming from the mortgage company (or some other source that means it will not be available until the date of completion), you may have to borrow the deposit. This will mean paying interest on the sum for the month between exchange of contracts and completion. It is worth trying to ask for a reduction in the deposit to reduce your borrowing costs.

The mortgage company will give your solicitor the cheque or banker's draft for the value of the house, just before completion. You will have to start paying interest on the loan from this date, and your lender will notify you of the first date of regular monthly payments.

There is also the stamp duty to pay. Stamp duty is a form of tax. When contracts on properties over a certain value are exchanged, they have to carry a stamp. The cost of stamp duty is a small percentage (1 per cent) of the value of the property.

Insurance

Once you have exchanged contracts, the house is in effect yours, although you have no right of access until you have paid the rest of the price. If it burns down, or is wrecked by squatters, you have to foot the bill. Insurance is essential. Most mortgage lenders will insist on comprehensive insurance from exchange of contracts. They may well stipulate a company, and the matter may be dealt with automatically.

In future years, it is important to check that the building insurance has kept up with current costs. It will have to cover complete rebuilding costs in case of major disasters such as fire or subsidence, as well as minor refurbishments

due to leaking pipes or storm damage. It should also cover you against the possibility of being sued for accidental injury to strangers (for example, if a tile blew off your roof and through the windscreen of a passing car).

Contents insurance comes later, once you have moved in, but you should be thinking about it now. Again, it is worth shopping about for a good deal: like car insurance, premiums will vary. The cost will depend on the value of your possessions; the type of property and how secure it is; the address of the property and so on.

You also need life insurance – indeed this may be automatic, a condition of the mortgage. If you get run over by a bus tomorrow, you don't want your partner saddled with mortgage payments for the next 25 years.

Moving in

Although you cannot move in until completion, once contracts have been exchanged your new home is in effect yours, and planning must begin in earnest.

The first thing to decide is your moving date. This is likely to be the same day as completion, particularly if you are selling and buying at the same time. However, if the property is in poor condition, if you want to rewire or replumb, or install a new kitchen, central heating system or bathroom suite, or if there are works to be done like damp-proofing or woodworm, it may be advisable to put off your move. Major works mean disruption to the household, and you may have to go without water or power for hours at a time, and find everything is covered with a film of plaster dust.

But bridging loans (which you need if you want to stay in your old property while you do up the new one) are expensive. Even storing furniture so that you can stay with friends or relatives costs money, and you will have to pay two sets of removal costs. So you may be forced to move in on the day of completion.

Before you move

Now you can start thinking about furniture and furnishings. You should have measurements of the rooms in the new home, but these will not give details of the width of alcoves, the size of windows and so on. Sellers are not obliged to give the buyers free access to the property, but if you approach them they are usually happy to let you in at least once to measure up in more detail.

However, they may be a bit put out if they are selling the house because of bereavement, or moving because they can't afford their mortgage payments, for example.

You can't always expect to have everything straight within a few days of moving in. Remember that made-to-measure curtains take time to organize; the vendor may be reluctant to let carpet fitters in to measure up; new furniture may take up to six weeks to deliver; and fitted kitchens even longer.

If you are having new flooring installed try to organize enough time between completion (usually at midday the day you move in)

and arrival of all your furniture.

If possible, you will want at least one room shipshape almost as soon as you move in. Decide which will be the easiest to make habitable first.

Contacting the contractors

Book a removal firm as soon as you can. At some times of the year they are very busy, and you may have to search for companies that can do the job. Get several estimates, and ask exactly what is covered in terms of insurance: if you have a lot of antiques or valuable pieces, you may have to pay extra. And you will also have to discuss how much work you are prepared to do in terms of packing things into boxes.

Some firms are no more than a man with a van – which is cheap if you only have a few boxes to move (if you are a first-time buyer, and don't have much furniture). They may also be prepared to collect any furniture you have recently bought as part of the deal. At the other extreme, some firms insist on packing all your possessions, down to the last wine glass, so that they know it is packed to the standard demanded by their insurers.

You will also have to arrange to take over the services of the property. In most cases you save by taking over the services, rather than having them cut off and reconnected.

Allow plenty of time for all these things, as you may have to give notice in writing, or visit the appropriate showroom.

The services in your new home

- **Gas: contact the gas board about a week before you move to make the necessary arrangements. Check that they will have someone to read the meter at the moment the property becomes yours. If necessary, make an appointment for a fitter to come and connect any gas appliances you are taking with you or having delivered at the time of the move.**
- **Electricity: again, contact the electricity board before you move and arrange for an electrician to connect appliances if necessary. With both gas and electricity it is advisable to take a reading yourself, the moment you get into the house, so that if there are any queries when your first bill comes in you will have a record of how much power you have used.**
- **Telephone: contact the telephone company; you may be able to transfer your existing number if you are moving within the same dialling code area.**

Organization

As soon as you have exchanged contracts, you can send out change-of-address notices to friends, relatives, bank, credit companies, insurance companies, tv licensing authority, car and driving license authority, pension companies and so on. These days, many people have access to word processors, and can print out as many copies as needed, or you can simply get them duplicated on a photocopying machine at your local newsagent. Remember to include details of account or policy numbers where appropriate.

On the day of the move, make arrangements for someone to look after the pets and children, if necessary. (With school-age children, there is no reason why they shouldn't go to school, if you are moving fairly locally, as long as they know the way to their new home!)

Check that your home contents policy covers moving (if you are not covered by a removal company), and that you have notified the policyholder of the new address: the rates may change if you are moving to an area with a different risk rating.

Organize a small box of things to transport yourself by car if possible. This may include some bedding (any baby equipment, such as food, bottles, carry-cot if you have a small baby), some of your children's favourite toys, any cooking equipment you are going to need for the night you move in, and – most important – tea- and coffee-making equipment for yourself and the removal men: it may be the last thing you need before moving out, and the first thing you need when you move in. If possible, buy takeaway meals, eat out or get invited round by friends, to save cooking on the day of the move.

Your first home

Most first-time buyers don't have much in the way of furniture, curtains, home accessories and so on. To start with, you may have to beg and borrow what you can from friends and relatives, or go for second-hand or inexpensive new furnishings. Most young people are happy to rough it a bit, improving their homes room by room, rather than over-extending themselves with credit arrangements to furnish their home. As long as you have your own, sound, property, the interior can wait.

Moving on

If you are selling and buying at the same time, the whole business of moving is much more fraught. First of all, there is the problem of being a link in a chain during all the negotiations of price and date for exchange of contracts. You may be able to reach agreement with the parties you are dealing with, but there may be a hitch somewhere along the chain – perhaps the people who are buying the property from the people who are buying your property find that they can't get a mortgage; or the people who are selling you their home find that the house they want to buy is riddled with woodworm. The longer the chain of sellers and buyers, the longer the process is likely to take. Moving home is one of the most stressful activities, so be prepared for frayed nerves.

Make your home as attractive as possible when you are selling. It may help to redecorate, but don't do anything costly. Plain, pale coloured paint is cheap, fresh, and less likely to put off prospective buyers than heavy patterns. Most buyers will be much more attracted by a clean, tidy house (whatever their habits are). Rooms will also look bigger, and people will get the feeling that the house is easier to run if it is tidy. Some people go as far as to make sure there is a smell of baking or freshly-brewed coffee, to give the house a welcoming, homely feel when prospective buyers come to view. If you are leaving the keys with an estate agent because you are out all day, you will have to leave the place tidy when you go out to work. Always check the position of the people who want to buy your home: have they got a property to sell? Have they found a buyer, or isn't their property on the market yet? Are they likely to be able to get the sort of mortgage they are after? They may not answer your queries, and they may be over-optimistic, but it's worth trying to find out.

Money matters

You may take out a mortgage with the same company on your new home, or you may approach a different company. In most cases, you will have to redeem the old mortgage and take out the new mortgage at the same time, which may incur extra charges. You will also have fees to pay on the sale, as well as the purchase, to the solicitor. If you are selling through an estate agent, rather than advertising privately, you will have to pay the estate agent's fees. It is worth shopping around as agents' fees may vary slightly. They may also offer better rates if they are 'sole agents', which means that you are asking them to sell the house, and not putting it with any other estate agents.

Moving day

Remember you will have to be ready to move out at the moment of completion of the sale of your property, which will also be the moment at which you complete the purchase of your new property.

If you have a lot of furniture, and the move is a long one, you may have to make the move over a couple of days: one day packing, one day travelling (the day of completion, in many cases) and another day unpacking. This may give you the chance to get flooring laid in the new home.

Do remember to make arrangements for handing over the keys at both ends of the move: you can't be in two places at once. Many a move has been disrupted because when the removal van has arrived at the new home, there is no one to unlock the house.

If you've got a lot of furniture, and a lot of rooms in the new home, plan where it should all go carefully. Scale drawings of the various rooms, with paper rectangles to represent the furniture, can be very useful, although some things (the position of pictures, arranging the coffee table and sofa so there is room to walk around the room easily) will have to be finalized when you move in.

Devise some system of labelling furniture and boxes (sometimes removal firms will take care of this): make sure the doors of the rooms in the new home are labelled to match, so that everything labelled 'Main bedroom' can go into what you have decided will be your bedroom, everything labelled 'Jane's room' goes into what will be Jane's bedroom, and so on.

Keep an eye on the men as they work. You want them to position heavy furniture exactly where you want it to save having to get some strong friends around to help you out later.

Making the most of your home

When you're making decisions about decorating your home, whether it's because you've just moved in, because your needs have changed, or simply because you want something different, it's worth having a good look at the way things are to start with.

It may take some time to get things right, even if you just want to change the existing decor, rather than making major alterations or improvements. If it's going to be a long job and the building is very dilapidated, it may be worth painting everything white (or some other pale colour) so it is clean and comfortable. Then start to think carefully about what major or minor improvements are necessary.

You have to get the structure right and be sure of how rooms should be furnished and decorated, before you can start working on details of decor. Although you want to make your hallway as welcoming as possible, it makes sense to leave carpets, walls and woodwork on the hall and stairs until last if you can, so that they don't get damaged by builders, decorators and furniture delivery men moving in and out.

Planning alterations

• Before having wiring done, think about the lighting (wall lights, recessed ceiling lights, power outlets for standard and table lamps; kitchen appliances (fridge, washing machine, dryer, iron, dishwasher, cooker, cooker hood or extractor fan, food processor, microwave, toaster, kettle, coffee maker – the list is endless); tv, video and hi-fi equipment; electric heaters; vacuum cleaner (you'll need an accessible socket in every room, and one in hallways and on landings); other special needs such as a sewing machine, home computer or hobby equipment.

• Before having central heating installed, think about the position and style of radiators: will they prevent you from putting prize pieces of furniture where you want them? Do you need a heated towel rail in the bathroom?

• Plan any replumbing at the same time as central heating: is the cold water supply in the right place for the kitchen sink? Do you need a tap in the garden? And what other taps will you need?

• Get the gas supply dealt with at the same time as the central heating, if it is gas. Do you need a gas tap by a fireplace to run a log-effect fire, or a gas poker for a real fire? Do you want to run any gas appliances – fridge, water heater?

• Before having walls knocked out and extensions built, plan the position of furniture: there's no point in knocking down a wall between a kitchen and dining room, only to find you don't have room for the fridge. Wide openings between rooms or out to extensions may use up valuable wall space, where you could have put shelves or a chest of drawers.

Major problems

If you have major works to be done, plan the order of work carefully. Damp-proof work may involve removing plaster and making good – a very messy business. And woodworm or rot treatments may mean replacing beams, floors and trims such as skirtings and window frames. Replacing windows almost always involves replastering.

Work, such as replastering, replumbing, rewiring, putting in a new central heating system, knocking down walls or building extensions, should be done as soon as possible.

Room-by-room planning

Look at how you are going to make the best use of the space in your home. It may be possible to change the way in which you use rooms, to make life more comfortable. Here is a list of suggestions.

The kitchen: Are you happy with the kitchen as it is? Would it be improved with new units (or just new doors)? Could you move the cooker, sink, or the positions of doors or windows, to improve the way it works? Could you extend it? Could you knock through to the next room? Would it be better to have the kitchen somewhere else in the house?

The dining room: Do you want a separate dining room (which may be essential for entertaining and useful as a playroom, or somewhere for teenagers to do their homework)? Is the dining room close enough to the kitchen? Would it be better to have the dining area in a corner of the kitchen, with the lighting arranged so you can 'switch off' the kitchen when you sit down to dine? Do you need a family eating area in the kitchen or living room, and a more formal dining room?

The living room: If you are not happy with the living room, is there another room that would be better – a dining room with a conservatory at the back of the house that is warmer and more accessible; a large bedroom upstairs at the front of the house that is more spacious or better proportioned? Could you knock the living room through to another room to make it more spacious? Could you add a fireplace to make it more homely?

A study space/sewing area/ home computer desk: Could this go in an unused corner of a living room or in the hallway? Could your dressing table double as a desk in the bedroom? Is there a small room that could double as a spare room and study?

Bathroom: Do you need to turn an existing bedroom into a bathroom, and if so which one

Living room plan

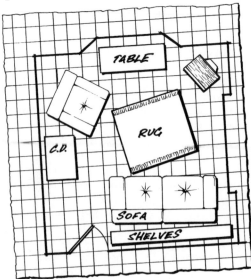

You can make a plan of a room using graph paper and paper shapes (which should be in scale) cut out and laid in place to represent the furniture.

would be best? Could you fit a second (or first) bathroom into a bedroom? Could you make an internal bathroom by taking some space from two adjacent bedrooms? Is it possible to fit a shower room under the stairs, or in an existing utility room?

Bedrooms: Could you divide any bedrooms up to make an extra bedroom? Rather than making the largest bedroom your bedroom, would it be better to let children use it and have a smaller one for yourself? Is there space for clothes storage elsewhere, leaving more room to get round the bed?

Remember that the furniture within a room can alter its use: a fold-away table means a living room or study can double as a dining room; a sofa bed turns a living room into a spare room, and a desk instead of a dressing table enables you to keep important papers and writing materials in the bedroom.

Ways with walls

The walls are the first thing to look at, once you've got the stucture of your home right. You'll probably choose a colour scheme based on some other aspect of your furnishing: the colour of the carpet, the curtain fabric, or the upholstery, for example. But you should attend to the walls and woodwork before you start laying the flooring and hanging the curtains.

If you live in a rented property, or are looking for cheap, quick cover-ups or improvements, here are some ideas to get you started.

Quick transformations

• Cover the walls with posters or pictures. Posters can be stuck up with Blu-Tack (on paint) or drawing pins (on wallpaper). Use proper picture hooks to hang pictures – they're stronger, go in more easily, and can be used over and over again if you handle them carefully.

• Hang fabrics – a length of woven or patterned cloth if your budget is low, or perhaps a patchwork bedspread if you can get hold of one. You can pin fabric straight to the wall, or nail battens in place and tack the fabric to them so it is stretched taut.

• It doesn't cost much to add a fresh coat of paint (over wallpaper or paint of an unsuitable colour). Simply wash down the walls (working from the bottom upwards) and check the plaster is reasonably sound. Then apply a couple of coats of water-based emulsion paint. A good quality emulsion may even cover in one coat, though it does depend on the colours you use. You will need more coats if covering one deep colour with another strongly contrasting colour or if using a silk finish.

• If plain painted walls are a good colour but look dull, consider adding a wallpaper border. These are available in a wide range of widths, colours and styles, from simple geometrics and imitation mouldings to stencilled effects and flowery patterns. You can use them to change the proportions of a room, by sticking them at picture-rail height, or the height of a chair rail, about 500mm above the floor;

or you can break up large expanses of blank wall by creating rectangular panels with the . borders. Or simply fit them around the top of the wall, at the angle with the ceiling.

Choosing a finish

Choose the final finish for your walls according to the function of the room. In a kitchen or bathroom, for example, you want a finish that will resist steam, and something that you can wash down. Hallways and stairs take a lot of wear, so the finish must be durable. In bedrooms and reception rooms, the finish can be more luxurious.

You must also consider the state of the walls: you may be able to paint over existing wallpaper, but it is always better to strip the walls back to bare plaster when

---

Options for wall finishes

• **Paint** is a cheap and easy option. Emulsion gives a serviceable matt finish, but silk or satin finishes may be more durable in bathrooms, kitchens or hallways.

• **Paint effects** are fashionable, and good for disguising lumpy walls. If you're prepared to take some time over the job, it is possible to learn how to do-it-yourself; professionals are expensive; it may be better to go for a paint-effect wallcovering.

• **Plain wallcoverings** are designed to give a better finish to the walls before painting – simple lining paper softens a bare plaster wall; woodchip is an economical textured paper for covering rough walls; moulded papers and blown vinyls add simple patterns; anaglypta gives a tough surface, but is more difficult to hang. Some of the modern plain coverings, white or self-coloured, have a finish that does not need to be painted.

• **Patterned wallcoverings** come in an ever-increasing range of patterns and finishes. There are traditionally-made wallpapers for areas of minimal wear; papers with a wipeable surface; paper-backed vinyl for a tougher finish; heavier vinyls, such as tile-effects for kitchens or bathrooms; paper-backed fabrics; hand printed, extremely expensive wallpapers – the list is endless. Many manufacturers produce ranges with matching borders and co-ordinating fabrics.

• **Tiling** is almost essential in some parts of the bathroom and kitchen: behind a sink, washbasin or bath, or you could completely tile the walls of a bathroom or shower. Small panels of tiling may be a useful option in some other situations: use it to give a neat finish to a window recess, or cover a damaged wall where a fireplace has been removed.

• **Panelling** with wood or wood-effect panels is a good way to cover damaged plaster without the expense of replastering. You could panel below a chair rail, or fit strips of tongued-and-grooved wood panelling within an alcove. Paint or varnish the wood for a durable and highly attractive finish.

redecorating. If there are lumps and bumps, they will be thrown into deeper relief by glossy wallcoverings. Gently mottled patterns and cushioned vinyl wallcoverings will help to disguise the defects.

Alternatively, make a virtue of the rough finish with a rough paint effect – a translucent wash of coloured emulsion will give a simple, country look to poorly finished walls. However, you should make sure that walls are sound, making good any damaged plaster and filling cracks.

Looking at floors

Even if you can't afford much in the way of furnishing, you'd be surprised at how much more 'furnished' a room feels once the floor has a good finish. Flooring can be a very expensive element of your decorating costs if you're after a good carpet or high quality ceramic or vinyl tiling. However,

there are cheaper options.

If you are buying fitted carpet, it will be labelled to indicate what type of wear it is intended for. Some carpets are not suitable for stairs, some are not suitable for kitchens or bathrooms, and some are intended only for use in bedrooms. For most living rooms, the best fibre for carpets, in terms of durability and resilience, is a mixture of 80 per cent wool and 20 per cent synthetic fibre. When

Ideas for floors

• Existing floorboards in reasonable condition can be sanded and sealed to give a durable surface. You can hire an electric sanding machine (which looks like a cross between an upright vacuum cleaner and a lawn mower) and do the job yourself: it's messy, and you must take certain safety precautions, but it's a reasonable option and produces good results.

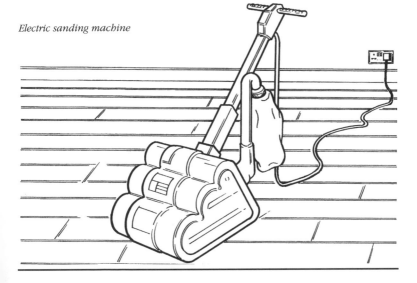

Electric sanding machine

Ideas for floors (continued)

• Stained or unevenly coloured floorboards can be recoloured with a special wood stain. There are several types on the market, suitable for use on floors.

• Cover (or replace) badly damaged floorboards with manmade boards: use hardboard over floorboards if you intend to lay carpets or tiles, or use chipboard or sheets of plywood for more solid flooring.

• Paint over plywood with good quality gloss or lino paint for a colourful finish.

• Varnish plywood or chipboard (which will come up looking like cork).

• Solid concrete floors can be painted with special lino paint, which comes in a small range of colours. If you just need to keep the dust down, seal the floor with a suitable clear sealer.

• Add a decorative touch to painted or varnished floors by stencilling a pattern around the edge of the room. Protect the paint with a top coat of flooring quality polyurethane varnish, or the same clear finish you have already used on the floor.

• Add a softer touch, or cover ugly carpets with small rugs. You could amass a collection, position one or two at strategic points, or invest in a room-sized carpet.

• Secondhand shops are a good source for larger carpets if you need to buy them cheaply. You can have them cleaned professionally if necessary. You'll also find smaller rugs, but do remember there's a difference between 'secondhand' prices and 'antique' prices.

• Many furnishing shops carry a range of lightweight dhurries and woven rugs from various parts of the world. These are an economical option, but do think about how much they will show the dirt, and how easy they are to clean. Make sure rugs don't slide about: a piece of underlay should help stop them slipping, and will certainly stop them from wearing so quickly.

buying look out for special deals, like free fitting, and get a good quality underlay to improve the look and wear of the carpet, as well as its feel to walk on.

Coir matting is an alternative to carpet. It is durable and neutral, and can make an effective background for rugs and carpets if you want to add them later. It is a bit rough for bedrooms.

Other options for flooring include ceramic tiles, like terracotta and quarry tiles, vinyl and cork tiles, and linoleum and sheet vinyl

floor covering. All have different merits, depending on whether you want a cool, clean finish, a rough country look, or a softer finish that is colourful and durable.

Window-dressing ideas

If you want something extravagant at your windows, but can't afford it, start simply, and add more drapes as you can afford it. A plain white or pastel blind looks good in any room, and you can add curtains, dress curtains ('mock' curtains that are not meant to be closed), frilled or flounced blinds, or lace net curtains, or all of these!

Roller blinds are available in simple kit form – you just have to trim them to fit. You can get them made to measure – or go to the other extreme and make them up from a basic kit, using your own, stiffened fabric.

Austrian, flounced and roman blinds create various effects: all are designed to be drawn up with a series of cords running behind the blind. Special kits are available, which make them easy to sew yourself, or you can have them made to measure – at a price.

Bamboo blinds are a reasonably priced option, but beware – they may not give complete privacy when closed at night.

Venetian blinds now come in a variety of widths in both metal and wood. Wooden venetian blinds are elegant, don't show the dust and provide good insulation when closed. Metal blinds are available in a wide range of colours and in matt, gloss or metallic finishes.

Paper and fabric pleated blinds are available in a wide range of prices.

Curtains are the most popular option. You can get them ready-made, make them yourself using ready-made curtain tapes to form the gathers, or have them made-to-measure. You will have to choose a

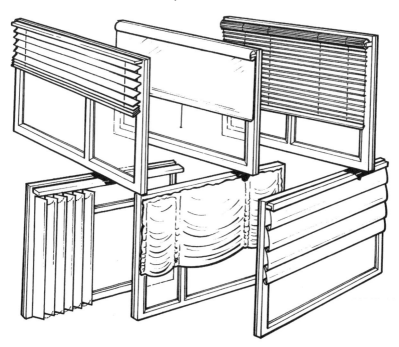

Blinds (from top left): Venetian blind, roller blind, bamboo blind; (bottom row): vertical blind, flounced blind, Roman blind.

track to suit the style and weight of the curtains.

Sheer curtains can be bought ready made, or you can buy lengths of curtaining with ready-made hems and headings, to suit a wide range of windows.

Get the lighting right

A good range of lighting adds atmosphere to any room. You should think about your needs and the function as well as looks of different types of lighting before you buy.

Quick transformations

If you live in rented property, you can always take down hideous curtains and drape something else in their place: Indian cotton bedspreads can be looped and pinned in place over existing tracks, or you can run up some simple curtains using economical fabrics. If you don't want to make gathered headings, you can stitch a simple casing across the top of the curtain and slot it on to a length of bamboo tied to hooks across the top of the window.

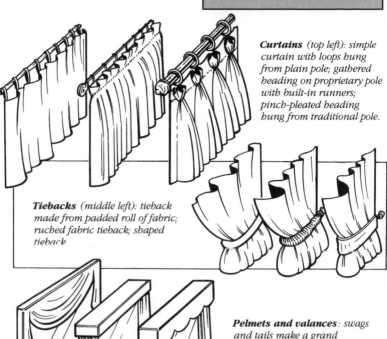

Curtains (top left): simple curtain with loops hung from plain pole; gathered heading on proprietary pole with built-in runners; pinch-pleated heading hung from traditional pole.

Tiebacks (middle left): tieback made from padded roll of fabric; ruched fabric tieback; shaped tieback.

Pelmets and valances: swags and tails make a grand statement; a simple pelmet gives a tidy finish; a shaped pelmet or valance adds extra style.

Options for lighting

If you want to add more than just a few free-standing lamps, you will almost certainly have to have some rewiring work done, so you should plan the lighting and have it installed before you embark on the redecorating of the rooms.

• Almost every room has some form of ceiling lighting. In a great many cases, this is just a hanging pendant. Could you make it more dramatic, with a new fitting or shade? Could you extend the electric flex and loop the light to one side – to hang over a dining table or near a bookcase, for example? Could you change it for a 'rise-and-fall' fitting, to give flexible lighting over the table in a family kitchen? Could you change it for a spotlight fitting? Or do you want to change it altogether, and fit downlighters or recessed eyeball lights at strategic points?

• Table lamps provide warm pools of light. There are traditional ceramic bases with fabric or card shades; brass lamps with brass or glass shades, angled lamps that you can adjust for reading and working, modern halogen lamps, which cast an unexpectedly bright light, and so on.

• Standard lamps bring more general background lighting, and some are also convenient for reading by. Again, there are traditional styles, as well as more modern lamps that almost double as sculptures.

• If you are prepared to do some rewiring or pay to have it done for you, you can add wall lamps: Victorian-style brass or wooden bracket lamps; picture lights to shine over your 'gallery'; simple, semi-circular dishes, to 'wash' light up the wall. Take a good look at the options, and plan positions of pictures and wall-hangings if possible before rewiring.

• There are many types of specialist lamps – to go beneath wall-hung cupboards in the kitchen, to fit around bathroom mirrors, to fit into shelving or alcoves – but again, you must think about the wiring at an early stage.

• You could install 'dimmer' switches which allow you to adjust the strength of the light according to your needs.

Storage plans

A fair proportion of the furniture you buy will be for storage purposes: clothes, hi-fi, video, dinner sets, tea sets, glasses, cutlery, kitchen utensils, cleaning and laundry equipment, medicines, books, ornaments: all these require

---

Ask yourself

• Have you got enough overall lighting, which you can turn on as you walk into the room?
• Do you need light on specific surfaces – for the cooker, sink and worktop in a kitchen; over a dining table; by a mirror, to light your face?
• Do you need adjustable task lighting – for reading and hobbies?
• Do you need extra lighting to bring dark corners to life?
• Are there any special features in the room that you want to illuminate?

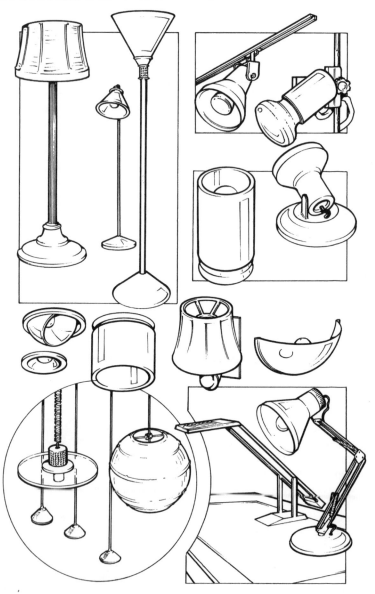

Lighting *(top left): traditional standard lamp with waisted shade gives general lighting plus task lighting; small standard for task lighting or spotlighting; standard uplighter; (top right): spots (these are on tracks) may be fitted to ceilings or walls; two styles of uplighter; (middle left): recessed and ceiling-mounted downlighters; (middle right): traditional and modern ceramic wall-mounted lights; (bottom left): adjustable pendant lamp and pendant lamp with paper shade which casts good overall light; single pendant spots; (bottom right): halogen and Anglepoise task lamps.*

storage space.
• Alcoves are useful storage areas: It is easy to build in your own shelves across alcoves, perhaps with built-in cupboards below, or consider using alcoves for wardrobes in the bedroom. If you want to buy free-standing furniture, make sure that wardrobes and chests will fit into alcoves where appropriate.
• There are many ranges of shelving in kit form that you can fit to suit your needs. Look out for adjustable track-and-bracket shelving, simple wood shelves with matching brackets, and unobtrusive strip supports for wood, melamine or glass shelves.
• Cheaply priced ready-made shelving units can be a bit unstable, so consider screwing them to the wall: you may have to cut away part of the back of the shelving unit to fit around skirting boards.
• Look out for reasonably priced secondhand furniture. It is often sturdier than new furniture at a comparable price. You can always give it a new look with a coat of paint and new handles.
• Improvise a work area: a pair of cupboards or filing cabinets with a length of melamine work surface laid across the top makes a sturdy desk or sewing table.
• Look at the wasted space in your home: could you fit a bookcase, just deep enough for paperbacks, perhaps, in the landing? Could you hang some kitchen cupboards on the wall in the bathroom? Is there room for shelves over the bath? Could you fill an awkward space between kitchen units with shelves

to display casseroles or storage jars?
• Is there a cupboard under the stairs? Could you use it to store hobby equipment, and move the unused suitcases to the loft or bedroom? Could you open up the cupboard and use it for shelves and a study area?

Decorative devices

To create a home, you need more than just furnishings and furniture – you need pictures or plaques to hang on the wall, cushions to soften sofas or armchairs, ornaments to add interest.

It is the individual accessories that will give your home your personal touch. You will have set the style with the decor and furniture you have chosen. Follow the theme through to suit your taste – you can start before you have bought all the major items if you want to.

If the style is pretty and floral, go for fabric accessories, piles of cushions or pillows, pretty floral prints, and fresh plants and flowers. For a country-style kitchen hang bunches of dried flowers, put colourful plates on the wall or dresser, and display earthenware pots and old-fashioned kitchen utensils. In a city-slick living room, go for a few, strongly shaped, minimal accessories – dramatic statues, stark prints on the walls, and serve the drinks from a chrome cocktail shaker!

The way you display your possessions is important. A few carefully chosen accessories can make more impact than lots of ornaments dotted around the room.

Try to group items of different shapes, sizes and textures following a theme: a wooden painted box, an enamelled dish and a wooden statuette, all from the Far East, give an ethnic note; a group of stones and some cacti in brightly coloured pots will bring a hint of Mexico; a bowl of pot pourri and a fabric-lined sewing basket in front of a framed sampler are reminiscent of Victorian tastes. You will find that grouping things in odd-numbers – threes or fives – often looks better than pairs or sets of four.

If you are a collector, display your collection. You could hang a collection of plates made by a particular pottery on the dining room wall; frame stamps, postcards, or even lace collars; arrange old glass bottles on glass shelves fitted across a window; stand a collection of salt-and-pepper sets on specially built narrow shelves in a hallway.

And if you have a constructive hobby, you can display your products: frame photographs you have taken and hang them up the stairwell; make tapestry cushions to scatter on the sofa; hang kites in the corner of a bedroom. Themes and thoughtfulness will add up to a distinctive effect – a stamp of personality in your new home.

INSIDE THE HOME

Time spent learning how your house is put together is never wasted. Once you know how your house is built and how the services work, you will be in a better position to carry out home improvement projects and, perhaps more importantly, know what to do if something should go wrong. Many potential disasters – a burst cold water pipe, for example – can be averted with a bit of forethought and many minor problems are easily solved if you know what to do. Unfortunately, houses, like children, need watching. Knowing what to look for and where to look are the keys to successful maintenance.

House structure

A stroll down any high street will reveal just how many different ways a house can be built. It is usual, however, to find that all the essential structures – walls, roofs, floors and so on – fall into identifiable categories. Roofs, for example, can be separated into pitched roofs and flat roofs. A double pitched roof is a valley roof; a flat roof may be concealed by an A-shaped façade.

The overwhelming majority of houses are made of brick, concrete and timber with either slates or tiles used as a roof covering. There are, of course, exceptions. Some houses are built from mud (cob) or stone and some houses may have thatched roofs but these exceptions are in such a minority that they do not warrant discussion here.

Walls

Walls can be divided into two broad categories – exterior walls that define the shape of a house and interior walls that divide the space inside into rooms. Exterior walls bear some, if not all, of the weight of the roof and floors and they also protect the interior of the house from the weather. As well as serving as room dividers, some internal walls can also be loadbearing.

Exterior walls are usually built of bricks, bricks and concrete blocks, or bricks and wood. They can be either solid or so-called cavity walls. Telling the two types apart is not always easy but the age of a building can often give a clue as to which is which.

Solid brick walls are found in buildings built before the 1920s and they are at least 225mm (9in)

Solid wall (exterior)

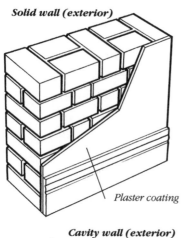

Plaster coating

Cavity wall (exterior)

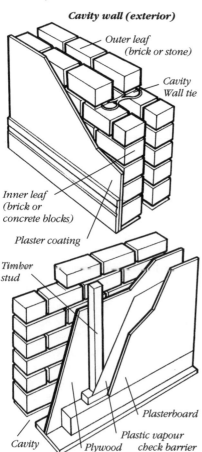

*Outer leaf
(brick or stone)*

*Cavity
Wall tie*

*Inner leaf
(brick or
concrete blocks)*

Plaster coating

*Timber
stud*

Plasterboard

*Plastic vapour
check barrier*

Cavity

Plywood

thick. They are often rendered on the outside with a cement-based mix to make them more weather-resistant, and on the insides are usually covered with two coats of plaster – a thick undercoat and a thin finish coat.

The main disadvantage of solid walls is that they are susceptible to problems caused by penetrating and rising damp – not all solid walls will have had damp-proof courses (DPCs) incorporated into them when they were built. The presence of a DPC can usually be seen by the naked eye – it may take the form of either a thin strip of bituminous felt or plastic inserted into a mortar course just above ground level, a row of filled holes (indicating the injection of a chemical DPC), or a row of impervious engineering bricks.

Cavity walls came into their own after World War I. They comprise two 'leaves' with a gap of 50mm (2in) in between. The outer leaf is invariably made of bricks and the inner leaf of bricks or concrete blocks. In timber-frame houses, which are often found on modern housing estates, the inner leaf is made of a wooden framework that is clad with plywood on one side and plasterboard on the other. It is the inner leaf, regardless of what material it is made from, that is the loadbearing part of the wall; the outer leaf acts as a protective shell and the gap between the two serves as a moisture barrier. The two leaves have either plastic or bituminous DPCs built into them at ground level.

Where bricks or blocks have been used to construct the inner leaf of a cavity wall, the interior surface is usually covered with two layers of plaster; with timber-frame walls, the plasterboard is covered with a single coat.

Interior walls can be either solid or hollow and both sorts can be loadbearing. Hollow walls can usually be detected by tapping with the knuckles or by drilling tiny holes through to the inside. Unfortunately identifying loadbearing walls, which should never be tampered with, is not always easy. However, a wall that is built on top of floorboards is most likely to be a partition wall that is non-loadbearing.

Solid walls are usually made of a single leaf of bricks, lightweight concrete blocks or hollow clay blocks. Such walls are between 125mm (5in) and 150mm (6in) thick and invariably finished with two coats of plaster.

Hollow walls in older houses (built before the 1920s) are usually lath-and-plaster stud walls. These comprise vertical studs (timber posts) to which are nailed narrow strips (laths) of wood which provide a key for a thick layer of coarse plaster. Modern stud walls are faced with plasterboard sheets and finished with a thin coat of plaster.

Stud partition wall (interior)

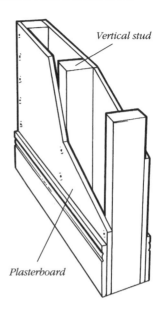

Vertical stud

Plasterboard

Lath and plaster wall (interior)

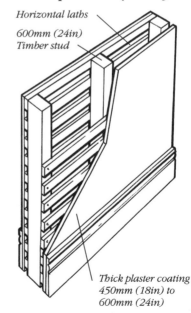

Horizontal laths

600mm (24in) Timber stud

Thick plaster coating 450mm (18in) to 600mm (24in)

WARNING

If you have a timber-frame house do not attempt to attach anything to the inside of the exterior walls as you may pierce the vapour barrier which lies behind the innermost sheet of plasterboard.

Possible problems

Loose fittings on walls usually indicate that an inappropriate fixing method has been used. If you want to fix into a solid wall either use screws (in conjunction with wallplugs) or masonry nails which must be driven into the brickwork or blockwork underneath the plaster. If you want to attach something to a lath-and-plaster wall, drive screws or nails directly into the vertical studs or into the horizontal 'noggins' that space the studs apart. Plasterboard can take the weight of moderately light objects provided special plasterboard fittings are used; heavy items, however, should be attached to the studs inside the wall using either wood screws or nails.

Damp problems on external walls are usually detected by stains or mould growths on the inside. Rising damp, at the base of a wall, indicates that the damp-proof course (DPC) in the wall has been breached or that there is no DPC at all. Clear away anything heaped against the outside of the wall that might be bridging the DPC and if the problem persists, call in professional help. Damp stains high up on a wall could indicate either penetrating damp or condensation. Penetrating damp is most common in solid walls and is usually caused by a leaking gutter or downpipe. If the problem continues after the damp has been dealt with, a coat of waterproofing silicone solution on the outside of the wall will deflect rainwater. Condensation problems are most common in modern houses and the problem is usually cured by increasing ventilation.

Sapped bricks, bricks that have started to flake due to old age or frost damage, should be replaced as soon as possible as serious penetrating damp problems could develop inside the house.

Pointing, the layers of mortar in brickwork, that has started to deteriorate can also lead to damp problems. The only solution is to hire a professional to rake out all the damaged mortar and to replace it with a fresh cement-sand mix.

Plaster that has broken loose from a wall often indicates damp although old age may have something to do with it. Solve the cause of the problem before getting a professional to patch or replaster the wall.

Problem areas (external walls)

Rising and penetrating damp problems are common in older houses that have solid walls. Tackle the cause of any such problems before redecorating the interior.

Roofs

Roofs are either flat or sloping (pitched) and they are wisely considered to be no-go areas by most householders. Ideally they should be checked once a year or so for damage but provided they are well maintained they should last for many years – ten or more for a flat roof, 20 plus for a pitched roof.

Pitched roofs have a series of triangular timber supports (rafters) which are joined together by horizontal battens. This framework

Problem areas (external walls)
Rising and penetrating damp problems are common in older houses that have solid walls. Tackle the cause of any such problems before redecorating the interior.

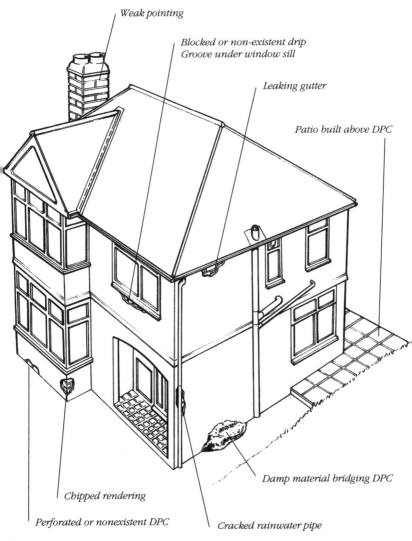

Weak pointing

Blocked or non-existent drip Groove under window sill

Leaking gutter

Patio built above DPC

Chipped rendering

Perforated or nonexistent DPC

Cracked rainwater pipe

Damp material bridging DPC

rests on timber wall plates sited on top of the exterior walls and on central loadbearing walls if there are any. The frames can be braced in a number of different ways – with horizontal 'purlins', with a ridgeboard, or with an arrangement of struts. A layer of bituminous roofing felt is usually sandwiched between the battens and the triangular frames for added protection against damp.

Pitched roofs are usually covered with tiles or slates. Tiles are either plain (flat) or interlocking and are held on to the roof by 'nibs' on the underside, which hook over the battens. To make sure the tiles are held securely, every third or fourth row is usually nailed to the underlying battens as well. Slates are nailed individually to battens as they do not have any nibs on the underside.

The top of a pitched roof is capped with ridge tiles, which are held in place with mortar, and flashing, which seals the roof where it buts against walls. Strips of bituminous felt, zinc and plain mortar are used as flashing, but by far the best material is lead.

Flat roofs should in fact slope slightly to allow rainwater to drain away. The supporting structure consists of a series of parallel joists which are topped with sheets of plywood or chipboard (decking). The decking is covered with at least three layers of roofing felt – the first layer is nailed down and the subsequent ones are usually bonded with hot bitumen. The top layer of felt is often covered with stone chippings, which reflect the sun's rays and prevent the felt from blistering in very hot weather.

Chimney stacks are sealed against the roof with flashing and the pots on top are held in place with mortar (flaunching), which is sloped for drainage. Chimneys that are no longer used are often capped with a half-round tile or something similar to prevent water from entering the flue.

Possible problems

Damaged tiles or slates should be replaced by a roofing specialist as soon as possible or else rainwater will cause havoc inside the house.

Condensation inside the roofspace (loft or attic) can cause considerable damage if it is left to accumulate. Check that insulation material is not blocking up the eaves where there should be a gap and make sure that any air vents are open.

Condensation in blocked-off chimney flues is not unheard of. This will show up as damp stains on the chimney breast and the likelihood is that the flue has been completely sealed up. The solution is to have a half-round tile (or something similar) installed at the top and a ventilator grille installed at the bottom.

Weak roofing frames can often be spotted from the outside – a slightly bowed roof indicates that all is not well. The chances are that the framework was originally designed to take slates and is currently supporting tiles, which are far heavier. Seek expert advice.

Damaged ridge tiles and damaged flashing should be replaced as soon as possible. Patching ridge tiles or flashing is

Roof structure

Slates and tiles on pitched roofs are fixed to horizontal battens, which are supported by rafters. Flashing is used to seal edges where they butt against walls.

Flaunching

Flashing

Roofing felt

Rafters

Slates nailed to battens

Battens

Ridge tiles

Metal valley

Flashing

Flat roof covered with three layers of bituminous felt, topped with stone chippings

Capping the chimney

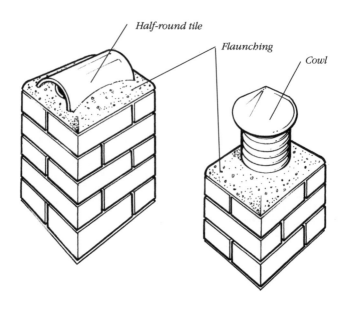

Half-round tile

Flaunching

Cowl

Airbrick

Unused fireplace
To prevent condensation when a fireplace is blocked off, an airbrick or ventilator must be incorporated into the brickwork or panelling. The top of the chimney should be capped with a half-round tile or special cowl.

Loft insulation

Heat will be conserved inside the house if the loft is well insulated. Lag pipes at the top and sides of the cold water storage cistern at the same time. Leave gaps at the eaves to encourage an air flow and be sure to wear gloves and a face mask if you do the job yourself.

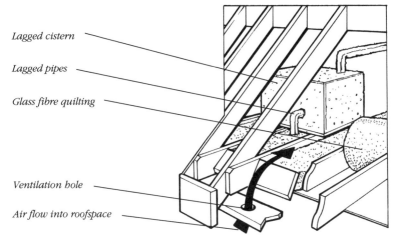

Lagged cistern

Lagged pipes

Glass fibre quilting

Ventilation hole

Air flow into roofspace

seldom satisfactory and the expense of a complete overhaul is usually more worthwhile.

Leaking flat roofs indicate that the felt has blistered and cracked. The only completely satisfactory answer is to have all the felt replaced as soon as possible, although temporary repairs can be effected with a rubber solution. Check the condition of the roof regularly and make sure that the chippings are evenly spread over the surface.

Heat loss through the roof can be dramatically reduced by laying down insulation material between the joists. If you do this job yourself using either polystyrene beads or glass fibre matting, wear a face mask and gloves. Do not lay insulation underneath the cold water storage cistern or under the boiler's header tank. Do, however, lag the sides and top of the cistern

and any exposed pipework with insulation material.

Floors and ceilings

There are two kinds of floor. Suspended timber floors are found in houses of all ages, and solid floors are found in basements and at ground level in modern or recently converted houses.

Suspended timber floors comprise 100 x 50mm (4 x 2in) wooden joists that support floorboards or flooring-grade chipboard sheets nailed on top. At ground level, the ends of the joists are either embedded into the exterior walls or are supported by squat 'sleeper' walls sited just inside the exterior walls. Upper storey joists can either be built into the exterior walls or can be slotted into steel joist hangers, which are fixed into the brickwork. Long joists are given extra support at ground level by additional sleeper walls and in upper storeys by loadbearing walls.

Ground level suspended timber floors must be well ventilated to prevent damp, so perforated air bricks, metal grilles or special ducts are incorporated into the exterior walls to ensure a continuous flow of air underneath the joists.

Solid floors are usually only found at basement or ground level although they sometimes form the upper storeys of modern houses and flats. Solid floors at ground level have several layers. The base layer consists of compacted hardcore laid over the earth. A concrete slab is laid over the hardcore and this is covered with a damp-proof membrane (DPM). The final layer, laid on top of the DPM, is a level screed of sand and cement.

Ceilings in modern houses usually consist of sheets of plasterboard nailed to the underside of the flooring joists or, at the top storey, to the underside of the roofing joists. The plasterboard sheets are often covered with a thin coat of plaster to make them uniformly smooth. In older houses, lath-and-plaster (see Interior walls section) ceilings are common.

Possible problems

Draughts whistling up through bare floorboards at ground floor level can be a nuisance as well as a drain on heating bills. The solution is NOT to block up air vents on the outside of the house; it is infinitely better to tackle the problem inside. You could either have the

floorboards relaid so that there are no gaps between them or else you could fill the gaps with slivers of wood. A fitted carpet will also put paid to the trouble.

Creaking floorboards are common in older houses where the fixings have worked loose. The problem can usually be solved by screwing – a better option than renailing – the offending boards to the joists.

Condensation is common on solid floors in kitchens and bathrooms where steam is created. Ventilating the room usually solves the problem or you could try turning up the background heating (warm air can hold more moisture than cold air). It may also be worth changing the floor covering from, say, ceramic tiles to carpet or cork tiles. Check that dampness on the floor is indeed condensation by bedding a clear glass in a ring of putty on the floor: moisture on the outside of the glass indicates condensation, moisture on the inside indicates a more sinister problem like rising damp.

Cracks in ceilings are most common in old houses where lath-and-plaster has been used. Small cracks can be patched with cellulose filler but large cracks caused by the plaster breaking away from the laths usually requires large scale remedial work, which is best left to an expert.

Hairline cracks are common in plasterboard ceilings where two sheets have shrunk and parted. Such cracks can be filled and painted. If plaster has 'popped' off plasterboard nails, cover the nail heads with filler and paint.

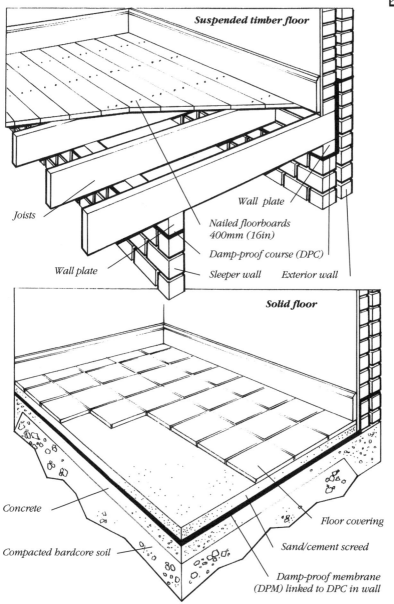

Suspended timber floor

Joists

Wall plate

Nailed floorboards
400mm (16in)

Damp-proof course (DPC)

Wall plate · Sleeper wall · Exterior wall

Solid floor

Concrete

Compacted hardcore soil

Floor covering

Sand/cement screed

Damp-proof membrane
(DPM) linked to DPC in wall

Types of floor

At ground level, suspended timber floors rest on wall plates that are built into the exterior walls or are supported on shallow sleeper walls; at higher levels the joists are either built into loadbearing walls or are supported by joist hangers. Solid floors are usually only found at ground or basement level.

Sash window

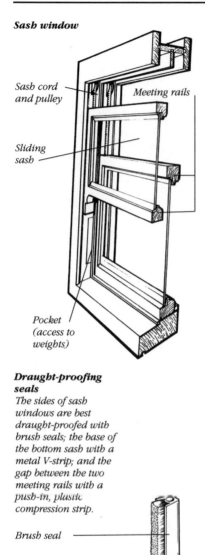

Sash cord and pulley

Meeting rails

Sliding sash

Pocket (access to weights)

Draught-proofing seals

The sides of sash windows are best draught-proofed with brush seals; the base of the bottom sash with a metal V-strip; and the gap between the two meeting rails with a push-in, plastic compression strip.

Brush seal

Metal V-strip

Push-in compression seal

Windows

All windows come in rigid frames that are slotted into openings and held in place with brackets (lugs) or screws. The frames are sealed against the weather with beads of mastic or mortar. Where they are installed in a wall, a lintel of concrete or wood stretches across the top of the opening and this takes the weight of the wall above. The base of the opening sometimes includes a concrete or wooden sub-sill.

Glass in old wood and metal windows is held in place by nails (sprigs) or clips, which are covered with a sealing bead of putty. Many of the latest plastic and aluminium windows, however, dispense with sprigs, clips and putty altogether and the panes are fixed with sealing strips of plastic or rubber. Leaded lights – tiny panes of glass held in a framework of lead – are a '40s revival of Tudor style.

Casement and sash windows remain the most common types, although pivot windows are popular in loft conversions. Wooden windows in particular need regular checking for chipped paint, which could let in water. It is also worth keeping an eye on seals around the edges to check that they are intact.

Casement windows have casements (the parts that open and close) mounted on hinges either at the top or at the bottom. They can be made from wood, steel, aluminium and plastic and many modern types have sealed, double-glazed panels (primary double glazing).

Sash windows have two sashes

that slide up and down (or in some modern windows, from side to side) within the frame. The sashes in traditional windows are balanced by weights, which are suspended on cords inside the sides of the frame. Modern sash windows, however, are usually balanced by springs to the sides.

Possible problems

Condensation on windows is common in kitchens and bathrooms. Double glazing or improved ventilation will cure the problem (consider a ventilator or extractor fan built into the window itself) but raising the background temperature of the room will also help.

If moisture condenses in the gap between panes of a double glazed window, try placing a tray of moisture-absorbing crystals in the middle (this is only practicable where secondary double glazing has been installed).

Sticking sashes are usually caused by an excess of paint, which has stuck them to the frame. Tape up the panes to prevent them from shattering and then try tapping a block of wood held against the side of the offending sash with a mallet. This should break the sashes free.

Broken sash cords are a common problem with old windows. The only access to the weights is via pockets at the sides of the frame and the only way to get to the pockets is to partially dismantle the window – a job for someone who knows what they are doing.

Damaged sills (or sub-sills), especially wooden ones, should be

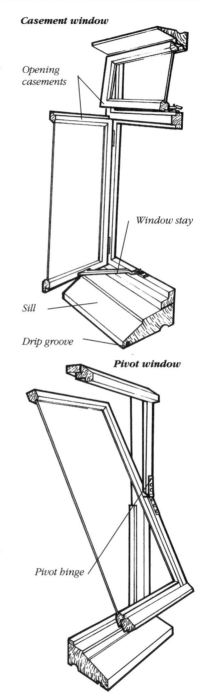

Casement window

Opening casements

Window stay

Sill

Drip groove

Pivot window

Pivot hinge

dealt with immediately before rot sets. It is possible to patch minor damage with exterior grade filler and paint but badly rotten sills are best replaced. Sills and sub-sills should have grooves cut along the undersides. These prevent water from running back to the wall, and if they get blocked up damp and rot problems can follow. Inspect them regularly.

Broken panes are best replaced by a glazier – handling glass can be dangerous and kneading putty into rebates is surprisingly tricky. It may be left up to you to paint over the putty (it will deteriorate unless painted) when it has hardened after two or three weeks.

Heat loss can be quite considerable through large windows and this can be prevented by installing secondary double glazing. Call in an expert for a quotation.

Noise from road or air traffic is only partially reduced by standard double glazing. If the problem is severe, get specialist advice before you make a move.

Draughts are particularly common with old sash windows, which tend to rattle at the same time. Fit brush draught excluders up the sides of the frame against the sashes; these will also reduce rattling. Special draught excluders can also be slotted into the gap between the sashes when closed.

Security locks fitted to windows are a wise precaution. There are any number of locks on the market but not all of them fit all windows. The Crime Prevention Officer from your local police station will be able to give you free, unbiased advice.

Window locks
Dual-screw bolts offer good security for sash windows and mortise bolts for either casement or pivot windows. Both types are operated with a special key.

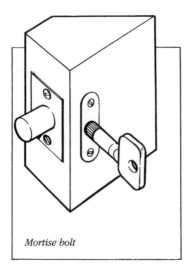

Mortise bolt

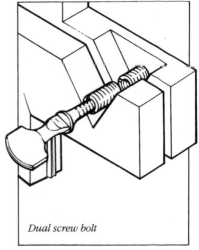

Dual screw bolt

INSIDE THE HOME

Doors

Doors can be divided into two main categories – panel doors and flush doors. Both types come in exterior and interior grades and both are hung in frames on hinges. Exterior doors and their frames need regular maintenance, particularly if they are painted softwood, and it is well worth touching up apparently minor chips and cracks before moisture can cause any damage.

Panel doors consist of two side pieces (stiles), a central muntin, and several horizontal rails. Housed between these elements are panels of solid timber, plywood or glass. Panel doors are made from hardwood or softwood and they are usually heavier and stronger than their flush counterparts.

Flush doors comprise a simple rectangular frame faced with plywood or hardboard. The inside is usually braced with horizontal rails and can be filled with packing.

Other types of door include aluminium doors, sliding doors and French windows. Of these, sliding doors are unique in that they run on rollers set into tracks top and bottom.

Possible problems

Sticking doors usually catch at the side or bottom, either because they have absorbed moisture and swollen up, or because they have had one too many coats of paint. The solution is to plane or sand down the offending edge until it no longer catches. If the problem is with a softwood external door, the shaved area must be repainted or else the problem will get worse.

Types of door

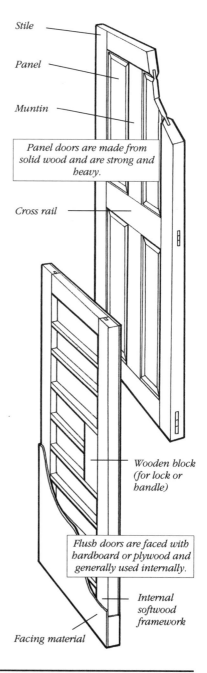

Stile

Panel

Muntin

Panel doors are made from solid wood and are strong and heavy.

Cross rail

Flush doors are faced with hardboard or plywood and generally used internally.

Wooden block (for lock or handle)

Internal softwood framework

Facing material

Dropped doors indicate that the hinges have worked loose. Tighten up screws and if the problem persists, call in a carpenter – the hinges may have to be repositioned or replaced.

Draughts under and around old front and back doors are common. The remedy is to fit draught excluders, of which there are many types. Draughts through a letterbox can be prevented by fitting a special letterbox draught excluder.

Damp seeping underneath an external door usually indicates the absence of a weatherboard along the bottom outside edge. A weatherboard has a built-in drip strip that drains water beyond the door sill.

Security locks are to be highly recommended on external doors – five lever mortise deadlocks are the best option. For free advice, you can contact the Crime Prevention Officer at your local police station.

Staircases

The commonest sort of staircase is the 'tread and riser' type, although 'open' staircases are found in a few new houses. Spiral staircases are familiar in public buildings, but they are only rarely incorporated into private properties.

Tread and riser staircases have two parallel pieces of timber (strings) running up each side, and to these are fixed the treads and risers. The string that lies against the wall is always closed (i.e. its top and bottom edges are parallel) and the treads and risers are slotted, wedged and glued into grooves cut into one side. The other string can either be closed or

open (ie. with a zig-zag top profile). With an open string the treads lie on the horizontal edges and the risers are fixed to the vertical edges.

Newel posts at the top and bottom of each flight support the handrail. The balustrade of most staircases consists of vertical balusters, which are attached to the underside of the handrail and either to treads or to the top of a closed string.

Possible problems

Creaking treads are common with old staircases and the problem can usually be solved from underneath. Remove any of the wedges that secure the treads and risers, reglue them with PVA adhesive and tap them back with a hammer. You may find triangular blocks joining the risers and treads together. Again, reglue any that have worked loose.

Weak or broken balusters should be replaced as soon as possible as a faulty balustrade could be dangerous. This job is best left to a

Storage space is often provided by enclosing the area below the stairs.

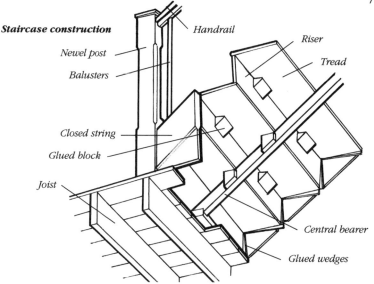

Staircase construction

Handrail

Newel post

Balusters

Riser

Tread

Closed string

Glued block

Joist

Central bearer

Glued wedges

joiner. Similarly, a wobbly newel post or a frail handrail should be checked by an expert.

Services

Services are taken for granted by the average householder and few people pay them much attention until something goes wrong. Many mishaps with one or other of the service supplies – burst pipes, or blown fuses for example – can be avoided or easily rectified, but more serious or persistent problems are best dealt with by qualified engineers.

Electricity

Electricity enters your home, usually underground, via a mains service cable. This cable runs to a 'sealed unit', which is connected to the meter by two cables ('tails'). If your system has been adapted to use cheap rate electricity for such things as night storage radiators, a

sealed time switch will be incorporated into the wiring between the service fuse and the meter. Up to and including the meter the installation is the property of the electricity board, thereafter it is the property of the householder. Modern electricity installations should last for 20 years or more and they rarely need maintenance. Old circuits, however, can be extremely dangerous and should be replaced immediately.

Fuses are deliberately weak links in the wiring system. If a fault should develop in a circuit, or if it is overloaded, the fuse will 'blow' and cut off the supply. Circuit fuses are found in the consumer unit ('fuse box'), which is connected to the meter by a pair of cables. Also mounted on the consumer unit is the mains switch, which can be thrown to cut off the supply to all the circuits. A typical consumer unit will carry two lighting circuits (upstairs and downstairs), two power circuits (for electrical sockets) and possibly several separate circuits for such things as the cooker and immersion heater. Circuit fuses are normally either thin wires or cartridges held in colour-coded fuse carriers. However, some modern consumer units carry miniature circuit breakers (MCBs), which are not strictly speaking fuses at all but work on the same principle and cut off a circuit if it is overloaded.

Socket plugs also carry cartridge fuses as a first line of defence should an appliance develop a fault. Some appliances such as extractor fans and storage heaters remain put in one place and these are often directly connected to the mains by fused connection units (FCUs), which are wall-mounted and contain fuses inside them.

Flex and cable are two terms that are often confused. Flex, short for flexible cord, is used to connect appliances to their plugs or FCUs. The wires inside flex consist of thin strands of copper twisted into 'cores'. These cores are sheathed in colour-coded insulation: brown for the live wire, blue for neutral and green-and-yellow for earth. Cable is more rigid than flex and is used for the actual wiring of the house. It usually contains solid copper cores that are coded red for live and black for neutral. The earth wire is bare inside the outer sheath but is usually covered with a green/yellow sleeve where it is connected to a terminal.

Possible problems

Blown fuses usually indicate that all is not well and the cause should be dealt with before the fuse is renewed. Check, for example, that a power socket is not being abused by having too many appliances plugged into it by way of adaptors. To replace a fuse in a consumer unit, turn off the mains switch and check the various fuse holders. Holders have a fuse rating (5, 15, 20, 30 or 45 amp) stamped on them or else they are colour-coded (white – 5 amp, blue – 15 amp, yellow – 20 amp, red – 30 amp, green – 45 amp). Replace the burnt-out fuse with appropriate fuse wire or with a new cartridge, re-insert the holder and turn the supply back on. With MCBs, a button or switch is thrown when a circuit is faulty or overloaded. All that needs to be done is to flick the switch back on, or to press the button back in.

WARNING

Electricity is potentially lethal and on no account should anybody tamper with electric circuits or appliances unless they are qualified to do so. Never take risks and ALWAYS turn off the supply at the consumer unit if you are repairing a blown fuse. Mains electricity can burn and kill.

Old circuits should be inspected by a qualified engineer as they may need replacing. If you have a dilapidated fuse board, have it checked. Rubber-sheathed cables and sockets that take round pin plugs also indicate old wiring, which should be renewed immediately.

When replacing a plug fuse, always use a fuse appropriate to the power output of the appliance. 13 and 3 amp fuses are the most common ratings – 13 amp fuses should be used for appliances with a power output of 700 watts or more.

Electricity bills can be cut if you have an immersion heater or storage radiators. Contact your Electricity Board – you may be able to run such items off cheap-rate electricity.

The fuse board

Up to and including the meter, the installation is the property of the Electricity Board; all the wiring from the consumer unit onwards is the responsibility of the consumer. Consumer units vary considerably in design – some have wire fuses, others carry cartridge fuses, and the very latest types have miniature circuit breakers (MCBs) which are easily reset. If your installation looks old, have it checked by a qualified electrician.

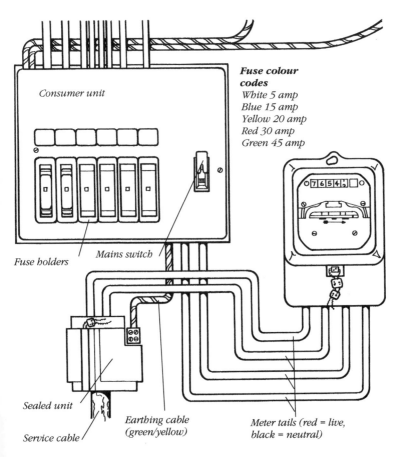

Consumer unit

Fuse colour codes
White 5 amp
Blue 15 amp
Yellow 20 amp
Red 30 amp
Green 45 amp

Fuse holders *Mains switch*

Sealed unit

Service cable

Earthing cable (green/yellow)

Meter tails (red = live, black = neutral)

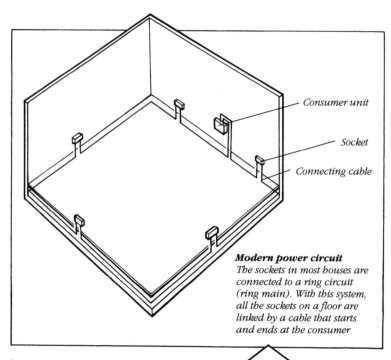

Modern power circuit
The sockets in most houses are connected to a ring circuit (ring main). With this system, all the sockets on a floor are linked by a cable that starts and ends at the consumer

Consumer unit

Socket

Connecting cable

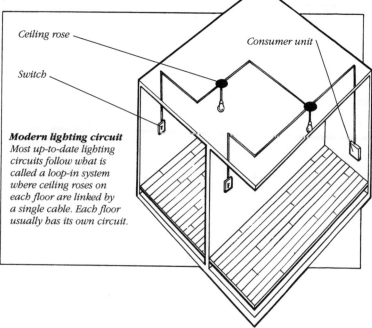

Ceiling rose

Switch

Consumer unit

Modern lighting circuit
Most up-to-date lighting circuits follow what is called a loop-in system where ceiling roses on each floor are linked by a single cable. Each floor usually has its own circuit.

Wiring a plug

It is important to connect flex cores to the right terminals in a plug. Do not strip the colour-coded sheathing back more than is absolutely necessary as a stray strand of copper could cause a short-circuit within the plug. Always secure the flex in the plug by tightening the cord clamp screws and check that a fuse of the correct rating is fitted. 3 amp (red) and 13 amp (brown) fuses are the most commonly recommended ratings – 13 amp fuses should be fitted where an appliance has a power output greater than 700 watts. 5 amp fuses are occasionally recommended for certain appliances such as computers.

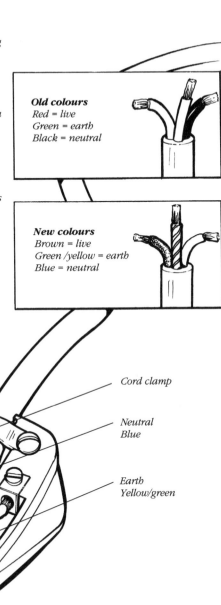

Old colours
Red = live
Green = earth
Black = neutral

New colours
Brown = live
Green /yellow = earth
Blue = neutral

Live
Brown

Fuse

Cord clamp

Neutral
Blue

Earth
Yellow/green

Water

Water enters your house, under pressure, via an underground service pipe. At some point along this pipe, most usually just outside the boundary to the property, there is the water company's stopcock, which can be used to shut off the entire supply. All the pipework after the water authority's stopcock, is the householder's responsibility. Very old systems have lead pipework and this should be replaced with copper tubes by a qualified plumber. New systems seldom give any trouble, although tap washers and such may have to be renewed every so often. It makes sense to insulate all exposed pipework, especially in the roofspace, and hot water cylinders and cisterns should also be lagged. Just in case a disaster should occur, it is worth knowing where you can turn off the supply (see valves in next column).

Cold water systems have two common layouts. In most properties the service pipe enters the house in the kitchen or under the stairs and it is then called the rising main. In the majority of houses the rising main leads directly to the cold water storage cistern in the roofspace and only one tap, usually the kitchen cold tap, is connected to it. This kind of layout is called an indirect system. At the base of the cistern there are two draw-off pipes – one supplies all the cold water taps and WCs in the house and the other feeds the hot water cylinder. With a so-called direct system, all the cold taps and WCs are connected to the rising main and there is just one draw-off pipe at the cistern for the hot water cylinder.

Hot water systems also come in two common forms. With an indirect hot water system, there is a coiled tube (heat exchanger) inside the hot water cylinder and water inside this coil is heated by the boiler; the heat exchanger therefore warms up the water stored in the cylinder. With a direct system, there is no coiled tube and the hot water is heated directly by the boiler. It is common to find immersion heaters in both types of cylinder and these are usually only used as a backup in case of boiler failure. If you do not have a boiler at all, then the water in your cylinder will be heated by an immersion element only.

A vent pipe at the top of the hot water cylinder is a safety device and ducts steam and hot air back to the cold water cistern in the roofspace. A branch off the vent pipe supplies all the hot taps in the house.

Valves on plumbing systems come in various shapes and allow all or part of a system to be isolated. Stopcocks (stop valves) are fitted to pipes that contain water under mains pressure. One is always fitted to the rising main, usually below the branch for the kitchen cold tap. Gate valves are fitted to pipes where the water is not under mains pressure. A common place to find them is on the draw-off pipes at the base of cold water storage cisterns.

Possible problems

Hot water bills can be dramatically reduced by fitting an insulating

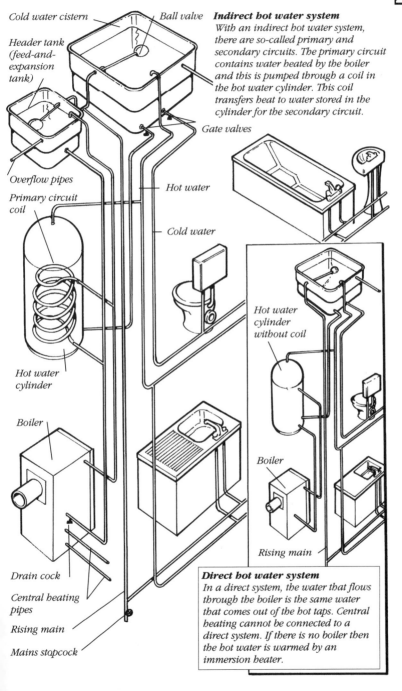

Cold water cistern

Ball valve

Header tank (feed-and-expansion tank)

Indirect hot water system
With an indirect hot water system, there are so-called primary and secondary circuits. The primary circuit contains water heated by the boiler and this is pumped through a coil in the hot water cylinder. This coil transfers heat to water stored in the cylinder for the secondary circuit.

Gate valves

Overflow pipes

Primary circuit coil

Hot water

Cold water

Hot water cylinder without coil

Hot water cylinder

Boiler

Boiler

Central heating pipes

Rising main

Drain cock

Central heating pipes

Rising main

Mains stopcock

Direct hot water system
In a direct system, the water that flows through the boiler is the same water that comes out of the hot taps. Central heating cannot be connected to a direct system. If there is no boiler then the hot water is warmed by an immersion heater.

Insulation

By insulating pipes, cylinders and cisterns, heat can be conserved and problems avoided in cold weather.

Cylinder jacket

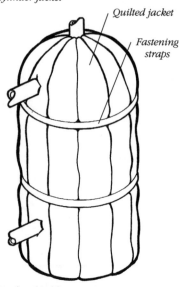

Quilted jacket

Fastening straps

Insulated cold water cistern

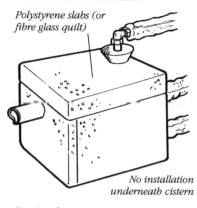

Polystyrene slabs (or fibre glass quilt)

No installation underneath cistern

Pipe insulation

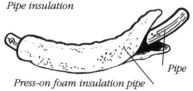

Pipe

Press-on foam insulation pipe

jacket around the hot water cylinder.

Bursts in cold pipes can often be prevented by insulating all exposed pipes with inexpensive foam sheathing. The cold water storage cistern should also be lagged (special kits are available). Do not lay insulation directly underneath the the cistern.

It is as well to have an emergency repair kit handy just in case a pipe does burst in freezing weather (inexpensive kits are available). If a pipe does burst, turn off the water supply and switch off the boiler. Seal the burst temporarily with a kit and get a plumber to make a permanent repair as soon as possible.

A dripping tap usually means that the washer inside has perished. Replacing a washer is not especially difficult, but the water supply to the tap may have to be temporarily turned off and it is best to get a plumber to do the job unless you know what you are doing.

Noisy systems are caused either by the rush of water through a series of bends in the pipework, or else by the expansion and contraction of hot water pipes. Clip loose pipes to walls or exposed joists; if the noise emanates from under floorboards, call in a builder or plumber. Water hammer, a particularly loud noise, is caused by a faulty ballvalve in the roofspace – get a plumber to replace it.

Drainage

Drainage water is divided into three categories – waste water

Two-pipe drainage system

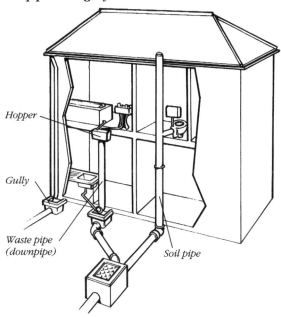

With this system, soil and waste water are kept apart until they reach the inspection chamber. The soil and waste pipes are mounted externally.

Hopper

Gully

Waste pipe (downpipe)

Soil pipe

One-pipe drainage system

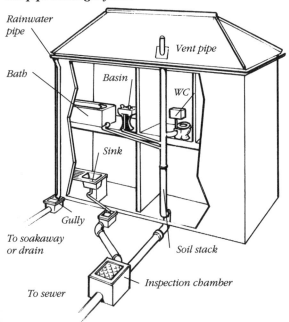

Rainwater pipe

Vent pipe

Bath

Basin

WC

Sink

Gully

To soakaway or drain

Soil stack

To sewer

Inspection chamber

In this system, waste from baths and basins and soil water from WCs flow into one soil stack that is often incorporated inside the house. Waste water from the kitchen is often piped to a separate gully.

(from basins, baths and sinks), soil water (from WCs), and rainwater. In the vast majority of cases, waste and soil water are diverted into a public sewerage system and rainwater is either ducted to soakaways or to a public drain. In a few cases septic tanks (miniature sewage works) or cesspools (underground tanks) receive foul water.

Modern drainage systems employ plastic, corrosion-free pipes and gutters that last almost indefinitely. Old systems, however, often have downpipes and gutters made from cast iron, which is both heavy and fragile, and such systems may need considerable maintenance. There are two common drainage layouts – the two-pipe system and the single stack system.

Two-pipe systems keep waste and soil water apart. A soil pipe outside the house receives water from WCs and this leads straight to an inspection chamber and from there the water is piped to the mains sewer. Waste water pipes from upstairs basins and baths pass through the exterior wall to a hopper head at the top of a waste pipe. This waste pipe empties into a gully, which often receives water from the kitchen sink as well.

Single stack systems have just one soil pipe (stack) which receives both waste and soil water. Kitchen sink water, however, is often ducted to a separate gully.

Possible problems

Gutters and rainwater pipes may be blocked by leaves. The simple answer is to retrieve the debris, but this is best left to a builder who is used to climbing a ladder.

A blocked waste water trap underneath a bath, basin or sink is usually easily put to rights. Plastic traps can simply be unscrewed but make sure that you place a bucket underneath first. With old-fashioned U-traps, an 'eye' at the bottom has to be unscrewed.

Blocked WC traps can usually be

Types of water trap
Traps prevent odours from the drains entering the house. WC traps are built in but basins, baths and sinks all have traps that can be dismantled in case there is a blockage.

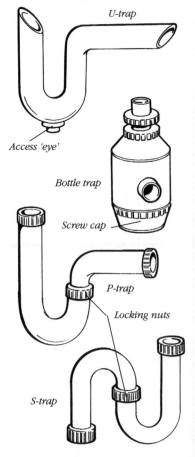

U-trap

Access 'eye'

Bottle trap

Screw cap

P-trap

Locking nuts

S-trap

cleared by using a special plunger which should be moved up and down over the entrance to the trap.

Gas

The underground supply pipe that feeds gas to your house terminates at the meter – everything beyond the meter belongs to the householder. A pipe from the

Possible problems

A smell of gas indicates a leak in the system or possibly that a pilot light or burner has gone out. Act swiftly. Check burners and pilot lights (including the one in the boiler) and open windows to allow the gas to escape. If a pilot light has gone out, relight it once the air is clear and check that it stays

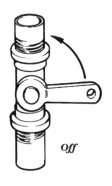   

Off   *On*

Mains gas tap
Your mains gas tap will be sited adjacent to the gas meter. Turn it off at the slightest hint of escaping gas and call the Gas Board.

meter ducts gas to various appliances around the house – such as cooker, boiler or gas fire – and on this pipe, usually adjacent to the meter, there is the mains gas tap, which can be used to cut off the supply if needs be. Gas installations require little maintenance as a rule, but appliances may need frequent cleaning or servicing to keep them operating efficiently. If any problems do develop with a gas appliance, or indeed with the pipework, do not attempt to deal with it yourself. Turn off the supply and call in a gas engineer or a specialist plumber.

alight. If you suspect a leak follow this procedure:
• extinguish cigarettes and naked flames;
• do NOT turn on any electrical switches (a spark could ignite the gas);
• turn off the gas supply at the meter;
• open doors and windows;
• call the gas emergency service (listed under Gas in the telephone directory).

An inadequate flow of gas could mean a number of things such as a damaged pipe or a faulty burner. Do not tackle the problem yourself but call in a plumber.

Alternative fuels

A number of alternative fuels to gas are used to power boilers, cookers and background heaters. All of them have advantages and disadvantages and the appliances for some may need considerable maintenance.

Oil is the major fuel for powering central heating boilers and cookers in rural areas. It is still relatively inexpensive but the main disadvantage of an oil-fired system is that the oil has to be stored in a large tank outside the house. Oil-fired appliances also need regular servicing.

Bottled gas or liquid petroleum gas (LPG) is most commonly used to fuel portable fires, which are extremely efficient. LPG, stored in a large tank outside the house, can also be used as an alternative to mains gas or oil. The main disadvantage of bottled gas is that it is relatively expensive.

Paraffin heaters are usually kept as a backup in case of a power or gas failure. The snags with these are that they are fiddly to use and they produce an enormous amount of water, which can lead to severe condensation problems.

Solid fuels such as coal and wood can be used with certain open fires, heaters, cookers and boilers. One of the disadvantages of solid fuel appliances is that they have to be perpetually stoked up or the fire will go out. Another is that fuel has to be stored somewhere, usually in considerable quantities. Furthermore, chimneys and flues need regular cleaning. In smokeless zones, special fuel has to be used and the price of this can sometimes prove prohibitive.

Telephone

Your telephone line enters the house by an overhead or underground cable and terminates at a master socket or junction box mounted on a wall. This installation remains the property of the telephone company and should not be tampered with. Until recently all equipment that used the telephone line had to be rented from the company but it is now possible to buy telephones and use them with the system provided they carry a green seal of approval.

A modern master socket allows new-style telephones to be plugged in and also enables you to add extension sockets all over the house (DIY extension kits are available). Old-style, lozenge-shaped terminal boxes can easily be replaced by the telephone company if you wish to use plug-in telephones or add extensions.

Telephone extensions
Modern telephone installations have a master socket to which a series of extensions can be added.

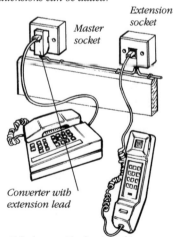

Extension socket

Master socket

Converter with extension lead

Telephone with plug-in cable

Two-pipe central heating
Hot water from the boiler is pumped around circuits that feed radiators. Cool water returns to the boiler and is reheated. The feed-and-expansion tank in the roofspace keeps the system permanently topped up.

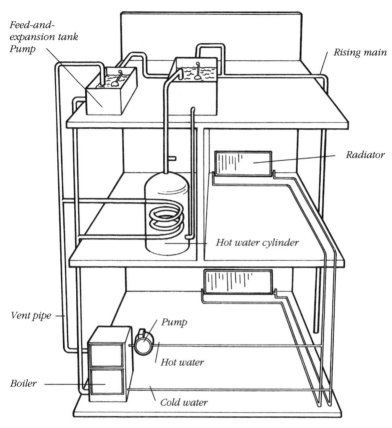

Feed-and-expansion tank
Pump
Rising main
Radiator
Hot water cylinder
Vent pipe
Pump
Hot water
Boiler
Cold water

Central heating systems

By far the commonest type of central heating is termed 'wet', meaning that radiators are heated by water. Other systems include storage heaters and ducted hot air. Storage radiators run on cheap-rate electricity and are a realistic option if a wet central heating system is not viable, but hot air systems are usually only found in blocks of flats.

Wet central heating in most modern installations has a two-pipe system. Water, heated by the boiler, is forced around circuits of pipes by an electric pump. Radiators or convector heaters are connected to these circuits by small-bore pipes that are usually hidden beneath floorboards. The boiler also heats water in the hot water cylinder and is kept permanently topped up by a 'feed-and-expansion' (header) tank in the roofspace.

Boilers of all types need regular servicing to keep them working efficiently but radiators and the central heating system itself rarely need to be drained down. Even if the system is not used for years, it should not be drained.

Timers, thermostats and valves are all used to control a wet central heating system. Nearly all systems have a timer, which can be preset to turn the boiler and pump off when central heating is not needed, during the night for example. Thermostats control the temperature of the system. A room thermostat can be set to a specific temperature and when the background heat rises above the preset figure, the boiler, pump or a special motorized valve in the system is turned off; when the temperature drops, the system is turned back on again. Room thermostats can be used to control the heat in individual rooms or in whole areas.

The water in the cylinder does not normally need to be as hot as the water flowing through the radiators. A thermostat clamped to the side of the cylinder will prevent water inside from getting unnecessarily hot by controlling a valve that controls the flow of water through the heating coil.

The water that flows through individual radiators is controlled by two valves. The valve that controls the inflow of water can be turned manually to cut off the water supply; the other valve (lockshield valve) controls the outflow and can only be operated with a spanner. Thermostatic radiator valves (TRVs) can be fitted instead of the standard manual valve and these control the temperature of each individual radiator.

Possible problems

Excessive heating bills can often be cut by draught-proofing the house. However, further reductions can be made by incorporating timers and thermostats into the system. Consult a heating specialist for advice.

Leaking radiators or joints in pipework are best left to a plumber who knows what he is doing.

Cold radiators can be caused by a number of different faults. If all the radiators are cold, the cause could be a broken pump, an airlock in the pipework, or a faulty thermostat. It is best to get any of these problems sorted out by a plumber. If some radiators are hot whilst others remain just warm, the system may need to be 'balanced'. This involves altering the outflow through the radiators by adjusting the lockshield valves. Again, let a specialist deal with the problem. If, however, just one radiator is cold or is hot at the bottom only, the chances are that it is only partially filled with water and needs 'bleeding'.

To bleed a radiator you will need a special radiator key (available from hardware shops). Switch off the pump and use the key to turn the small square nut that you will find at one of the radiator's top corners. Do not remove the nut but turn it just enough to allow trapped air to hiss out. When the hissing stops, water will begin to dribble out. Tighten up the nut and switch the pump back on.

Bleeding a radiator

Turn off the pump and twist the small, square-headed nut located in one of the top corners of the radiator a quarter turn or so using a special radiator key. When the hissing stops and water flows out, tighten up the nut once more. Keep a cloth handy to mop up any drips.

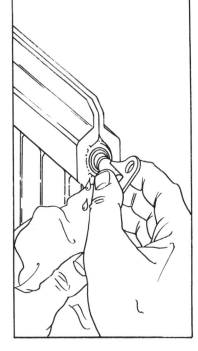

Outdoor space

With most properties, the outdoor space can be divided into two areas – the back garden and front garden. Of the two, it is usually the back garden that is larger and gets most of the attention, but both need regular checking – boundary fences or walls need to be maintained, hedges clipped and so on.

Planning a garden

Often the first decision to make is to choose between a paved garden or a lawn. Size is a crucial factor as a large expanse of paving will look barren and a miniscule patch of grass will not be worth the bother. It is of course possible to compromise if space permits by having just part of the garden paved. Either way, it helps to plot out your ideas on grid paper before you start setting to with a spade.

Paved gardens have the advantage of requiring very little upkeep. Precast slabs laid over a bed of sand are the commonest option but alternatives include crazy paving and bricks. It is reasonable to have flowerbeds around the edge of a paved garden or patio, but alternatively you could put plants in pots or brick planters.

Lawns are undoubtedly attractive but they do require regular mowing and attention during the spring and summer months. If you want a path across the lawn, leading to a shed for example, plan its course before you sow any seed (autumn or spring) or lay turves. A stepping stone path diagonally across the lawn may look nice but it could cost you dear in replacement motor mower blades.

Garden sheds are invaluable for storing gardening equipment and other paraphernalia and they come in a huge range of sizes and shapes. Wooden sheds should be made from pretreated timber or red cedar (which contains a natural preservative) and should ideally be positioned on a concrete slab. An alternative to a shed is a greenhouse but they are not usually well suited for storing mowers and heavy equipment. Avoid siting a shed or freestanding greenhouse next to the house – debris could collect behind it and cause damp problems.

Stocking a garden requires considerable forethought. Before buying any plants find out what sort of soil you have as this will determine what kind of plants will grow best. Is it acidic or alkaline? Clay, sandy, or chalky? Testing kits are readily available. The golden rule when planting out is to put tall shrubs and flowers at the back of a bed and to have shorter ones to the front.

Timing is crucial to most plants – if you plant bulbs or sow seeds at the wrong time of year, growth will be limited or nonexistent. Shrubs, roses and trees are best bought from garden centres when they are already approaching maturity – it is best to consult an expert before transplanting them into your garden as timing can again be important.

Planning a garden
When planning a garden from scratch, it helps to plot out ideas on squared paper before you start digging. This will enable you to spot pitfalls in advance.

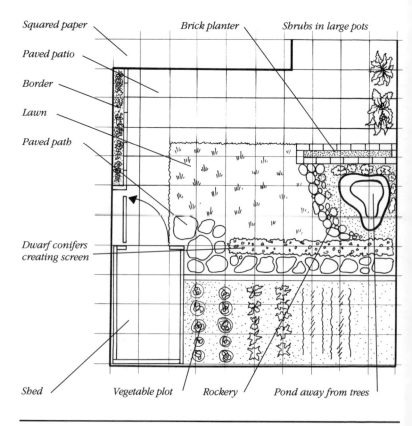

Squared paper

Paved patio

Border

Lawn

Paved path

Dwarf conifers creating screen

Brick planter

Shrubs in large pots

Shed

Vegetable plot

Rockery

Pond away from trees

HOME IMPROVEMENTS

Most homeowners dream of improving their homes, and many make their dreams come true by calling in professionals or by doing the work themselves. The types of improvements involved run from basic decorating and maintenance jobs to ambitious projects such as replacing a window, installing a new kitchen or building a conservatory. Whatever improvements you intend to make, the secret of success lies in the planning — in working out what you want to achieve, how best to go about it and how to minimize disruption while the work is going on. In this section you will find information on improving the exterior of your home, making internal alterations to fixtures and fittings, updating services and finding more living space. Planning options are clearly spelt out and any potential pitfalls are highlighted, but the final choice of what to buy and how to use it are for you to decide.

The most important thing to aim for is a balance between improving your lifestyle for a modest and manageable outlay, and increasing your home's market value. Some improvements such as a modern fitted kitchen or bathroom, a well-planned home extension or a loft conversion will always add immediate value to the property; others, such as inappropriately styled replacement windows, stone cladding on external walls (a capital offence in the eyes of architectural purists) or an expensive luxury such as a swimming pool may actually detract from its saleability.

And if selling is uppermost in your mind, there is some advice on how you can make your home seem more appealing than the competition without spending a fortune on it.

IMPROVING THE EXTERIOR

Fitting replacement windows

The most important criterion in choosing new windows is to pick a type and style similar to those you are replacing.

You can approach the job in two ways. Window frames are widely available from builders' merchants, timber yards and even some DIY superstores in a range of traditional 'standard' patterns and sizes, and you can either do the installation work yourself or call in a local builder to do it for you. This is the cheaper option, but may leave you stuck with single glazing and a recurrence of your existing maintenance problems in a few years' time.

The second option is to go for replacement windows that combine the latest design and constructional techniques with materials that promise minimal maintenance, and which include the bonus of having sealed-unit double glazing and built-in weatherstripping.

Choosing this option is likely to cost a lot more than the first one, but you will at least ensure that your windows are the best that money can buy.

Whichever option you choose, there is clearly little point in planning to fit replacement windows without including double glazing as an essential ingredient. The cost is not high; standard sealed units cost about twice the price of an equivalent-sized pane of plain glass.

Window types

Replacement windows are made in timber, aluminium, steel and plastic (unplasticized polyvinyl chloride, or uPVC for short). These materials are sometimes used in combination – aluminium windows may be set in a timber sub-frame, for example.

Timber windows are made either from preservative-treated softwood or a rot-resistant hardwood such as mahogany, and many have high-performance specifications that include integral weatherstripping and sealed-unit double glazing.

Aluminium windows are usually fitted into a timber sub-frame (hardwood, in preference to softwood: there is little point in fitting an indestructible window in a frame that could rot in ten years) and come with either a silvery anodized finish or a factory-applied colour coating in a limited range of colours.

Steel windows are often forgotten when new windows are being considered, but may be the perfect replacement in houses originally built with them. They are factory-galvanized to prevent corrosion, and many are also available with factory-applied coloured finishes that need no decorating. However, they can generally be fitted only with very slim sealed units, and some cannot be double-glazed at all.

Plastic windows are the most recent arrival on the replacement window scene, although they have been widely used on the Continent for around 25 years. They usually incorporate internal steel members for extra strength, and because of the relatively large cross-section of the various stiles and rails they often make an appropriate replacement for existing timber windows.

Window styles

As already mentioned, choosing replacement windows that suit your house is one of the most important points to consider. Thankfully, there is now a wide range of window styles available in the various materials, enabling you to choose windows with conventional casements and top lights, or with top-hung, horizontally-pivoting and tilt-and-turn panes. You can also get double-glazed vertical sliding sashes, so matching the style of your existing windows should not be a problem.

Whichever style of window you choose, ensure that it has at least one casement or sash that can be easily opened to provide an exit in case of emergency. Check, too, that it is fitted with lockable catches for security.

The type of glass also comes into the 'looks' category. Most replacement windows are fitted with clear glass, but you can also have obscured, patterned or coloured glass if you want – usually to special order. Equally important for vulnerable areas is the availability of safety glass – toughened or laminated. The most recent development is the growing use of solar control and low-emissivity glass, which helps to retain heat in the winter and to prevent unnecessary solar gain

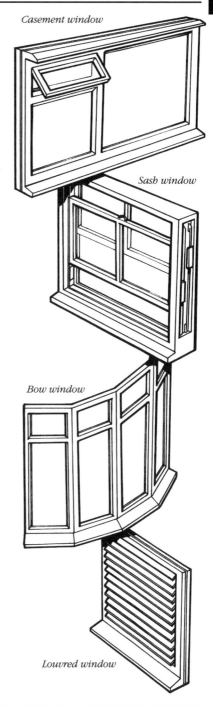

Casement window

Sash window

Bow window

Louvred window

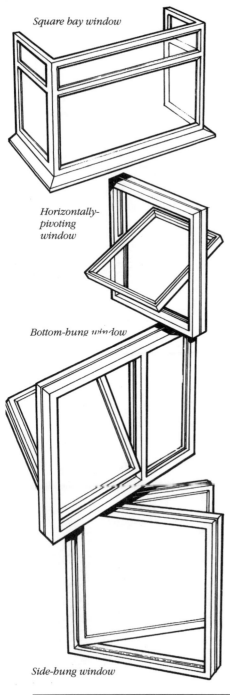

Square bay window

Horizontally-pivoting window

Bottom-hung window

Side-hung window

during the hot summer months.

You can also choose sealed units that give your windows the small-paned Georgian look or the appearance of leaded lights in square and diamond formats, with none of the cleaning problems – the glazing bars and lead strips are set in the gap between the outer panes for easy maintenance.

Window installation

There are literally thousands of firms offering a supply-and-fit replacement window service nowadays, and choosing the best one for your home can be difficult, especially if your requirements are at all unusual. Personal recommendation is still the safest method of selection, but you can rely on members of the Glass and Glazing Federation (GGF) to abide by the federation's code of practice. Clients of GGF member firms are also protected by an indemnity fund in the event of the firm going out of business before your installation is carried out.

If you want to save money and fit your replacement windows yourself, some firms now offer a supply-only service. In some cases the firm will do all the measuring up; others rely on the customer to do this tricky job.

Fitting new exterior doors

As with replacement windows, fitting a new front or back door involves choosing not only the right type but also the right style for your house. You also have the same options as far as installing it is concerned. You can buy a door from a timber merchant or DIY superstore and hang it yourself or get a carpenter to do it for you, or call in a firm to supply and fit a tailor-made door for you – they are usually the same companies that supply replacement windows. The latter option will be the more expensive, but you may choose it because you are having replacement windows fitted and can have a new door too as part of the package.

Door types

The vast majority of exterior doors are timber – either softwood, intended to be painted or stained, or hardwood, which is usually varnished or otherwise treated to enhance the natural colour of the wood. They may be solid or glazed, and come in a range of standard sizes; the commonest are 2032 x 813 mm (6ft 8in x 2ft 8in), 1981 x 838mm (6ft 6in x 2ft 9in) and 1981 x 762mm (6ft 6in x 2ft 6in). Doors for exterior use are always around 45mm (1in) thick so that they are not weakened by the fitting of locks and other security devices.

You can also buy aluminium-framed doors in a range of standard sizes, complete with matching door frames, for do-it-yourself installation. Aluminium or plastic-framed doors are the types most commonly offered by replacement window installers, and are made to measure.

Door styles

Doors – especially timber ones – are available in a huge range of styles, from simple flush-faced types to ornately carved panelled models. They can be solid, or may contain one or more glazing openings into which clear, coloured or patterned glass can be fitted to admit more light to the hall and also to allow you to check the identity of callers before opening the door. As with windows, it is important to choose a style that suits your house's architecture; many a humble terraced Victorian cottage has had its looks ruined by the fitting of a wholly inappropriate style of door.

Aluminium and plastic-framed doors offer less style choice than timber ones. The former are usually part or fully glazed; the latter may be glazed or solid and come in a range of panelled styles.

Either type of door should be fitted with a five-lever mortise deadlock made to British Standard BS3621 specification. A cylinder lock can be added for convenience, and hinge bolts and a door chain or limiter can also be fitted for extra security.

Door installation

Fitting a new timber door requires good carpentry skills if it is to fit well and close properly. You may have to cut the door down in height or width first if you have a non-standard door opening; then you have to attach the hinges, fit a lock and handle, cut a hole for the letter box and perhaps add some decorative door furniture such as a knocker or house number. Since the house will be 'open' until the job is completed, you may prefer to call in a professional carpenter to

Anatomy of a door

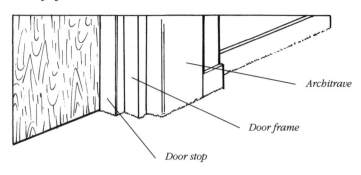

Architrave

Door frame

Door stop

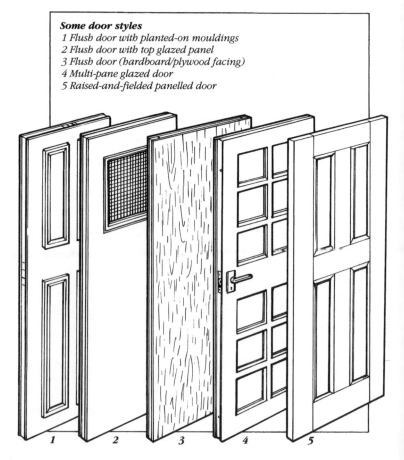

Some door styles
1 Flush door with planted-on mouldings
2 Flush door with top glazed panel
3 Flush door (hardboard/plywood facing)
4 Multi-pane glazed door
5 Raised-and-fielded panelled door

1   2   3   4   5

do most of the work in case you do not complete the job before nightfall.

By contrast, hanging an aluminium or plastic-framed door is simplicity itself, since the door will come complete with all its fittings, ready to be hinged to its new frame. All you (or the installer) will have to do is drive in the hinge screws and position the lock keeper on the frame.

Fitting new patio doors

Sliding patio doors are the most popular type of 'garden' door, linking one of the downstairs rooms in the house with the great outdoors and acting as a giant picture window when the door is closed. They are also a popular replacement for old-fashioned French doors.

A patio door

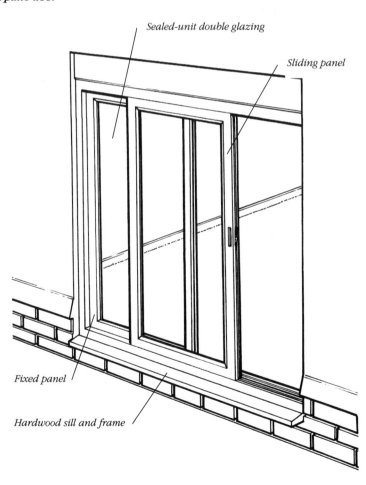

Sealed-unit double glazing

Sliding panel

Fixed panel

Hardwood sill and frame

Patio doors are available with timber, aluminium or plastic frames, and nowadays are always fitted with sealed-unit double glazing. In addition, it is vital to specify doors fitted with safety glass – either toughened or laminated – to eliminate any risk of injury should the glass be broken in a collision; not all doors on the market are. Most patio doors come with adequate security devices already fitted; check that they are lockable, and fit additional security bolts if you wish.

If you plan to install new patio doors yourself, they are available in standard sizes from builders' merchants, door and window manufacturers and some DIY superstores. They are also made to measure, supplied and installed by the same firms offering replacement windows.

Improving wall finishes

If you have brick walls, check that the pointing is in good condition. If it begins to crumble, water can get into the bricks and frost may then cause the surface to break away. Rake out any loose pointing you find, and repoint with new mortar shaped to match the profile of the

Repointing brickwork

If pointing is crumbling, hack the mortar out with a chisel and club hammer.

Brush away dust and debris from the joints with a stiff brush.

Moisten the joints by flicking water with a paint brush.

Mix up the repair mortar and take some to the wall on a board.

Press the mortar with your trowel into the vertical joints first.

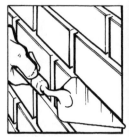

Then fill the horizontal joints and smooth them off with your trowel.

existing pointing. You can buy small bags of dry ready-mixed mortar, ideal for localized repairs. Treat porous brickwork with a coat of clear silicone water repellent to stop damp penetration.

If your walls are rendered or pebble-dashed, look out for cracks across the surface. Tap any you find, and listen for a hollow sound, which indicates that the rendering has lost its adhesion to the wall behind. Hack off any loose areas, back to a sound edge, and patch

the hole with fresh mortar using the surface of the surrounding rendering as a guide to level. Add some PVA building adhesive to the mortar to help the repair to stick. If you're trying to match a pebbledash finish, simply press pebbles into the mortar while it is still soft, using your float to bed them in securely.

Help keep rendered walls weatherproof by painting them every four or five years with a good quality exterior wall paint.

Patching rendered walls

Tap rendering with a hammer or other tool to locate loose areas.

Cut back the loose rendering to a sound edge with a chisel.

Wet the wall with a paint brush to improve the mortar's adhesion.

Use a plasterer's float to fill the area with repair mortar.

Use a timber batten to scrape off excess mortar so that it is level with the surrounding render.

Fill hollows and finish the patch smoothly with the float.

IMPROVING THE INTERIOR

Fitting a new kitchen

A new kitchen is one of the most tempting home improvements around, and there has never been a bigger choice of equipment available. But fitting one can be an expensive job, so to get yours right you must plan every stage of the new installation with some care.

First steps

First of all, stop and think whether some simple structural alterations might make your kitchen a better place to work in. For example, moving or blocking off an awkwardly sited door, repositioning the boiler or fitting a larger window might be worth considering, and on a larger scale knocking down a dividing wall or adding a small extension could let you create the kitchen you always wanted. It is also a good idea at this stage to think about reorganizing services such as gas, electricity and plumbing.

Choosing a layout

The shape of your existing or remodelled kitchen will lead naturally to one of five basic kitchen layouts.

The in-line kitchen suits long, thin rooms, and has all the major equipment ranged along a single wall. It is easy to plan and economical to fit.

The L-shaped kitchen has fittings ranged along two adjacent walls. It suits many awkwardly shaped rooms, especially those with two doors, and leaves room for a table in square or rectangular kitchens.

The U-shaped kitchen, as its name implies, has fittings along three walls, and allows the maximum flexibility in positioning individual pieces of equipment, especially in large kitchens where one side of the U can form a breakfast bar or room divider.

The galley kitchen has units on two opposite walls, and is used in narrow rooms or kitchens where there is an outside door at the far end. It is a far from ideal layout, though, because work has to cross a traffic route.

Lastly, the island kitchen adds a central 'island' to any of the other four basic layouts, often containing a hob and even a small sink. It can be incorporated only in relatively large rooms.

Work zones

Kitchen activity breaks down into three main tasks – the storage and preparation of food, its cooking and the inevitable washing up. You need a fridge, a freezer and some cupboard space for the first; a cooker for the second and a sink and draining board (and perhaps a dishwasher) for the third.

To speed up the work sequence (and to avoid the risk of accidents), these three zones should be linked by stretches of work surface and located at points forming the corners of a triangle (except, of course, for in-line kitchens), and the smaller this triangle is the better, so you do not spend all day walking about your kitchen.

Which appliances?

Next, work out which kitchen appliances are essential, and which ones you would like to include if space permits. You may be keeping some from your existing kitchen, and replacing or adding others; make sure you know the precise size of each one. If you want built-in appliances, your choice may be limited by the compatibility of individual appliances with different ranges of kitchen units.

How much storage space?

Most kitchens contain a lot of unnecessary bits and pieces, and now is the time to clear out unwanted or unused china, glass, utensils and gadgets to sell or give away. Do this, and you'll be surprised at how much cupboard space you do not really need.

Next, try to arrange for storage of regularly used equipment to be between shoulder and knee height, so you do not have to stretch or stoop for it. High or low-level storage can then be reserved for things you seldom use. Make the most of cupboard space by planning to include slide-out baskets, revolving carousels and door-back shelves wherever practically possible.

Above all, think about food storage. Being prepared for nuclear war is all very well, but today's shopping facilities mean that most people do not need to keep large food stocks in the house. Cut down

on the amount you store and you will need less cupboard space.

Choosing the units

Now you have worked out exactly what you want your kitchen to do, you can start thinking about choosing the units.

You can buy them flat-packed – usually from DIY superstores and the like – and assemble and fit them yourself. This is the cheapest way, but also generally the least flexible in terms of the choice of unit size and type available.

You can buy the units ready-assembled, either fitting them yourself or having them installed by a specialist fitting firm. This is more expensive, but offers more choice and greater flexibility.

Lastly, you can buy them custom-made to your precise requirements, and again have them professionally installed. This will of course be the most expensive option, but is the perfect solution if you have special requirements or an awkwardly shaped kitchen to cope with. It is also likely to last a lifetime!

As far as the look of the units is concerned, there is a huge choice of designs available, but they break down into two groups – plastic faced boards or natural timber. The former are generally the cheaper of the two, and offer a more streamlined look, while the latter have a softer 'country' style that is becoming increasingly popular – the sterile kitchen that resembles a hospital operating theatre seems to be a thing of the past.

However, the final choice is really as much a matter of personal taste as anything; you can find

Work triangle

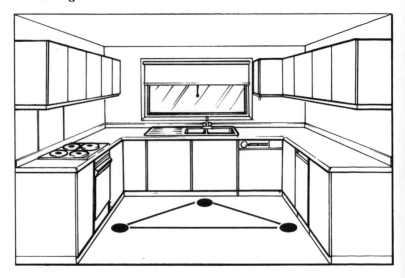

Standard kitchen units

Base units may have doors
or drawers; corner units
have one door. They are
designed to fit under a
standard worktop (600mm
deep x 900mm high).

Wall units usually have
doors, but may also be
open. They are
approximately 500mm deep
and come in two heights
(600-700mm, and 900-
1000mm).

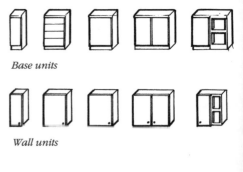

Base units

Wall units

Special units can accept
sinks, appliances, hobs and
ovens. Tall units provide
extra storage, while
bridging units fill gaps.

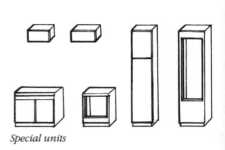

Special units

cheap timber units and expensive laminate-faced ones. The answer is to look at as many as you can – either in showrooms or in catalogues – before making your choice.

Planning the installation

What happens next depends on who is installing the kitchen. If you are employing a professional firm, you can leave the finer points of planning the job up to them, but if you are doing it yourself detailed planning is a must.

Begin with a floor plan of your kitchen, drawn accurately to scale on squared paper. Mark in the positions of fixtures such as door and window openings, boilers, radiators and water, gas and electricity service points. Then use scale cut-outs of the various units and appliances to work out the best arrangement, and draw them in when you're happy with their positions.

Add wall-mounted cupboards as dotted outlines on your plan, and then draw up elevations of each wall to help you visualize how the finished kitchen will look. Many manufacturers offer planning packs to help you with this stage; others offer a complete planning service. As you work out the plan, try to ensure that doors on floor units will not clash with room doors, and position tall units at the ends of runs so they do not interrupt worktops. Above all, keep hobs away from windows, so draughts cannot blow out gas burners and you do not have to lean across hotplates, risking burning to open

or close the window.

When you are happy with the arrangements, double-check all your measurements, and remember to allow at least 25mm clearance at either side of free-standing appliances. Then place your order and wait for your new kitchen to arrive.

Planning a new bathroom

The trouble with bathrooms is that you are rather restricted as far as choice of contents is concerned; unless your home's architect or builder took a quite radical view of the typical family's bathing requirements, it will contain one bath or shower, one washbasin and one WC. If you are lucky, there may be a bidet too. Any floor space remaining is meant for you, and there is often precious little of it for you to move about in.

Bathroom designers work from guidelines as to how much room is needed in a bathroom for using each of the pieces of equipment it contains. For example, there should be a floor area alongside the bath measuring 1100 x 700mm (roughly 3ft 6in x 2ft 3in) where you can stand to dry yourself. In front of a basin there should be a clear space 1000mm (3ft 3in) wide extending out by 700mm (2ft 3in), while for a WC this space should measure 800mm (about 2ft 7in) wide and 600mm (2ft) from the front of the pan.

The trouble is that these areas are allowed to overlap, on the grounds that two adjacent fittings are unlikely to be in use at the

Bathroom plans

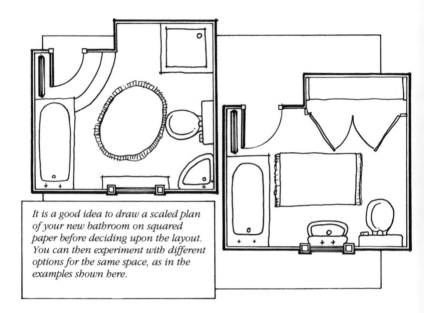

It is a good idea to draw a scaled plan of your new bathroom on squared paper before deciding upon the layout. You can then experiment with different options for the same space, as in the examples shown here.

same time. Bathroom designers have obviously not been in a small family bathroom during the busy morning rush hour!

If you are replanning your bathroom, there are several approaches you can take to make the best possible use of the available floor space.

Replacing fittings

You may be able to gain a few valuable inches by considering replacing one or more of the bathroom's fittings. The basin is probably the easiest to switch, since the plumbing connections are simple to disconnect and reconnect, and there are a number of slimline basins – particularly wall-hung types – now on the market that project from the wall

by as little as 250mm (10in).

However, before changing over to one, check in the showroom that the basin is not too small to be practical if, for example, you are used to washing your hair in it.

The average WC projects from the wall by about 700mm (2ft 3in), but you may be able to set it back a few inches by changing over to a slim-line cistern. However, this will mean remaking the soil pipe connections, and the space gained may not be worth the trouble involved.

The bath represents the biggest problem in small bathrooms. Because a typical bath is around 1700mm (5ft 6in) long, there is generally only one wall in the average small bathroom against which it can be positioned, and this

Bathroom plan

Each appliance in the bathroom needs space next to it for access and ease of use. In a small room these may overlap, on the grounds that only one is likely to be in use at a time.

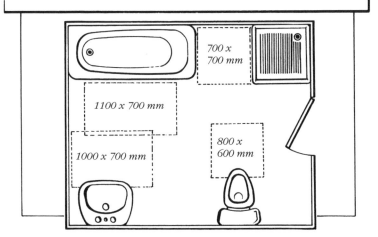

then governs where everything else has to go. If you are prepared for a fairly radical redesign of the bathroom, there are two options you could consider.

The first is to fit a corner bath. This may sound impractical, but the smaller types need a free corner measuring only about 1300mm (4ft 3in) along each wall, so one could well fit into a small room, with the washbasin or WC repositioned on the long wall against which the standard bath was originally fitted. The curved front of a corner bath also seems to free more floor space, although this is actually an illusion; a corner bath of this size takes about 10 per cent more floor space than a conventional bath. It is the shape that helps make better use of some small bathrooms.

The second possibility is to replace your standard-sized bath with a small 'sitz' bath. These are designed primarily for use by elderly or disabled people, and have a moulded integral seat at one end so you wash in a sitting rather than a lying position – no more long soaks, but still perfectly practical, and ideal for small children too. These baths measure around 1100mm (3ft 7in) long and 700mm (2ft 3in) wide, so could be placed along a wall too short to accommodate a full-sized bath.

Turning the room round like this could free a lot of extra floor space, making it easier to use the washbasin and WC. The bath could even double as a shower cubicle if a curtain or hinged shower screen were fitted alongside it.

Bath or shower?

The last step to consider, and by far the most drastic, is to do away with the bath altogether. The Building Regulations stipulate that every dwelling must have at least one room with a fixed bath or shower; a bath is not essential, and if you can live without one your bathroom will be turned at a stroke into a truly spacious shower room, since even a large shower cubicle takes up only around 900 x 900mm (just under a 3ft square). This may then allow you to reposition the washbasin or WC to make better use of the remaining floor space.

There are other advantages too. The main one is that you will cut your water heating bills dramatically, since a shower takes only around one-seventh of the amount of hot water required to fill a bath. Since you can take a shower in minutes, having one speeds up the traffic flow in busy bathrooms. You can wash your hair in them, and they are more hygienic than a bath because the 'final rinse' is with clean water. They are even easier to keep clean.

The only potential problem with this changeover is if your bathroom has a full-width window and the shower cubicle has to stand against the outside wall. This will simply mean having to install an opaque or solid side to the cubicle where it adjoins the window.

Fitting built-in furniture

Built-in furniture is becoming increasingly popular for both bedrooms and living rooms. In the bedroom, you can tidy away all your clothes in a neat run of fitted units, while in the lounge or dining room built-in wall units provide a neat combination of storage and display space for everything from books and ornaments to home entertainment equipment such as stereos and televisions.

The main advantage of built-in furniture is that since it is tailor-made, it makes the maximum use of the available space. Its drawback is that while it is generally less expensive than its free-standing equivalent, you cannot easily take it with you when you move house, or alter its position if you want to rearrange the room layout in the future.

Fitted bedroom furniture is similar in principle to kitchen units, with a range of different cupboard and drawer units available to suit your individual storage needs. Matching door and drawer fronts give the run a unified appearance and infill panels hide any gaps. You can either buy the units 'off the peg' and fit them yourself, or call in a fitted bedroom supplier who will both make and install the units for you although this is obviously more expensive.

A variation on the built-in theme is to have ceiling-height sliding doors concealing the storage racks and rails within. This type is much cheaper than rigid units, since the room's walls form the storage compartment, and is more flexible in its provision of various types of storage space.

Living-room units tend to be a combination of floor-standing and wall-mounted units linked together

Bedroom plan

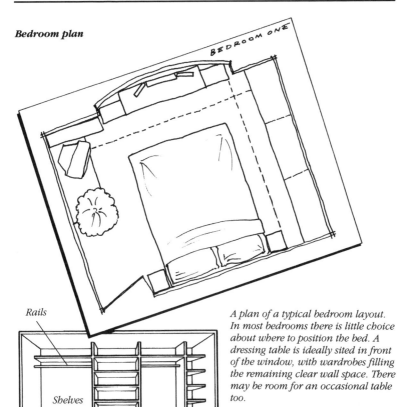

BEDROOM ONE

Rails

Shelves

A plan of a typical bedroom layout. In most bedrooms there is little choice about where to position the bed. A dressing table is ideally sited in front of the window, with wardrobes filling the remaining clear wall space. There may be room for an occasional table too.

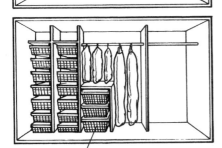

Wire baskets

Wall-to-ceiling sliding doors allow you to use the room's walls to form wardrobes. A wide range of interior storage fittings is available.

to provide complete runs of storage and display space along one or more walls of the room. You simply select the individual units you require to fill the space available. Most types can be moved relatively easily if required to give your room a new layout.

IMPROVING THE SERVICES

Improving the electrics

If you are considering carrying out any improvements to your home's wiring, ask yourself two questions. Firstly, is it in good working order? Secondly, am I confident that I can do the work safely and correctly? If the answer to either question is no, call in a professional electrician to put things right and to carry out any extra work you want done, such as fitting additional sockets or decorative lighting.

As far as the point about the system's condition is concerned, you should not try to extend any system with old-fashioned round-pin plugs or rubber-sheathed circuit cables (check the latter at your fuse box). Such a system is thoroughly outdated, may be dangerous and should be completely rewired with PVC-sheathed cable and modern wiring accessories.

Fitting new accessories

As part of your interior decor, you may wish you had more attractive light switches, socket outlets and other visible parts of the system such as ceiling roses. There are now plenty of wiring accessories available in metallic and coloured plastic finishes as well as the standard white finish. Replacing old accessories is a simple job, involving disconnecting the old and then connecting up the new.

Turn off your system at the main on/off switch before you start, and leave it off until you have finished the job. Then unscrew the old faceplate and ease it away from the wall. Loosen the terminal screws and pull out the cable cores after making a note of which went where. Remember that the live core is colour-coded red, the neutral is black and the earth is covered with slip-on green-and-yellow plastic sheathing. Then reconnect the cores to the same terminals on the new accessory, fold the cable back into the mounting box and attach the faceplate. Finally, restore the power supply.

Fitting new lights

If you have standard ceiling roses with a pendant lampholder and shade, you can replace them with modern two-part roses, which allow the lampholder flex to be disconnected like a plug from the ceiling rose. The new rose is screwed directly to the ceiling below a joist, and the circuit cables are connected into it just as they were at the old rose. Turn the power off at the mains before disconnecting and replacing the existing rose.

Wiring out of doors

If you want mains-voltage lighting or power supplies out of doors, you should call in a qualified electrician to do the work for you. If you use electrical equipment such as a lawnmower or hedgetrimmer, always plug it in via a special adapter containing a residual current device. This is a safety device that cuts off the power supply in the event of an electrical fault or accident, and could save your life if, for example, you cut through the appliance flex and then touched the cut end.

Improving the plumbing

As with your home's electrical system, you may want to improve the appearance of the plumbing system's visible parts, or to extend the system. The work is generally not difficult, and requires few specialist tools. However, if you are not a DIY enthusiast, you would do well to call in a plumber.

• You can improve the look of sinks, basins or baths by replacing the existing taps.

• The commonest extension you are likely to make to your plumbing system is to provide water for a washing machine or dishwasher. Some need just a cold supply, others both hot and cold.

• Another simple task you may want to carry out is the installation of an outside tap, and you can buy plumbing kits for the job.

• If your home has any lead piping, it is wise to consider having it all replaced with new copper or plastic pipe. Old lead pipework is often almost totally furred up, especially in hard water areas, and can cause unacceptably high levels of lead in the water supply. This is also an opportunity to have old galvanized iron water tanks replaced, and to modernize old plumbing fittings throughout the house. However, it is a major job best left to a qualified plumber.

Improving the heating

If you have full central heating, there is not much you can do yourself to alter the way it runs. However, you can replace, reposition or add radiators to the system, and also fit more sophisticated controls to help you run it more efficiently. If you are not sure of your ability to carry out the work, call in a plumber or heating engineer to do it for you.

Modern convector radiators are far more efficient than old panel types, and fitting them will improve the heat output quite noticeably.

Assuming that your system is already controlled by a room thermostat and a simple programmer, you could run it more efficiently if the system was fitted with more sophisticated controls.

For example, thermostatic radiator valves allow the temperature to be varied and closely controlled in individual rooms of the house. Motorized valves and a more sophisticated programmer would allow you to heat different zones of the house to different temperatures at different times, and fitting a cylinder thermostat will give you better control over your stored hot water.

Fitting a new boiler

Modern boilers are far more efficient than their ancestors, and you will make considerable savings in your heating bills by fitting one. The installation is a job for a plumber or heating engineer, however, to ensure compliance with the safety requirements of the Building Regulations and the fuel suppliers.

MAKING MORE LIVING SPACE

<u>Rearranging the layout</u>

If you want more living space, you may actually need to do little more than rearrange the way you use the space you have. Two examples of this are creating one large through room by knocking together two small adjoining ones, and subdividing existing rooms by building partition walls.

Internal alterations

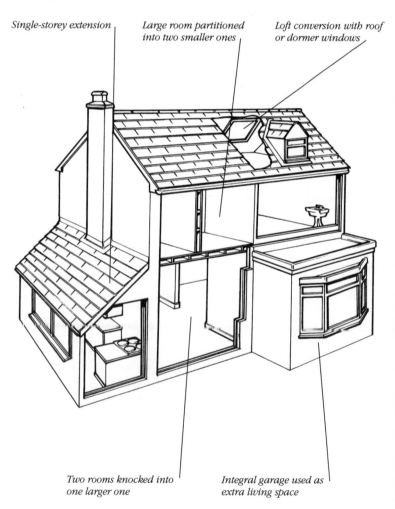

Single-storey extension

Large room partitioned into two smaller ones

Loft conversion with roof or dormer windows

Two rooms knocked into one larger one

Integral garage used as extra living space

Creating through rooms

Knocking two rooms into one can help give a cramped floor plan a much greater feeling of space and freedom of movement. Most people choose to knock lounge and dining room together to create a large open-plan living space, but in theory you could just as easily combine the dining room and the kitchen, or the lounge and the entrance hall (only if you have a separate porch – no one wants the lounge door opening straight on to the street). At the same time you may also be able to block off a redundant door, so improving traffic flow and freeing an extra stretch of wall against which to arrange your furniture.

The feasibility of the conversion depends on whether the wall to be removed is loadbearing, and if it is, whether a suitable beam can be built in to carry the load of the floor above. You need the help of an architect or structural engineer to assess your exact technical requirements, and a builder to carry the work out. Note that you will also need to apply for Building Regulations approval for the work.

Partitioning rooms

The other way of reorganizing your floor plan is to subdivide large rooms to create two smaller ones. The commonest situation is to provide an extra bedroom, or to create an en-suite bathroom for a large bedroom. Whatever you want to achieve, the task is much simpler than knocking rooms together; all you have to do is to erect timber-framed partition walls to create the new room shapes you

want. Line the frames with a double layer of plasterboard and fill the cavity with loft insulation to create walls with an acceptable degree of soundproofing.

Care must of course be taken over providing access to the new rooms; generally part of the floor space will be taken up in providing a passageway leading to the new room's door from the existing door position, since having access through an existing room is rarely satisfactory. It is also important to ensure that each new room has adequate natural light; rooms are not allowed to share a window, so you may have to consider putting in a new window if the existing room has only one.

No official permission is needed to create an extra room in this way, although if it contains any washing or bathing facilities you will need Building Regulations approval for the extension to the house's waste water system.

Extensions, porches and conservatories

If rearranging the existing room layout does not give you the extra space you need, you will have to consider a home extension. Extending your home is far more economical than moving to another, larger one, since almost every penny spent will give concrete results – no stamp duty, estate agents or solicitors to pay, and the opportunity to finance it with a simple increase in your mortgage. Whether you need just a new front porch, a conservatory in which to soak up the sun or a full-blown brick-built extension, your planning must be meticulous – from first thoughts, right through to laying the first brick.

First thoughts

The first thing you have to work out is how much extra space you need, and where you are going to put it. Much will depend on how big your plot is, and how you use it at present; for example, building a side extension may block off access to the back of the house, while adding rooms at the back of the house may take up too much precious garden space.

It is generally easy to plan the addition of extra living space at ground level. For example, a kitchen extension will lead quite naturally off the existing kitchen; a kids' playroom or a conservatory could well adjoin the living room. In these cases, traffic in and out of the new rooms will not take up much existing floor space and access from the rest of the house will be fairly easy to organize.

External alterations

Outbuildings rarely need planning permission or Building Regulations approval.

Loft conversions seldom need planning permission (except in Scotland) but always need Building Regulations approval.

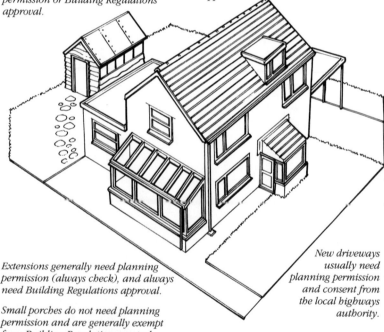

Extensions generally need planning permission (always check), and always need Building Regulations approval.

Small porches do not need planning permission and are generally exempt from Building Regulations control.

Conservatories may need planning permission (always check), but are exempt from Building Regulations if less than 30sq m in floor area.

New driveways usually need planning permission and consent from the local highways authority.

Garages and carports may need planning permission if close to the house; attached garages need Building Regulations approval, but detached ones do not.

Life becomes more difficult where two-storey extensions are concerned, because providing access to an extra bedroom or bathroom can mean lopping space off existing rooms to form corridors.

Upstairs or downstairs, you must also consider what effect the new work will have on natural lighting and ventilation to existing rooms.

If you already have an existing single-storey extension (or perhaps an attached garage) it may be possible to add a second storey on top of it. It is worth investigating the strength of the existing structure and its foundations.

While you are going through this process, it may help to solve an apparently insoluble problem if you are also prepared to re-plan the existing layout. For example, it may be better to build a new kitchen and turn the existing one into a dining room, or to turn an existing bedroom into a bathroom instead of putting a bathroom in the new extension.

PERMITTED ALLOWANCES FOR EXTENSIONS

House type	Extension size
Terrace or end-of-terrace	50cu m or 10% of the end-of-terrace volume of the original house up to a maximum of 115cu m
Any other	70cu m or 15% of the volume of the original house up to a maximum of 115cu m

The original house means the house as first built, or as it stood on 1 July 1948 if built before then. Any previous extension work counts against the stated allowance.

• For houses in National Parks, Areas of Outstanding Natural Beauty or Conservation areas, the limits are as for terrace houses.

Getting professional help

Remember that you don't have to tackle this planning all on your own. You can always employ a professional adviser – an architect or surveyor – to help you with the design stages, and if you will be employing a local builder for the actual construction work, his advice can be extremely useful at this point too.

Once you have decided what sort of extension you need and roughly where it is going to go, you can then start thinking about the layout and construction in more detail.

You should also give some thought to what the exterior of the extension will look like; it should look as though it's part of the original house or, if this cannot be achieved, it should at least match the architectural style and be constructed with similar materials.

Rules and regulations

The extension must satisfy the requirements of the Planning Acts and, in most cases, the Building Regulations; these mean that you do not have a completely free hand as far as the looks and the construction of the new work are concerned, so it helps to have a general idea of what you can and cannot do.

First, planning permission. You will need to apply for it unless your extension meets the following requirements:

• It does not increase the volume of the house by more than the permitted amount (see table on previous page).

• It is no higher than the highest part of the roof of the original house.

• It does not project in front of the forwardmost part of the house that faces the highway, or come within 20m of the highway, whichever is the nearer.

• If it is more than 4m high, it is at least 2m from the property boundary.

• It does not result in more than half the original plot area being covered by buildings.

Conservatories are treated as home extensions for planning permission purposes. Porches are treated separately; permission is not needed to build one so long as:

• Its floor area does not exceed 3sq m.

• No part of it is more than 3m above ground level.

• There is a distance of at least 2m between it and any boundary bordering a road or public footpath.

If you need to apply for planning permission for your extension, contact your local authority planning department. You will be given various forms to fill in, and will be told what plans and drawings have to be submitted for scrutiny. You will also have to pay a fee. You should receive notification of the outcome of your application within eight weeks, but work cannot begin until planning permission has been granted.

Secondly, Building Regulations approval is necessary for almost all extension work; the only projects that have been exempted in the current edition of the Regulations are ground-floor extensions involving the erection of a conservatory, a porch, a carport (which must be open on at least two sides), a covered way or a greenhouse with a floor area not exceeding 30sq m. A conservatory is defined as an extension with a transparent or translucent roof.

The Building Regulations include statutory requirements for building materials, site preparation, damp-proofing, fire resistance and safety, thermal and sound insulation, ventilation, stairways, drains and waste disposal and the installation of heat-producing appliances.

Your local authority Building Control Officer or District Surveyor will often be able to give help and advice on particular aspects of your proposals, but unless you have a good knowledge of building practice you would be well advised to enlist professional help in ensuring that your extension complies with the Regulations.

As with obtaining planning

permission, you apply to your local authority for Building Regulations approval – again, filling in forms, submitting plans and paying a fee. However, in this case you can either deposit full plans and wait for approval to be given, or else you can give what is called a Building Notice.

This gives brief details of your proposed alterations and a site plan (which must also show any new drainage works). As soon as this Notice has been deposited with the local authority, along with the necessary fee, work can begin; there is no need to wait for formal approval to be granted. However, you will have to notify the authority at various stages of the construction so that site inspections can be carried out.

Who will do the work?

Most homeowners are likely to call in a local builder to put up a home extension or a large conservatory, or at least to carry out the major structural work. However, small conservatories and porches are well within the scope of the competent do-it-yourselfer.

If you do decide to employ a builder, personal recommendation is the best way of finding a good one. Failing that you could contact the Federation of Master Builders (14 Great James Street, London WC1N 3DP) for names of member firms in your area.

Ask at least three firms to give either a tender – an offer to carry out the work for a definite price, or a quotation – a detailed breakdown of the work to be done, priced section by section. An estimate is no more than that – it is not a firm price, and if there is more work than the builder realized, he will be entitled to charge you more than his estimate.

Once you have accepted a tender or quotation, you have a binding contract. However, it is worth having a written contract signed by both parties covering things like start and completion dates, payment schedules, variations on the original plans and insurance cover while the work is going on. Obviously, if you are employing an architect, he will take care of all this for you.

Restrictive covenants

As if all this were not enough, there is one last point to check – the deeds of your property, which might contain restrictions (called restrictive covenants) on what you can do to the building. If they do, consult a solicitor for his advice on having them set aside.

The final step is to tell your insurance company and your local service authorities (if work is being carried out on the gas, electricity or water supplies). Then work can finally begin.

Loft conversions

If you need more living space and you've found that a conventional extension isn't the right solution, the answer might be a loft conversion. Whether one is possible depends on two factors: one is the type of roof construction you have; the other is whether access to the new storey can be provided without the loss of too much space on the floor below.

The roof structure

Most roofs in older houses are built up from individually cut timbers assembled in one of a number of traditional designs. It is generally possible to create space within such a roof by repositioning some of the timbers (although expert advice must be taken on how this is to be done).

Modern houses usually have roofs built up from prefabricated frames called trussed rafters, and every component of these frames is vital for the strength of the roof; it is seldom possible to remove any of them, and so a loft conversion is unlikely to be feasible.

Providing access

Next you must think about access. If the new rooms are to be an extension of your living quarters, you need a fixed staircase to reach them in comfort and safety, and this will have to be positioned so as not to take up too much room in the floor below. In a two-storey house it is often possible to build it as an extension of the existing staircase (perhaps with a dormer window in the roof slope to provide the necessary headroom above the new flight). Otherwise it will have to rise from one of the existing rooms – a loss of space that should be made up by the space gained in converting the loft.

Providing natural light

Next your thoughts should turn to providing natural light in the new loft rooms. If the loft has one or more gable end walls, it may be possible to install windows in these. However, most loft

Loft conversion options

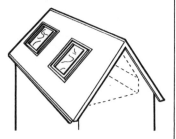

Roof windows are fitted between the roof rafters and are flush with the roof surface.

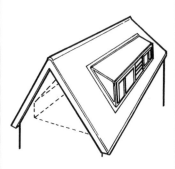

Dormer windows are built out from the face of the roof and can give extra headroom in the loft.

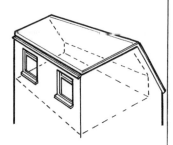

If the house walls can take the extra weight, one wall can be built up to create an extra storey.

conversions need extra windows in the roof slope – either sloping roof windows, or dormers projecting from the roof slope towards (or even right out to) the eaves.

Services in the loft

One more point is worth considering: what the rooms will be used for. At the very least they will need an electricity supply and some form of heating; you may also want to install washing, bathing or WC facilities. You therefore need to find out whether your existing services can practicably be extended, or whether wholesale alterations to the plumbing, electrics and central heating system will be necessary.

Rules and regulations

Any major structural alteration of this sort will have to comply with the Building Regulations. The current edition has done away with the former minimum headroom requirement (it used to be 2.3m; now any 'sensible' headroom is allowable) but it has tightened up considerably on the fire safety and means of escape requirements for loft conversions in two-storey houses.

Since the Regulations also control alterations to the roof structure, the strength of floors (an existing loft floor will generally need strengthening), sound and thermal insulation, ventilation and a number of other important points, it is essential that you get professional advice in drawing up a detailed specification for the conversion. The actual building work can be carried out on a do-it-

yourself basis if you have the necessary skills, but it must still satisfy the Building Regulations in every respect.

You may also need planning permission to convert your loft. Although the work is theoretically exempt because it does not substantially increase the volume of the house, in practice the addition of dormer windows may require permission. The best thing to do is to contact your local authority planning department for advice at an early stage.

Getting professional help

Expert advice in planning a loft conversion is essential on two grounds. Firstly, meeting the technical requirements of the Building Regulations is no job for a layman. Secondly, it will enable the best use to be made of the available space, and is likely to result in a better planned and better looking extension to the house. This in turn means that its value and saleability will be increased: an amateurish job, on the other hand, will have the opposite effect.

You can turn to an architect or surveyor for help, trust a local builder (ideally one with considerable experience of loft conversion work who is also personally recommended to you), or employ one of the many specialist loft conversion companies. Which you select will depend on how complex the conversion will be, and on whether you want to do the actual work yourself or not.

Your chosen expert will produce

the necessary drawings for submission to the local authority. Remember that work cannot start until you have received planning permission (if it is needed) and full Building Regulations approval. The only exception to the latter is for a loft conversion in a single-storey building; in this case the 'Building Notice' method can be used to save time. You simply give notice of your intentions and deposit simple plans with the local authority. Work can then start immediately; the Building Control officer will inspect the work at regular intervals to ensure that the Regulations are complied with.

If you decide to employ someone to convert your loft, get at least three quotations from different sources. When you have selected one, draw up a simple written agreement that specifies the price to be paid, whether payment will be made in stages, the completion date (and what will happen if it is overrun), how any variations on the original plans will be dealt with and what insurance arrangements have been made for the duration of the work.

Converting basements and cellars

If you have a basement or cellar, you may be able to convert it for use as extra living space – a playroom for the children or an office, for example – or to provide extra storage space. The biggest problem you are likely to face is damp, with rot in any basement timbers coming a close second. Headroom may also be restricted, but at least the space and access to

it already exist, so the job of finding some extra living space is half done. You simply have to complete the conversion.

The easiest method of waterproofing a basement, assuming that it is structurally sound, is to lay a new damp-proof membrane on the floor and link this to a coating of liquid damp-proofing applied to the walls. If the walls are seriously damp, however, you may need expert help and the installation of full-scale tanking to keep ground water at bay.

Depending on the outside ground level, it may be possible to excavate a well against the outside wall of the cellar so you can install a high-level window for light and ventilation. Otherwise you will have to rely on artificial light and mechanical ventilation via extractor fans. You will also have to consider either extending the heating system or providing individual heaters.

The existing staircase down to the cellar will probably have to be renovated extensively.

You will need Building Regulations approval to carry out a basement conversion, but planning permission is not needed unless there is a change of use involved – use of the basement as business premises, for example.

Converting integral garages

If your house has an integral garage, it may be possible to convert it for use as an extra ground-floor room.

Check with your local authority about whether planning permission is needed for the change of use.

IMPROVING TO SELL

Improving the exterior

If you are planning to sell your house, it is essential that it makes a good first impression on would-be purchasers; there is nothing more off-putting than a house that looks scruffy and neglected from outside, however smart the interior may be. So go and stand on the pavement outside your house, and cast a critical eye over it as a potential buyer would. Here are some points to look for, and some tips on what action to take.

First, make sure all the windows are clean. Wash down exterior paintwork, and touch in any obvious blemishes. Spruce up painted rendering by washing it down with a high-pressure hose; this will remove a surprising amount of dirt, and the result looks less suspicious (and costs less) than applying a fresh coat of paint. Use the spray on discoloured brickwork too, then repoint any areas where the pointing is crumbling or missing.

Make good any other obvious structural defects such as slipped or missing tiles and slates on the roof, sagging gutters and rotten wall cladding or damaged tile hanging. Straighten up that drunken tv aerial too! Attention to detail helps.

Next, tackle the front door, which is the first feature of the home a visitor will see at close quarters. If it looks at all scruffy, give it a fresh coat of paint or varnish, and polish up or replace the door furniture.

For evening callers, make sure the outside light works and that the house name or number is clearly visible at night.

Finally, make sure the approach to the house is neat and tidy. Leave your car out in the road, then sweep drives and paths and clean up oil patches from the drive surface. Hide the dustbin.

Improving the interior

Next, turn your attention indoors. First of all, ensure that the entrance hall is well lit and welcoming and that the rest of the house is reasonably (but not obsessively) tidy when viewers call. Vacuum-clean the carpets and add personal touches like vases of fresh flowers here and there. Make sure that windows are clean inside as well as outside.

As far as the internal decoration is concerned, remember that would-be buyers are likely to redecorate as a first priority, so unless your decorations are in really poor condition it is not worth wasting money on extensive redecoration. Instead, wash down wall and ceiling surfaces and paintwork, and touch in obvious blemishes. Use decorator's mastic to fill obvious cracks round ceilings, window and door frames and on staircases.

Make sure that sinks, basins, baths and toilets are clean and free from lime scale; an hour's work with a proprietary scale remover will be time well spent.

Lastly, check that everything works – that doors and windows don't stick, that lights work and so on. Attend to any minor maintenance jobs now – the sort of defects every family learns to live with and ignore, but which a visitor may quickly spot. However, do not be tempted to deceive; tricks such as fitting modern power points to conceal an old wiring system are definitely below the belt, and will be discovered by a surveyor and cause you embarrassment later on.

Improving the garden

The last area you should attend to is the garden, both front and back. Obviously how much you can do will depend on the season; you can hardly be expected to mow the lawn or cut the hedge in midwinter (nor should you do so), but you can at least make sure it looks tidy, by sweeping up leaves and lightly digging over flower beds.

In spring and summer, however, when your garden looks at its best, keep lawns mowed and hedges carefully trimmed, and weed flower beds as frequently as you can. It may even be worth employing a temporary gardener during the selling period to keep the garden in good order.

Lastly, clean patio and path surfaces with a high-pressure hose, and attend to any maintenance jobs that need doing, such as fixing loose paving stones and repairing sagging fences. Above all, make sure the For Sale board is secure!

FAMILY FINANCES

When looking at our finances it is easy to focus on the big items of expenditure – the car, the mortgage or rent for example – and blame them for a low bank balance. It is often surprising however to find that although costly, these things are just a few pieces in a much larger jigsaw of our spending habits.

Everyday money

Working out a family budget

Drawing up a family budget is the only way to form a true picture of where your money comes from and where it goes. If you are always in the red, the budget will help identify areas you can cut back on. If you have a fluctuating bank balance, a budget will help plan more efficiently and avoid the bank charges that even a small and rapidly paid-off overdraft brings.

Income Start by writing down the money that comes in. If you are paid on a monthly basis, and your major outgoings are on monthly standing orders, it makes sense to use monthly totals for all your budget figures.

Write down your and your partner's gross monthly wages or salary (see your pay slips), interest from investment accounts, and money such as family allowance or contributions towards food costs from older working children.

Expenditure Breaking your spending down into distinct areas is a great help when it comes to making sure you have included everything. There's no need to be too precise over what you call the areas; they are simply a guide for your thinking. For example, you may find it easiest to list your spending under the following headings:

• deductions from gross salary (see pay slip)
• standing orders and direct debits
• car expenses
• other travel
• general domestic
• clothing
• hobbies and activities
• entertainment
• Christmas/birthdays
• holidays

Under each heading you may have three, four or a dozen or so entries. It does not matter as long as all your spending has been covered and you have been honest with yourself – do you have one, or three, bottles of wine with a meal out for example – and have remembered items such as the television licence.

For variable items, such as the gas bill, total up the last four quarters and divide by 12 to give a monthly average. It may seem strange making a monthly allowance for one-off items like holidays, but this is the best way to get your spending under control.

The difference between your monthly income and expenditure is the amount you are managing to save each month or the rate at which your overdraft is growing. If the figure does not seem plausible, check through your entries and your cheque book stubs. Have you forgotten to make an allowance for the cost of replacing furniture or failed to include earnings from occasional bar work for example. Talking through your budget with your partner is a good way of spotting the elusive items.

Once you have finished the budget, check it against your receipts on a regular basis to make sure your estimates have been realistic and if not, adjust them as necessary.

Sticking to your budget

Few people can resist temptation and few control their money with ruthless efficiency. If you have trouble sticking to your budget, try some of the following:

• Pay off and cancel any credit or store cards

• Make use of saving stamp and budget schemes wherever possible. You can pay your car tax and tv licence like this, for example

• Limit yourself to one or two withdrawals from the bank each week

• Try alternative hobbies or pastimes. Some sports work out a lot more expensive than others for no greater degree of enjoyment.

• Investigate opening a bank budget account. Although you pay for this service it can help with all your regular bills. You simply add up the annual cost of the bills you want paid, agree these with your bank and pay one-twelfth of the total into your budget account each month. The bank pays the bills as they come in and at the end of the year the bank lets you know whether you need to increase or decrease your monthly payments for the next year.

Opening a cheque book account

Even if you have had a bank account for years, now may be the time to change to another type. Despite interest-paying current accounts having been available for several years, a large proportion of people have not switched over to them. Although the interest rate is kept relatively low, at least your money is working for you while sitting in the account.

Which bank or building society you should choose to open a cheque book account with depends on a number of factors – their opening hours and proximity of branches to you for example – but there is no reason why you should not have more than one. The main thing is to shop around and choose the account that offers the service most suited to your needs. Make sure you read all the small print however. While interest-paying cheque book accounts are fine for those who are always in credit, if you slip into the red you'll pay higher overdraft charges than you would normally.

You and your bank manager

Banks frequently promote themselves as organizations whose staff have a strong personal interest in your affairs. For many people, this runs counter to their own experience. Why the discrepancy?

The answer probably lies in communication, or lack of it. For a bank manager to be of assistance to you, you need to ask for help having first paved the way by explaining what you are planning. If you are heavily indebted with a poor payment record, an overdraft request may well be refused. On the other hand, if you keep your bank manager informed of your plans before you execute them, you are more likely to win his or her support.

If you have a complaint about your bank or its services take the following steps:

• Speak to the staff at the branch concerned. This may be the manager or one of the bank's experts in the field of your complaint. If the problem is not one that can be put right straight away, expect the bank to let you know what they are doing on a regular basis.

• If you are not satisfied, or for more serious complaints, contact the bank's area or regional manager (your branch should give you the details). You may be referred from here to the bank's head office.

• The last resort for anyone with a complaint against their bank is the banking ombudsman. This is a free service designed to provide arbitration and judgment once you have exhausted the bank's own complaints procedure. The building societies have a similar scheme.

Avoiding cheque fraud

Cheques offer a great deal of convenience when it comes to paying for things but they are frequently the subject of criminal abuse. Take the following steps to protect yourself:

• Always carry your cheque card separately from your cheque book – in different compartments of the same bag is not good enough.

• Never give your personal identification number (PIN) to anyone else. Banks and credit card companies advise never to write it down too. If you have no memory for figures and feel you must make a note of the number, disguise it heavily – as part of a genuine looking telephone number for

example – and avoid standing by a cash machine reading your disguised PIN number. Note that if you do forget your PIN number, a telephone call to the institution concerned will soon have another PIN on its way.

• Take care to destroy receipt slips from cash machines – they have your account number on.

When writing a cheque:

• Write the words and figures all as one word. Gaps can be used by the clever thief to amend the amount.

• Sign the cheque only when it is complete.

• Keep a record of all your cheques and compare this with your statement. If you write a lot of cheques and only receive a quarterly statement, ask for a monthly instead.

• Cross the cheque 'account payee only'. This means that the money cannot be diverted to someone else's account.

• Tell your bank immediately if you lose your cheque book or cheque card.

When accepting payment by cheque:

• Make sure it is filled in properly, dated and signed.

• Check the limit of the guarantee card and its expiry date.

• Compare the signature on the cheque with the signature on the card.

• Write the card number on the back of the cheque.

• Write the payer's address on the back of the cheque.

• Ask for proof of identity if you are suspicious.

Stopping a cheque

If you buy something by cheque and then decide you do not want to pay for it, you can stop the money coming out of your account provided that:

• The cheque has not already been paid.

• You did not use your cheque card to guarantee the cheque. By its very nature your guarantee card means that the amount will be paid.

• You tell your branch the details – date, payee, amount, cheque number – as soon as possible and complete a form.

Note that you are likely to be charged by your bank for stopping a cheque.

Credit, charge and store cards

'Paying with plastic' boomed during the 1980s and although their popularity has diminished, credit, store and charge cards still remain a convenient way to buy goods with money you may not have. Each works in a different way:

Credit cards The most common of these are Access and Visa. Each month you receive a statement showing the amount you have spent and a request to pay off a certain amount of this – the 'minimum payment'. Paying off the full amount within the specified time is the wisest course as it means you will not incur interest charges; letting your debt roll into the next month can be a very expensive business.

You will probably have to pay an annual fee for the use of the card although there are occasional special offers that waive this. Note that in certain cases a retailer (who pays a commission to the credit card company for each sale he makes this way) is entitled to charge a credit card customer more than he would a cash or cheque customer – to ask before paying is the best protection against this.

Store cards These work in a similar way to credit cards but their use is restricted to the store or group of stores that issued the card. They are often heavily promoted with the vision of being able to walk out of a shop with hundreds of pounds' worth of goods and paying for them later. What many people fail to appreciate however is that they may well incur heavy interest payments for this privilege.

Charge cards A restricted form of credit card. Each month's statement must be paid in full so there is no opportunity to let the debt accumulate.

Savings and investment

Putting aside some of your money in a savings account serves two purposes: firstly, it keeps money you are not spending in a secure environment; secondly, your money grows in value with time. But before you put any money away, there are a number of things to consider.

Can you afford to save?

Even if your bank statement shows you are overdrawn each month, you may not be too far away from becoming a regular saver. But the first step for anyone wanting to save is to gain control of their money by writing a household budget. This will show one of three things:

• Your income is greater than what you spend. First check through your figures, bills and cheque book stubs because most of us live up to, if not beyond our means. If everything tallies, now is the time to begin saving regularly. More money than you actually need to pay up-and-coming bills left sitting in a current account, even one that pays interest, can be regarded as money wasting away.

• Your income and expenditure are equal. In this case you need to cut your spending by the amount you wish to save or earn more

money, by taking a part-time job for example.

• You are spending far more than you earn. You won't have needed to write a household budget to discover this, you no doubt receive regular letters from your bank and creditors reminding you. Do not despair however. Use your budget to identify areas that cost you more than you thought and then cut back. After a while, your books will balance and, with care, you should soon find yourself swinging back into the black.

Liquidity versus higher interest

Liquidity is the technical term for how accessible your money is. Cash is the most liquid asset you have because you can simply take it out of your pocket and buy something with it. Long term bonds, where you agree not to touch your money for a period of five years for example, are not a very liquid asset.

In general, the more accessible your money is, the lower the rate of return you'll get for it. Wise savers spread their money so that some, perhaps most, is always in an instant access account in case of emergencies, a smaller proportion is in an account paying higher interest but perhaps requiring 90 days' notice for a withdrawal, and any money left over may be in a long term investment such as National Savings certificates.

Who should I save with?

There is so much competition for savers' funds that it can be difficult deciding who to go to. For most savers however, the choice lies between the high street banks, building societies and National Savings via the Post Office. Which to use is largely a matter of personal choice but there are several things to ask yourself:

• Are there convenient branches? You are likely to want to pay in and withdraw near your home and your place of work if this is some distance away. Some institutions are more localized than others so you will not be able to get at your money if you are holidaying at the other end of the country for example. On the other hand, when you are at home you are likely to find queues at local institutions shorter than those for nationwide organizations.

• Are the opening hours convenient? There has been greater harmonization of opening hours in recent years but make sure they suit you.

• What other services are there? This includes things like the provision of loans and the use of a card for out-of-hours access to your account.

Once you have worked out how much you can save and have narrowed your choices of who to save with, you are ready to look at particular accounts. There are similarities between many of them but the key points to look for are:

• Access – how quickly can you get your money out and will you lose interest if you do not give notice in advance? Also check the withdrawal limits.

• Entry level – what is the minimum amount required to open the account?

• Interest rates and thresholds – does the interest rate rise each time your account reaches a new height? And what happens as the balance falls? It is worth noting here that some accounts give a very poor return on what are considered small balances and accounts with less than say £10 in may not be paid any interest at all. Always shop around for the best rate.

Everyday schemes on offer

Individual savings schemes on offer from different organizations vary in detail (make sure you read all the conditions and benefits before opening your account) but most come under the following broad headings:

Instant access You can take your money out on demand without loss of interest. The entry level is as low as £1 and the interest rate rises each time your balance reaches a pre-set threshold – typically when you have saved £500, £2,500, £5,000, £10,000 and £25,000.

These accounts are very flexible and offer an incentive to save. But many will find the higher thresholds set at unattainable levels. Check the daily cash withdrawal limits.

Investment account £500 is normally the entry level for this type of account. You may need to give 90 days' notice if you want to withdraw without loss of interest although some accounts offer one or two free 'on demand' withdrawals per year. Again, the interest rate rises at particular balance thresholds, and you should check what these are.

High interest cheque accounts A high entry level is set for this type of account, typically £1,000, but it pays double the rate of interest of an interest-paying current account. There may be a minimum amount you can write cheques for, £100 for example, and the interest rate rises with your balance in the same way as other savings accounts.

Longer term schemes
To get the best out of TESSAs, PEPs and Unit Trusts, you must be able to lock your money away for several years.

TESSAs A Tax Exempt Special Savings Account is well worth considering if you can afford to save regularly and tie the money up for five years. The maximum you can put into a TESSA is £9,000. TESSAs pay a good rate of interest with the added advantage that they are tax free.

If you are considering a TESSA, read the literature from more than one supplier – terms and conditions vary widely.

PEPs Personal Equity Plans are a tax efficient way of investing in stocks and shares if you can tie your money up at least for the medium term. You can invest up to £6,000 in your own selection of shares or have a fund manager select them for you. Dividends from the shares are tax free as are any profits made when you sell the shares. There are many variants on offer so shop around and, if you are at all uncertain, seek professional advice.

Unit Trusts These are run by professionals who use your contribution, and the investments

made by thousands of others, to buy parcels of shares. In this way, the money you put in, and the risk you take, is spread across a far greater range of shares than you could achieve on your own. Unit trusts are not a short term investment but need to be monitored regularly – a sudden peak in profits would enable you to sell to your advantage.

National Savings
National Savings offer a wide range of saving schemes. As always, compare rates of return before you open an account or invest money.

Ordinary account A basic savings account paying a low rate of interest. This is enhanced if you keep a certain amount in the account for a whole year.

Investment account One month's notice is required to withdraw from this account but the interest rate is much better than for the ordinary account. An ideal account for those with small amounts that they do not need instant access to – children for example – because the interest rate is the same whatever your balance.

Savings Certificates These are sold in £25 units. There are two types – fixed interest and index-linked – and both pay out tax free. For fixed interest certificates, check the interest rate on offer before buying – you may lose out if you buy and interest rates then soar. Index-linked certificates rise in value in line with inflation and pay an extra amount on top.

Yearly plan In this scheme, you make a commitment to save regularly for one year and leave the amount accumulated in the plan for four more years. At the end of the five years, your return is tax free.

Income bonds Interest from these bonds can be paid into your bank or building society so that your capital is producing a regular income. £2,000 is the minimum investment and you can add to it in £1,000 blocks. Three months' notice is needed to cash the bonds in although there is a severe interest penalty for withdrawing in the first year.

Capital bonds Again a long term investment. The minimum investment is £100. At the end of the five year term you get your money back plus the amount of interest fixed at the time you bought the bond.

Guaranteed growth bonds Introduced in the summer of 1992, these bonds offer a fixed rate of interest for a year at a time. £1,000 is the minimum investment and the interest, after deduction of tax at 25%, is added at the end of the year – when the bond can be cashed in without penalty.

Government stock Known as 'gilts', shorthand for gilt-edged securities, these are ideal for people wanting to lock their capital away but get an income from it. Gilts pay a guaranteed rate of interest throughout their life and pay out gross (tax payers must declare this). A curious feature of gilts is that they can be bought and sold during their lifetime for a profit or loss in much the same way as shares.

Premium bonds Probably the best loved and most well known product on offer from National

Shares

The privatization of nationalized industries in the 1980s gave many people the chance to make a quick profit, but the value of shares can plummet just as quickly as it rises. If you do invest in shares, you need to be quite confident that you really can afford to lose all your money.

Redundant accounts

Banks and building societies introduce new savings schemes all the time, often offering better terms than the ones you are getting. In the last year or two there has been much criticism of this practice from customers who thought they were getting the best rate of interest only to find that their particular account is no longer available and their money is earning less than they thought. Keep an eye on the financial pages of your newspaper and change your account as soon as a better one comes along.

Avoiding fraud

Investment frauds are commonplace and often on a large scale. In general it pays to save or invest only with a reputable institution. Always view with suspicion the offer of profits or an interest rate larger than that generally available.

Children and other non-taxpayers

Many people, such as children and the elderly, do not earn sufficient income to pay tax. If you are a non-taxpayer, or are thinking of opening an account for your children, make sure that you receive gross interest. National Savings investment accounts pay gross interest to everyone (taxpayers then have to declare it as part of their income) but for other institutions you'll need to fill in Inland Revenue Registration Form IR85. If you do not do this, 25% of your interest goes straight to the government instead of you.

Savings. This is despite the fact that the prize payout is equal to an interest rate of just 6.5% per year and if you don't win a prize, your money has not grown at all. Of course, there is always a chance that you will win the monthly big prize of £250,000 (tax free, as are all premium bond prizes) but to put this into perspective, one bond should come up once every 1,000 years!

Getting extra help

Even the boom years of the 1980s failed to clear the unemployment register. And the recession that followed threw the spotlight on what can happen to a family's affairs when high mortgage rates and redundancy put a squeeze on their finances.

But you don't need to own your own home or be out of work to run into financial difficulties. Below you'll find an outline of the main benefits available to help.

Low income families

Even people on good personal salaries may qualify for help if they are the family's breadwinner and their partner is not working. It is not necessarily how much you are paid that counts – what is also taken into consideration is how far that money has to go.

Income support This benefit is for people working less than 16 hours a week. It is designed to bring their family's income up to a government set minimum. Each family member is allocated a weekly personal allowance and there are additional allowances to cover certain circumstances. Set against these allowances is the family's income after tax. If your income is less than the government set minimum, you receive the difference.

One of the key points about income support is that it helps with those housing costs not covered by housing benefit. It pays, for example, half of your mortgage interest for the first 16 weeks of your claim and the full amount of mortgage interest thereafter.

Family credit This is for people who have at least one child and are working for at least 16 hours. Each person is allocated a particular amount and the family receives the total figure if their income after tax is less than £66.60 per week. If their income is more than this, they lose about 70 pence off the full amount for every pound they go over. Unlike income support, family credit does not help with housing costs.

Housing benefit Local councils give help to people finding it hard to pay their rent. Like income support, the amount you get depends on the size of your family, your income and your outgoings in terms of rent.

Community charge benefit This will pay up to 80% of your community charge bill. People claiming income support are given a community charge benefit form at the same time – anyone else should apply direct to their local council.

Social fund This is a catch-all fund to cover one-off payments such as buying equipment for a new baby or paying for a funeral. Usually you already need to be in receipt of another benefit.

Other benefits There is a range of other benefits designed to help the less well off, covering anything from free milk to help with the costs of travelling to hospital.

If you are unemployed

The first step, if you think you are about to become unemployed, or have already lost your job, is to check your entitlement to a redundancy payment. On the first day out of your job, get in touch with your local unemployment benefit office or Jobcentre – any benefit you receive will start from this date so do not delay. In addition to the benefits outlined above, you may receive the following:

Unemployment benefit This is paid at £43.10 per week for a single person and £69.70 for a

couple (1992/93 figures). To get it you must have paid enough Class 1 National Insurance contributions (so the self-employed are usually excluded) and be ready and available for work.

A point worth noting is that if you leave a job of your own free will, rather than being made redundant, you can be disqualified from receiving benefit for the first 26 weeks of your claim.

Claim – it's your right

Many people fail to make a claim when they know or think they are entitled to a state benefit because pride holds them back. This is understandable. But, remember, if you have paid tax and National Insurance contributions throughout your working life, you may have more than covered what you will receive in benefit.

Free advice

There are many sources of free advice on claiming benefits.
• Your local council's welfare rights advisers will have dealt with many cases like yours.
• The Post Office stocks a range of helpful leaflets.
• You can visit your local Social Security office.
• You can telephone Freeline Social Security for general advice on 0800 666555. Although there is no charge for this call, the number is very busy.

Child benefit

Child benefit is a weekly sum that you can have paid direct into a bank or building society account. It is paid at the rate of £9.65 for the first child and £7.80 for each further child. Every parent should apply for this as soon as they are able – delay may mean missed payments.

Tax and local authority charges

Income and other taxes are set by the government to pay for a vast range of the nation's services. From a new car to a tankful of petrol, a bottle of sparkling wine to the new home you'll be toasting with it, the number of transactions on which you are being taxed is endless – and that is after a 25% chunk has been taken from your earnings.

You are also taxed by your local authority to pay for services nearer to home such as libraries, leisure centres and the costs of running the authority itself.

Below, you'll find the main taxes payable and a breakdown of how they might affect your particular circumstances.

Income tax and allowances

Income tax works on the basis that the more you earn from your job and things like savings, the more you pay. Most people have this tax deducted from their wages or salary by their employer under the PAYE (Pay As You Earn) scheme; the self-employed have to tell the Inland Revenue how much profit they have made and are then taxed under what is known as Schedule D.

You do not pay tax on everything you earn – there is a range of tax free allowances. The basic two at 1992/93 rates are:
• Personal allowance: £3,445
• Married couple's allowance: £1,720.

There are increases in both of these for the over-65s. In addition, there are allowances for widows, blind people and those who are bringing up a child under difficult circumstances. Your local tax office can supply you with a full range of leaflets explaining your entitlements.

Once your income rises above your tax free allowance, it becomes what is known as taxable income and is taxed according to these rates:
• 20% on the first £2,000 of taxable income
• 25% (known as the 'basic rate') on taxable income between £2,000 and £23,700
• 40% (known as the 'higher rate') on your taxable income over £23,700.

National Insurance

National Insurance contributions go towards paying for a whole range of state benefits – from unemployment to the state retirement pension. There are four classes:
• **Class 1** Once your earnings from a job reach a certain level, both you and your employer have to pay Class 1. The more you earn, the more you pay.
• **Class 2** A flat rate contribution

payable by the self-employed, or those who do some work for themselves, unless their income is below about £3,000.

• **Class 3** Another flat rate contribution. You can elect to pay Class 3 if you are exempt from Class 2 but wish to build up your entitlement to a state benefit or your contribution record in general is not good enough for you to qualify.

• **Class 4** Payable by the self-employed, Class 4 is directly related to income between a lower and upper earnings limit. It is payable at the rate of 6.3% of qualifying earnings.

In general, people who work for an employer pay just Class 1. The self-employed pay Classes 2 and 4.

Capital Gains Tax – CGT

CGT is a tax on total profits above £5,800 that you make from selling investments or a second home (it is not payable on profits made from selling your main residence).

If you think you might be in a position to make this kind of profit,

---

Income tax and married women

At one time, a wife's income was treated for tax purposes as part of her husband's – there was no tax privacy. Nowadays, couples are assessed independently. What women in particular saw as the last injustice was removed in the budget of March 1992. The Chancellor of the Exchequer announced that from 1993/94, the married couple's allowance can be given entirely to the wife, partners can agree to split it or the wife can request half of it whatever her husband's wishes.

---

seek financial advice – you may be able to legally rearrange your affairs to avoid CGT.

Inheritance tax

You may not be able to take your money with you when you die but that is no reason to leave it to the government. Inheritance tax is payable on the value of a deceased person's estate over £150,000 (1992/93 figure) unless they have taken steps to reduce the liability. There are two ways of doing this:

• By distributing your estate in your will in such a way that your surviving spouse receives an inheritance-tax free amount and so does everyone else.

• By giving some of your money away before you die. However, if you die within seven years of making the gift, and it amounted to more than the inheritance tax threshold, your heirs will still have to pay some tax. This is calculated

---

Company cars and other perks

Many companies provide certain staff with cars, pay for petrol, contribute towards transport costs or offer other perks which you might not consider as salary. However, the Inland Revenue attaches a financial value to all of these benefits-in-kind and taxes you on the total. So, perks to the value of £3,000 will add £750 to a basic rate taxpayer's bill.

on a decreasing sliding scale for each year you survived.

Especially if you own your own home and it has little or no mortgage left on it, seek advice about reducing your liability to inheritance tax. If you do not pass on your money wisely, some of it will be lost to the state.

Local authority charges

To pay for the system of local government, your local authority levies an annual charge. At one time this was called rates, but it is now the Community Charge (more commonly known as poll tax) and each scheme has used a different system to calculate how much you need to pay. Rates were based,

---

VAT and other taxes

You pay VAT on a huge range of goods and services at the rate of 17%. Some things such as clothes for children have no VAT on them but there are plenty of other essentials on which it is charged. VAT is administered by HM Customs and Excise as is a range of other duties. In the 1992 budget, increases in these duties added:

- 13p to a packet of 20 cigarettes
- 28p to a bottle of spirits
- just over 1p on a litre (5p per gallon) of unleaded petrol
- £10 to your car's road tax.

Small though some of these amounts are, the price of many of these items is already largely made up of duty and you are paying for these things out of income you have already been taxed on.

Tax on retail goods

Tax on retail goods is composed of Value Added Tax and duty.

Leaded petrol

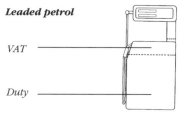

Tax = 67.2% of retail price

Cigarettes

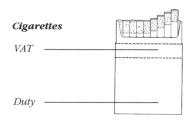

Tax = 75.6% of retail price

Beer

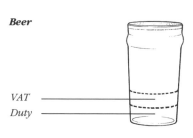

Tax = 33% of retail price

Whisky

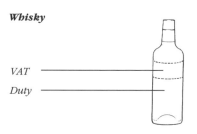

Tax = 68.1% of retail price

notionally anyway, on the ease with which you could let your home no matter how many people lived in it. Community Charge is levied on adults over 18 on the electoral register and Council Tax will use the current market value of your home to decide how much you pay.

It is likely that there will be further changes in the structure of local authority charges in the years to come. For instance, the Community Charge will become the Council Tax from 1993/94.

Making a will

You need to make a will to ensure that after your death your property goes to the people or organizations of your choice, and that your assets are correctly managed by the executors of your estate. If you do not make a will your estate will be divided and distributed according to law, and this may not benefit people important to you. Making a will avoids unncessary heartache for your family.

The first thing you need to consider when making a will is whom you should appoint as your executor. This person (or persons) will carry out your instructions and administer your affairs. The executor must be over 18 years of age and you should let him or her know where to find a copy of your will. You can keep your will anywhere but it is best to keep it where it will be found easily after your death, for example with your solicitor or at your bank.

People commonly make wills when they set up home together or

A valid will must:

1. Be in writing (handwritten, typed or printed).
2. Be signed by the testator (the person who is making out the will) or by some other person in the testator's presence and under his or her instructions if the testator is unable to sign.
3. Indicate clearly that by signing, the testator intended to give effect to the will. (The testator may instruct someone else to sign the will on his or her behalf if he or she is unable to do so.)
4. Be signed in the presence of two or more witnesses who must also sign the will. Beneficiaries should not be witnesses.
5. Long wills should be signed on each page by the testator and each witness.
6. Be dated. The last will should revoke any wills written before, so it is important to date a will.

buy a property, when they marry, have children, split up or divorce, or when grandchildren are born, but in fact anyone over 18 who is of sound mind and understanding can make a will at any time. Under-18s can make a will in special cases, such as if they are soldiers at war. A solicitor will have details of all such exceptions from the minimum age rule.

The will should be witnessed by non-beneficiaries and kept in a safe place. It will be revoked (legally cancelled) if it is burned, torn apart or otherwise destroyed by the person whose will it is. There are also other circumstances in which a will may be revoked. Getting married may revoke a will, unless you specify in the will that marriage will not affect it. Divorce does not revoke a will, but the divorced spouse cannot benefit from the will. It is advisable to make a new will as soon as you divorce, marry or remarry. The existence of a new will may revoke all previous wills, which is why it is always vital to date your will.

THIS IS THE LAST WILL AND TESTAMENT

of me *Sarah Smith*

of *10 King Street, Manchester*

I hereby revoke all previous wills and codicils I have made. This is my last will.
As executor(s) of this my will I appoint: *my husband Peter Smith of 10, King Street, Manchester; and my brother Roger Bean of 20 Queen Street, London.*

I direct that all my debts and funeral and testamentary expenses be paid as soon as is convenient after my death.

I leave all my estate to my husband Peter Smith of 10 King Street, Manchester. If he does not survive me I leave all my estate to my two children Karen Smith and James Smith, both of 10 King Street, Manchester, to be divided equally between them.

Dated this *25th* day of *September* 19 *91*

Signed by the testator / testatrix in our presence and by us in his/hers

.... (1st witness)
of *310 High Street, Reading*

.... (2nd witness)
of *12 Wood Close, Basingstoke.*

An example of a standard will

Preparing a will

Once you have chosen your executor, you should draw up a list of all your property and assets, including those jointly owned. Property includes your home, car and other valuable possessions; assets include bank and savings accounts, insurance policies and stocks amd shares. Estimate the value of each item and calculate the total, then you can decide how to distribute your estate.

Many people simply leave everything to their spouse, but you may prefer to leave special gifts, such as jewellery or other valuables, to other people close to you, and leave the residue to your spouse. You should write an accurate description of each gift and give the beneficiary's full name and address. You can also explain their connection to you ('friend', 'son-in-law' etc.) to make sure there is no confusion.

Once you have made all your specific bequests, including donations to charity and other institutions, you should state who is to get the residue (what is left) of your estate. You may want to leave this to one person (your spouse, for example), or to divide it equally between two or more people (such as your children). You should name a second beneficiary in case your first choice of beneficiary does not survive you.

Remember when you are making your will to keep the language simple, and don't try to use legal terms when plain English would suffice. Although making a will is easy, it is advisable to use a form to avoid complications.

Debt and how to control it

There are two types of debt – managed and runaway. If you can afford to repay them, some debts can make good financial practice. A sensible mortgage on a good home and interest-free credit on a fairly priced hi-fi system are just two examples of debts worth taking on.

If such managed debts begin to account for too much of your disposable income though, things can soon get out of hand. And the dangerous thing about debt is that it is all too easy for this to happen. A drop in overtime at work, an unplanned baby, repairs to the roof – these are just some of the everyday things that can turn your finances topsy-turvy.

Debt action plan

If you are having problems with your money or are beginning to

Things to avoid

Keep your debt problems simple by being aware of or avoiding the following:

• **Debt collectors:** creditors can ask collectors to get money off you but the collectors must work within the law. If they harrass you or get in touch with the firm you work for, contact your local consumer advice centre.

• **Borrowing more:** this can be tempting especially when you see adverts promising to take over all your debts. However, all you will be doing is swapping a series of small debts for one big one.

wonder how you are going to manage later in the year, take the steps outlined below now.

1. Write a household budget. Debts or no debts, a household budget provides the framework for all your financial affairs. You'll find guidelines to writing one elsewhere in this chapter. The key points to remember are:

i) List all your income including interest from any savings account and things like child benefit or any other form of social security benefit you might be receiving.

ii) Be honest with yourself about your spending.

2. Identify non-essentials you can cut back on.

3. Sell things you no longer need. If your children have grown, you may have an unused playpen or cot in the loft, or you may have some sports equipment left over from an abandoned hobby.

4. Check your entitlements to things like family credit. Claim or seek advice if you are in any doubt as to your right. Income Support, for example, can help with your mortgage costs. Check that you are not paying too much tax by asking your local Inland Revenue office for an explanation of your coding.

5. List your debts and then sort them into order of importance. Creditors you must give priority to are those who have a right, because of the nature of your relationship with them, to take your home, cut off your power and water etc., or take you to court quickly for non-payment of things like poll tax and hire purchase instalments.

6. Contact all your creditors and explain your situation (doing this in writing – keep copies of all letters – formalizes the arrangements you make). Although you cannot avoid your debts, many companies offer customers reduced instalments on the basis that some money is better than none.

One thing to remember when contacting your creditors is that being in debt can be embarrassing. But no matter what your situation,

Repossession

If you haven't kept up hire purchase payments, you may have the goods repossessed. This is because under HP agreements you don't actually own your new tv, or whatever, until you make the last payment.

A more serious, and increasingly common, form of repossession can happen if you fail to keep up the mortgage payments on your home. As with HP, you don't actually own your home until the mortgage is paid off. And the only reason a company lends you enough money to buy a home is because they can take it off you and sell it to get their money back if you default.

If you think you may face difficulty with HP agreements or your mortgage payments, get in touch with your lender immediately – it does not matter if you later solve your problems without difficulty. Your lender may agree to cut your repayments to a level you can manage for a while or adopt some other strategy to help (if not, contact your local consumer adviser straight away).

the chances are that the company has dealt with it, and a lot worse, before.

Buying on credit: what to look out for

A skilfully written credit deal can look an absolute bargain. But beware, making low payments over two years or so may be adding hundreds of pounds to the price you pay.

Whenever you are buying on credit, look out for the APR figure. APR stands for Annual Percentage Rate of charge and is an accurate way of gauging the difference between deals. It takes account not just of the interest rate quoted but also of things like the amount of deposit payable and the size and period of repayments. In general, the lower the APR, the better value the credit you are being offered.

Protecting your interests

No matter how hard you work in life, or how well paid your job, all your efforts can be ruined by a stroke of fate. And if you survive your first three score years without mishap, what are you going to live off for the next ten?

Pensions and tax

There are tax advantages to paying into your own pension. Income and capital gains from your fund are tax free and the payments themselves qualify for tax relief.

Life after debt

Some people find difficulty getting credit again once they have emerged from a period of debt. If this happens to you it is likely to be because a credit reference agency has been consulted and the company granting the loan has decided you are a bad risk. This may be justified but may not. If you are refused credit and feel there is no good reason why, check your own credit references.

1. Contact your local consumer advice centre for the addresses of the four main agencies.

2. Write to the agencies enclosing a fee of £1. Give your full name and address and, if you have been at your present address for less than six years, any other addresses you have lived in during this time.

3. The agency then has a week from receiving your letter to send you details of your file or tell you there is nothing on the file.

If your details are incorrect:

1. Write to the agency telling them why and saying how you want the entry corrected.

2. If you hear nothing within 28 days, you can send the agency a 200 word statement of correction. The agency must add your comments to your file or explain to the Office of Fair Trading why they will not do so.

What are you worth?

Whatever your finances, you should plan now for a secure financial future. In general, the earlier you do this, the better, but

before rushing out to insure your life for a million pounds, there are certain things you should consider:
• Who will miss me if I die? A single person with no dependents may need to do little more than insure the fabric and contents of their home and car and make sure they will be entitled to a decent pension when they retire. As long as they leave sufficient money to

Getting financial advice

You can arrange much of your insurance yourself but for things like a pension or life assurance, you may want to take professional advice. Sales staff get commission on their deals so do your homework first to narrow your choice and speak to more than one adviser. For any financial adviser, check the following:
• Are they independent? If so, they can sell you products from more than one company and are duty bound to get you the best deal.
• Are they tied to one particular company? If so, you may not be getting the best advice as only one company's products will be presented to you.

One word of warning, don't enter into any deal without fully understanding it. Ask for time to think it over if necessary. Take care however, that you don't simply use this as an excuse to put off arranging to cover yourself for another few years.

Are you covered?

It is not impossible to have more insurance cover than you really need but most people have too little. Use this checklist to see if you and your family have full protection.
• Mortgage protection to cover your commitments if you die or to take care of your repayments if you hit financial difficulty.
• Buildings insurance to pay for things like subsidence damage.
• Home contents insurance.
• Car insurance – and are the car's contents on the policy?
• Health – policies are available for private medical treatment, to cover you if your earning capacity is reduced or to compensate you for a major illness.
• Pension. Check the terms of any occupational pension you have. Back it up with a personal pension if necessary.
• Life assurance. If anyone is dependent on you, or you them, make sure you or they have life assurance. Dying without such cover can leave your family with little protection against the ravages of poverty.

pay for the funeral of their choice, who is going to miss them, financially speaking, when they are gone?

The financial consequences of the loss of a family's breadwinner can be devastating however. Under the terms of your mortgage, this may be paid off if one of you dies – but who is going to pay for the upkeep of the home, the children's care and welfare, finance holidays and major items of expenditure and provide whatever else you spend your income on? It is especially difficult for a single parent to support under school-age children because of restricted work opportunities.

• Supposing I live – but am incapacitated? Many people do of course survive major illness and go on to lead a very productive life. But it is possible that your earning potential may be severely reduced and you need to be sure your family will not suffer financially. There are policies that cover you for this eventuality.

Income after retirement

It is no exaggeration to say that you cannot begin planning for your retirement soon enough. The basic state pension will never be enough to support a good standard of living and occupational pensions often fall short of ideal too. Take the following into account when thinking of your life in the years after work:

• What kind of lifestyle will you want? Few people can accept a drop in their standard of living but age may restrict some of their more expensive activities.

• Your mortgage may be paid off by the time you retire but will your house give you an income? Many people plan to sell up and move to a smaller, cheaper place to free up their money.

• What money will you be entitled to from existing pension provisions? If you are within a decade or so of retiring, making what are called additional voluntary contributions before you retire may boost a meagre pension into a decent one.

Boosting your income

Most of us feel we could do with more money in our pockets. First thoughts turn naturally towards extra overtime or promotion but these are not options available to all. And in any case, before overloading yourself with work, the first thing to do is make sure your financial affairs are working for you, rather than against you. You may be surpirsed at what you find.

Financial checklist

If you feel your income needs a boost, run through the following checklist before you do anything else.

• Do you know exactly what your income is and what you spend it on? No? Write a household budget. You may spot areas you can cut back on and gain money that way.

• Do you know roughly what your current account balance is at any one time? No? This means one of two things; you may be incurring costly account charges by needlessly running up occasional overdrafts, or, you may keep a larger balance in your account than you need for monthly expenses. This extra could be earning valuable interest in an instant access savings account. And make sure your current account is an interest paying one.

• Do you avoid paying off your credit card because you don't want to dip into your savings? This is not uncommon but remember – credit card interest may be costing you 25%; your savings are probably earning you less than 10%. Your priority therefore should be to keep your credit card under control.

• Do you know if your tax code is correct and have you checked your entitlement to state benefits? Also, if you are getting state benefits, whether in the form of Family Credit or a pension, do you know how much you can earn before your benefit is cut?

• If you have children and one of you is going to stay at home, which of you has the greatest earning power in the short, medium and long term?

If one or a combination of the above does not give you enough, then earning some extra money is your only option. Outlined below are some typical situations with points to be aware of.

Returning to work after children

The arrival of children makes a substantial dent in most people's income. Household earnings can be halved or worse, and expenses mount up no matter how supportive friends and relatives are. At some stage you may decide to return to work but take the following into account first.

• Is it worth it? Your earnings will be reduced by the cost of tax, national insurance and childcare – very few companies give assistance with this. There may well be an increase in the rate of your emotional wear and tear too, as you cope with both job and family commitments. Might you be better off registering with your local authority as a childminder and earning money helping yourself and others at the same time?

Part-time work

Part-time work can be of a casual or more formal nature. Whatever, you must declare your earnings to the Inland Revenue and to the relevant department if you are receiving state benefits.

Where tax is concerned, you have a personal tax free earnings allowance of £3,445 (1992/93). State benefits may be reduced by £1 for every £1 you earn over a certain limit.

Jobs of less than 16 hours a week give reduced entitlements to things like redundancy pay. Be wary of taking such employment and then being asked to work regular overtime – the overtime doesn't increase your rights.

Freelance work

You may have a hobby that makes you money or a professional skill which you can turn to profitable use. Keep records of all the work you do, payments received and expenses incurred. You may need to pay tax on your freelance income but, if it is not very great, your expenses will reduce your liability.

Check your liability to pay Class 2 National Insurance contributions. You are liable for these once your income from part-time or freelance work rises above about £3,000, even if you work mainly for an employer and pay Class 1 contributions.

Letting a room

Letting a room can be an ideal way to bring in some extra money; but it can also prove to be a disaster. Aside from making sure you get on personally with your sharer, there are several other areas to consider:

• Lodger or tenant? If you are not careful, the person sharing your home may end up with more rights than you intended. A lodger, someone for whom you provide meals and who shares your home as part of the family, has few legal rights and the agreement can be ended with ease. This is especially the case where the agreement is written and you both sign and keep a copy.

However, you may have two bathrooms, for example, and out of a desire for your own privacy and respect for your lodger's, suggest you have one each. Once you do this you are muddying the water of the agreement between you and may be creating a position where your lodger has Housing Act protection.

The legal ins and outs of letting even a single room can be complex – if you are planning to do this, even for someone 'just staying while they find a place of their own', seek advice from your local Citizens' Advice Bureau. An attitude of 'better safe than sorry' may save you a lot of distress.

• Your tax position: letting a room for money renders you liable for tax if what you receive takes you over your personal allowance. Most people's income in these circumstances will be treated as investment income and they will be allowed to set certain costs, such as food and heating, against it. Keep full records.

If you let a part of your home that is self-contained, you may be able to set some of your mortgage payments against your income. If this applies, beware – you may also be setting yourself up to incur capital gains tax when you sell the home. Once again, before letting, seek professional advice.

• Your mortgage company: check with your mortgage company that you can let a room. Remember, they have a vested interest in your property.

• Your insurance: check with your contents insurance company that you will not be invalidating your policy by having someone come to live in your home.

YOU & YOUR CAR

This section of the book provides a comprehensive guide to owning and running a car. Beginning with learning to drive, it takes you through the pitfalls of buying and selling a car, with advice on how to check out a worthwhile purchase and spot a dodgy dealer. It explains motoring offences and how the endorsement system works. It sets out maintenance schedules that will save garage fees and help avoid unexpected breakdowns, and there are plenty of tips for driving abroad and in bad weather conditions. Finally, it tells you how to cope in an emergency, with particular advice for women travelling alone.

Learning to drive

Passing your driving test can be one of life's most rewarding experiences. Learning to drive should be safe and enjoyable but can prove frustrating unless you take as much time as you need and have proper instruction.

Getting an instructor

There are over 33,000 Approved Driving Instructors around the country most of which advertise in local papers and directories. The best way to choose one is by talking to friends and colleagues and making your initial selections through personal recommendation.

Meet and talk to more than one instructor. You will be working closely on a regular basis so must feel happy that you have got a good teacher and someone that

you will be comfortable with on a personal level too.

All professional instructors must by law display a green eight-sided symbol (signifying that they have passed their examinations and are regularly monitored by the government's inspectors) or a pink triangle (showing that the instructor is still in his training period but is entitled to give tuition).

To qualify, instructors must pass a written exam, a special driving test of much higher standard than you will be taking and a test of their ability to teach.

If you start lessons with an instructor and then feel you do not get on, talk it over and if necessary change to a different instructor. Do not feel it is your fault – learning to drive is a two way experience and remember, you are the one paying the money.

Lessons from friends and family

Your family and friends can play an invaluable role in helping you learn to drive by accompanying you when you go out to practise in between formal lessons. These practice sessions let you perfect the techniques you have learned with your instructor and also do some 'real' everyday driving – whether just to the local shops or for a day out.

Some words of warning:

• Choose who accompanies you with care – not all family members are good teachers or can take the strain of being with a learner driver. And keep the number of people in the car to a minimum.

• Avoid the temptation to drive for too long or on just one type of road.

• Be careful not to pick up bad driving habits from your companion.

• Your companion must be over 21 and have held a full driving licence for at least three years.

What it costs

One of the things that frequently puts people off learning to drive or causes them to abandon learning altogether is the cost. Going out with friends and family is one way of keeping costs to a minimum but very few people get by without formal tuition too.

Many driving schools work on the basis that an average learner needs 25-30 hours of formal tuition backed up by regular outings with a friend or relative. Another rule of thumb often used is that you need 1-1½ hours of formal tuition for every year of your life – this formula acknowledging that as we get older we are slower to learn. One useful tip for keeping learning costs down is to find out how long the waiting lists for driving test appointments are in your area (telephone numbers on the back of

---

Use this example to work out what it could cost you to learn to drive. Driving school fees are typical for a reputable company. Petrol priced at 46p/litre (£2.10/gallon).

Provisional licence	£21
25-30 hours of driving school tuition @ £15.50 per hour	£387.50-£465
Cost of fuel for informal 'lessons' – 25-30 hours @ 4.55 litres (1 gall) per hour	£52.50-63
Driving test fee	£21.50
<u>Example total</u>	<u>£482.50-£570.50</u>

Note: on top of these amounts you may also need to pay to put yourself on someone else's insurance or, if you are running your own car, bear all the costs of maintenance too. Don't forget that while you may need fewer hours of formal tuition than given in the example, your driving test is likely to involve using the driving school's car for a pre-test lesson and the time of the test – so you will need to budget for this on top of the test fee itself.

driving test application forms available from your local Post Office). Booking in plenty of time will save you paying for lessons just to keep your standard up until your test date arrives.

Taking your driving test

If you've had plenty of practice and your instructor thinks you are up to test standard, you may find your test nerve-wracking but it should not be an ordeal. It's well worth having a pre-test warm-up lesson and getting to the test centre in plenty of time.

Many people complain that their examiner was unfriendly. Unlike your instructor, he is not there to be friendly, just to assess if your driving is up to standard. A good instructor will have prepared you for this.

Drive normally on your test and if you make a mistake, correct it if possible and then carry on unless the examiner tells you to stop. Once you have passed your test, do not forget to send away to have your provisional licence converted to a full one – this is free.

Motorways

Learner drivers are forbidden from motorways so it can be a daunting experience tackling one for the first time. Despite adverse publicity when reckless drivers crash in fog or as a result of following the car in front too closely for their speed, motorways are remarkably safe roads because they have very few side turnings, no parked vehicles on the carriageway and of course everything always travels in the same direction. Some tips for the novice:

• Re-read the Highway Code section on motorways before driving on one and make sure you know what your braking distances mean. As the car in front passes under a bridge, for example, say out loud 'only a fool breaks the two second rule'. If you pass under the bridge before you have said this, you are following too closely for your speed. You can use this rule on any road too.

• Make sure you know where you are getting on and off in plenty of time.

• When you join a motorway, give yourself time to adjust to the speed of other cars before overtaking any yourself.

• Use your mirrors frequently and return to the inside lane whenever you reasonably can. Never hog the middle or outside lane.

Learning-to-drive holidays

One– or two–week intensive learning-to-drive courses with a driving test at the end have become very popular as they combine a holiday with a practical achievement. For around £300 for one week (accommodation and food extra) you can drive with a tutor and another pupil from 9-5.30 Monday to Friday and if you're up to standard take your driving test at the end. Consult the holiday advertisements of the national papers for details or contact the tourist board of the area in which you would like to learn.

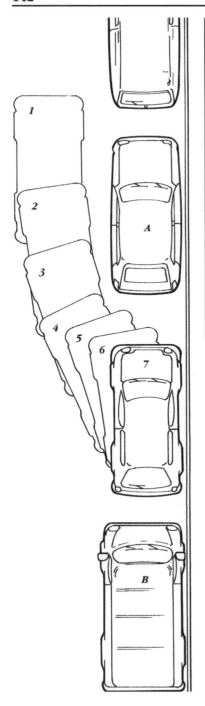

Parking

The most efficient way to park in a tight spot is to reverse in.
Study the diagram, then practise.
(1) Stop parallel to the parked car (A) and then reverse with the steering wheel turned slightly left.
(2) Continue reversing, watching the corner bumper of the parked car (A).
(3) Begin to straighten the front wheels as you move clear of the parked car (A).
(4) Lock your wheel fully to the right.
(5) Swing to the kerb, moving slowly and watching the parked car (B).
(6) Take off some of the right lock so the car does not swing in too far.
(7) Finally, check that your car is positioned correctly to the kerb and the parked cars.

Night driving

Driving at night demands extra vigilance because cars, cyclists and pedestrians are masked by shadows and other cars' lights can dazzle you. Before setting off, make sure all your windows are clean and give your lights a wipe over. If it is raining, clear all your windows and exterior mirrors of water before starting to greatly improve your vision. Always use dipped beam even in towns. On long journeys rest frequently, keep a window open for fresh air and avoid looking directly into oncoming cars' headlamps. If your interior mirror is adjustable to deflect light coming from behind, use it. Do not drive far at night if you feel tired particularly on long stretches of road such as dual carriageways or motorways.

Buying and selling a car

Whatever your budget, buying a car will take a significant chunk out of it. Because of this, and because buying a car forms only part of the cost of owning one, it makes sense to ensure that what you buy is a good buy.

Choosing the right car for you

We all have our dream car be it sleek, red and fast or a comfortable 1950s classic. Dreams need to be tempered with reality though. Run through the following checklist to help you form a more practical profile of the car that's right for you:

• What do you really want a car for?
• How many miles a year do you drive?
• What sort of roads do you drive on?
• How many people do you regularly, and occasionally, carry?
• Do you need to carry large/awkward loads or pets?
• How much money can you afford to buy and run a car?
• Do you really want a new car or will secondhand do?

The checklist will guide you in the direction of two doors or four, saloon versus hatchback and so on. To narrow your choice to a particular make and model, run through the following:

• Which cars that fit your profile do you like?
• Is there more than one local dealer for spare parts and service back-up?

• What is the car like to actually use, including driving, operating all controls and loading and unloading? (There is no substitute for personal experience in this. Arrange at least one test drive before making your choice.)
• What are the car's running costs including servicing and insurance?
• What reputation does the car have?

Buying new

Buying new from a dealer should be the ideal way to buy a car. Make sure you know what the price quoted includes however. Number plates, delivery and getting the car ready for you in what is known as a pre-delivery inspection are often charged as an extra.

New cars are covered against faults developing in the first year by the manufacturer's guarantee but note that where corrosion warranties are provided, you may need to submit the car for an annual check and have any rust spots that have occurred eliminated. Failure to do either invalidates the warranty.

Buying secondhand

Although buying new is not without its potential problems, buying secondhand is where many people come unstuck. There are three ways of of buying secondhand; from a used car dealer, in a private sale, and at auction.

Used car dealers These vary from the excellent to the highly unscrupulous. To find a good one ask around. In general, good

Fuel and the environment

A fuel-efficient car makes sense in terms of your running costs and will do less damage to the environment. Your car will burn less fuel for the same mileage if you:

• Avoid aggressive acceleration and brake in good time.
• Check and adjust the tyre pressures regularly.
• Use the choke sensibly.
• Keep your top speed to around 50mph. Many engines are at peak efficiency in top gear at this speed. Above it, wind resistance increases to such an extent that for just an extra 20mph in speed your car will burn almost one-third more fuel.
• Have your car regularly serviced.

Three main fuels for cars

• Unleaded petrol: Lead in petrol is harmful to the development of children and unleaded petrol sales have now reached about half of all sales in the UK. Unleaded petrol also has a price advantage over leaded which offsets any slight increase in fuel consumption.
• Leaded petrol: Cars are now being manufactured to run on lead-free petrol and most existing cars can be converted to use it. Leaded petrol will eventually cease to be sold.
• Diesel fuel: Rapidly gaining in popularity. Diesel-fuelled cars have shed much of their 'taxi' image as the engines have become quieter and manufacturers have improved soundproofing, winter starting and acceleration. A diesel-fuelled car may easily achieve more than 45 miles per gallon against the 30 miles per gallon of a petrol-fuelled counterpart and also emits less pollution. Diesel fuel costs less than both leaded and unleaded petrol.

dealers will be on well established sites and may well belong to the Motor Agents Association or Retail Motor Industry Federation which investigate complaints and lay down codes of practice. Many dealers have their cars inspected by one of the motoring organizations prior to putting them in the showroom – this is a good sign. When you buy from a dealer you have the backing of the Sale of Goods laws in three important respects:

• The car must be of 'merchantable quality' – that is, in a condition fit for its normal use.
• The car should be 'as described' – so 'very good condition' should not mean that there are dents in the bodywork or faults with the

engine, brakes, steering etc.
• The car should be 'fit for the purpose it was sold for'. So if you told the dealer you regularly drive over unmade roads and wanted a good four-wheel drive vehicle for that purpose, your new car should do the job.

Make sure you know exactly what is included in the price of the car – it may come with a limited mileage guarantee – and don't be afraid to haggle over the price. Even if the dealer won't come down, he may well include some extras for the same price. It all depends on the state of the car market at the time.

Private sale You will always be able to buy cheaper in a private sale than from a dealer but you need to act with care. Private sales do not come with Sale of Goods legal protection or a guarantee and you are not buying from a trader who has his reputation to think about. Only if the seller lies to you, about the mileage, for example, can you get compensation.

When buying this way, do much of your work over the telephone to avoid wasting too much time visiting unsuitable cars.

Auctions Bargain basement prices are the attraction of auctions but they are probably best avoided unless you or a companion are fairly knowledgeable about cars and feel fully confident about your prospective purchase. There are no test-drive opportunities and as with all auctions, it is easy to get carried away into bidding for something unsuitable.

Protecting your interests

No matter what rights of complaint you may have, it is better to avoid an unsatisfactory purchase in the first place. Taking the following precautions whenever you buy a car and before parting with any money will help avoid coming to grief:

• Ask to see the Vehicle Registration Document ('log' book). Check the name and address of the registered keeper (note that this need not be the owner) and be wary if this is not the seller or their partner. 'I'm selling it for a friend' is a much used confidence tricksters' phrase which means they may take your money for a sub-standard or even stolen car and you are left with no proof of who you have bought from. Also check

the vehicle details and question any discrepancies. Make, model, type, colour, engine and chassis numbers listed on the document should all match up with the car. You'll usually find the engine and chassis numbers on a prominently positioned plate in the car's engine bay – look for signs of tampering.

• If the car is more than three years old it should have a valid Department of Transport Test Certificate ('MOT'). Check how long the certificate has to run and the recorded mileage detailed on it. Compare the recorded mileage to that on the car's mileometer and ask yourself if the two are plausible. Also ask to see previous test certificates and check the recorded mileage on those. If a car is being sold with little time left to expire on the test certificate, it is worth asking the seller to have it tested so that you know the car is up to standard now.

• Ask to see all receipts and documents relating to repairs and servicing of the car. These form a potted history that should confirm everything the seller has told you.

• Do not be afraid to contact the previous recorded owner of the car (their name and address appears on the Vehicle Registration Document) particularly if you have doubts about what the seller has told you. Ask them to confirm mileages and the general history of the car.

• And if you can, arrange for an independent engineer to test drive and inspect the car.

Remember, an honest seller should have no objection to any of the above if you are showing a sincere interest in buying their car. Check that the price being asked is reasonable in the specialist car buying guides and by looking at similar cars.

Pre-purchase vehicle inspections

No matter how competent you are mechanically, it is always advisable to take someone along with you when buying a car. Arranging an inspection by a qualified engineer is a lot better. The motoring organizations carry these out for members and supply a comprehensive written report based on a thorough visual inspection and a test drive. Depending on the price of the car, you may see the inspection as a handy insurance policy against buying a car with expensive faults that you had failed to spot. Although these inspections cost getting on for £100, you can easily recoup some if not all the price by using the results of the report to negotiate a better price for the car. Less expensive inspections can be had by scouring the small ads of your local paper where you are sure to see 'vehicle engineers' offering their services. Always check their qualifications before asking one to make an inspection for you.

Cash or cheque?

Whether you're buying or selling, it's as well to know where you stand with the money side of things.

• Paying by cash may be the only way a seller will let you drive away the car there and then. Make sure you get all the documents, that the seller retains their section of the Vehicle Registration Document and that you get a signed receipt from them for the money detailing their name and address, full details of the car and stating that the car is indeed theirs to sell. A full descriptive receipt means you can prove to the police, if necessary, that you own the car and may also help you get compensation if the car proves to be not as good as you had been led to believe.

• Do not let a buyer drive your car

Spot the 'dodgy dealer'

Trust your instincts when buying a car. If things do not ring true you may be better off avoiding the deal. Below are some of the more common 'tricks' used by the unscrupulous in both private and trade sales.

• Showing a car with a valid Road Fund Licence ('tax disc') but actually selling it without for the same price. Dealers can make a tidy sum claiming refunds on unexpired licences.

• 'Clocking'. This is winding back the mileometer to present a high mileage car as a lower mileage one. If no MOT or service documents with past recorded mileages are available for you to check, be suspicious. Contact the last recorded keeper of the car (name and address on Vehicle Registration Document) before parting with any money. Look at the car's control pedals, seats – particularly the driver's, tyres, paintwork and engine bay area to see if the level of wear and tear on these is greater than you would expect.

• Advertising as a private seller when in fact a dealer. This is to avoid buyers getting Sale of Goods law protection. Look out for the same phone number appearing in the 'For Sale' columns.

• Steam cleaning and valeting. This may be an absolute bonus to you but both can conceal a car's history. A steam cleaned engine bay or suspension system will show no oil leaks so you will need to give the car a long test drive and look for leaks closely afterwards. Valeted upholstery can look as good as new and help mask a high mileage or particularly heavy use.

• Showing a car fitted with a radio and other accessories and selling it without or with replacements of inferior quality. Be quite clear about what is included in the price of the car when you first view it. Avoid the deal or negotiate a reduction on the spot if you are not satisfied when you come to pay for the car.

• 'Selling for a friend'. When the seller and the details on the Vehicle Registration Document don't tally, be wary. Reputable dealers on permanent sites are obviously going to sell vehicles that do not have their name on the Registration Document but an alarming number of stolen or poor quality cars are sold this way too. If in doubt, contact the last recorded keeper to check. An honest seller should not object to this.

away on the basis of a personal cheque alone. It will take at least three working days for the cheque to clear and for you to be reassured that the money has indeed gone into your account. If a buyer is keen and only has a cheque book with them, take a deposit by cheque but keep the car until you know that the cheque has cleared. Take the balance of the money in cash. Alternatively, take a cheque for the full amount and hand the car over when your bank confirms the money is in your account. This last method is risky if you are the one buying as there is a chance that you may lose the money and the car. If you buy this way, ask to take all the car's documents and a receipt for your cheque with you.

• Bank warrants are a form of payment as good as cash without the dangers of carrying cash around. For a small fee, a bank will give a buyer a warrant and the seller can be fully confident that he can hand the car over. Building society cheques work in a similar way but there has been controversy due to stolen cheques being used. As a precaution against this if you receive payment in this way, your buyer can arrange for you to telephone the bank or building society concerned at the time of the deal to confirm that a warrant or cheque was indeed issued to the buyer.

The golden rule

Do not part with money or car until you are absolutely certain that the other side of the deal is genuine.

Mechanical/bodywork faults to look for

When buying a car, take a friend and make sure you view in good daylight – dusk and darkness bring a sparkle to the dullest paintwork. Listen to what the seller has to say but do not deviate from the following checklist.

• Walk around the car noting dents, scratches, chipped windows, damaged tyres (sidewalls and treads), missing parts or trim and anything else that does not look right. Bubbles in paintwork may mean a poor respray or rust working its way to the surface.

• Ask the seller to demonstrate that all the lights are in working order – side, head (dip and full beam), indicators and hazard flashers, reversing, brake and any auxiliary lights such as fog, spot and high intensity rear lights.

• Look in the engine bay for any obvious faults such as dripping oil or water, low fluid levels in the battery or brake and clutch reservoirs, loose parts and wires.

• Look in the boot checking the condition of the spare wheel and tyre and accessories.

• Inside the car, sit on all the seats, adjust them forwards and back, operate all the windows and all of the controls (you may need the engine running) not forgetting the heater, windscreen wipers and the horn. Try all the accessories such as the radio/cassette and sunroof too. Open and close all the doors, the bonnet and the boot.

Checks to make when buying a car

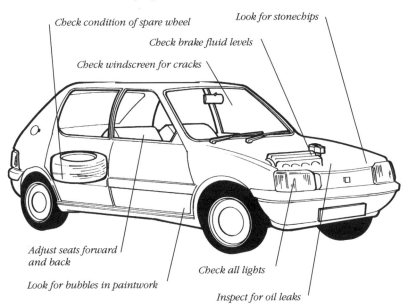

Check condition of spare wheel

Look for stonechips

Check brake fluid levels

Check windscreen for cracks

Adjust seats forward and back

Look for bubbles in paintwork

Check all lights

Inspect for oil leaks

The test drive

Only now should you be thinking of having a test drive. There is no substitute for driving the car yourself — make sure you are insured to do so. Include a stretch of straight fast road in the drive.

During the test drive, ask yourself the following:

• Does the car start easily from cold? Also check that it starts easily when warm.

• Do the brakes work? Test the pedal pressure before pulling away and try the brakes firmly as soon as it is safe to do so. The car should stop in a straight line with no pulling to either side.

• Does the car work well for you and sound and feel right? The gears, including reverse, should be easy to engage, there should be no unusual noises and the car should

steer in a perfectly straight line with barely any pressure on the steering wheel.

• Do I like this car? A purely personal but very important consideration.

After the test drive, leave the engine running and look in the engine bay again for water or oil leaks. Have the seller rev the engine while you listen for any unusual noises and look for puffs of smoke from the exhaust which could show that the engine is worn and burning oil.

If all is satisfactory, ask to see all the documentation and repair and servicing records. You should now be able to form a fairly accurate impression of the car and can arrange to have this backed up by an engineer's inspection for further peace of mind.

When things go wrong

Private sales These offer little protection unless the seller has lied to you about the vehicle (which is why a receipt detailing mileage and condition is so important – it may be valuable evidence). If you have second thoughts about a car's suitability for you once you have bought it, there is nothing you can do; the seller does not have to give you your money back. If you discover that the car needs a major repair you had not previously spotted and the seller had not lied about, you can always try going back and asking for some money back but the seller is under no obligation to do anything.

If you think that your private seller was really a dealer, you should inform your local Trading Standards Department.

Trade sales These offer all the protection of the Sale of Goods laws. If you have a problem, contact the dealer first to see if he will put things right. If you remain unsatisfied, your ultimate sanction is to seek compensation through the Small Claims Court but your first port of call should be your local consumer advice centre or Citizens' Advice Bureau.

The car and the law

Keeping yourself on the right side of the motoring law will not only save you a lot of inconvenience, it is likely to save you money in insurance premiums too.

Documentation

Keep this in order. Entering expiry dates in your diary at the beginning of each year will avoid driving without insurance for example. If you are stopped by the police, you will be asked to show your documents (with the exception of the tax disc which should always be displayed). If you do not have your documents with you, you can choose to show them at a police station of your choice within seven days of being stopped.

Each car or driver must:

- have a valid driving licence that is signed.
- display a valid Road Fund licence (tax disc) even if the car is only parked on a public road.
- have a valid 'MOT' certificate if over three years old.
- be properly insured.

Insurance types

You have two main choices when insuring your car – Third Party, Fire and Theft cover or Comprehensive insurance cover.

Third party, fire and theft Covers you for damage you cause to someone else's property, for damage by fire to your car and for the theft of your car. If you dent your own car while driving, or someone else damages it and does not leave their details, you have to pay for the repairs to your car yourself.

Comprehensive Depending on the type of policy, comprehensive cover matches third party, fire and theft and adds payments for damage to your car even if it was your fault, for loss of personal possessions and personal injury. It is by far the best cover if your car is worth a lot of money but the premiums may well be twice as much as for third party, fire and theft.

The MOT – how to pass first time

About 40 per cent of cars fail their MOT due mainly to poor routine maintenance and the lack of any pre-test inspection by the owner. The following are the items tested:

- Steering
- Foot and hand brakes
- Seatbelt condition, mountings and operation
- Horn
- Windscreen wipers and washers
- Front and rear lamps
- Headlamps and beam aim
- Brake lights
- Rear reflectors
- Indicators
- Tyres – correct ones fitted and in good condition
- Wheel condition
- Shock absorbers
- Transmission shafts
- Wheel bearings
- Suspension
- Exhaust system
- Exhaust emissions

(In addition to the above, other items such as locks and bodywork will be added in future years to bring the MOT into line with European requirements.)

Where headlamp aim, tyres and exhaust emissions are concerned there have been changes to the law that still catch people out. The law now says:

Headlamp aim The break point for headlamp beams where the beam is of the pattern shown and the lamps are no higher than 850mm/33in from the ground should fall within the area shown (see diagram below).

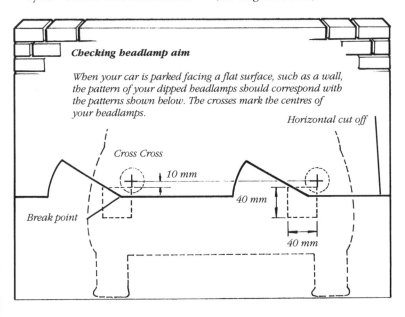

Checking headlamp aim

When your car is parked facing a flat surface, such as a wall, the pattern of your dipped headlamps should correspond with the patterns shown below. The crosses mark the centres of your headlamps.

Horizontal cut off

Cross Cross

10 mm

40 mm

Break point

40 mm

Checking tyre tread depth

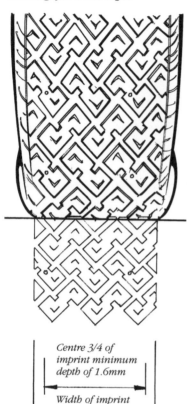

Centre 3/4 of
imprint minimum
depth of 1.6mm

Width of imprint

Tyre tread depth New standards
were introduced on 1 January 1992.
Tyres must now have a tread depth
of at least 1.6mm right across the
central three quarters of their width
and right around their
circumference.

Exhaust emissions From the
beginning of November 1991 levels
of both carbon monoxide and
hydrocarbons in the exhaust have
been tested and cars are failed if
not up to scratch. Keeping your car
properly tuned will avoid this.

While you may not feel
sufficiently mechanically competent
to check your car's transmission

shafts or wheel bearings, all too
often cars fail their MOT simply
because a bulb is not working or the
exhaust system, which may be
difficult to see but is easy to hear,
has a hole in it.

To make sure your car passes its
MOT first time (the full fee of £20
is payable again unless you leave
the car where it is to be repaired
and retested, have it retested after
failures on specific relatively minor
faults such as a malfunctioning
bulb or return it the next day for a
retest), you should carry out much
the same inspection as for when
buying a secondhand car and
taking into account all the
components listed above. With a
partner, it should take you little
more than 20 minutes to check
your car over.

And don't forget if you are a
mechanical novice, many tyre and
exhaust centres offer a free opinion
on these parts of your car and
sometimes the headlamp alignment
too. (Note: it is always wise to
compare the advice of two
independent centres.)

Rear seatbelts and child restraints
Compulsory wearing of front seat
belts was introduced at the end of
January 1983 and has saved an
estimated 200 lives and 7,000
serious injuries per year since.
Many motorists remain confused
about child restraints and the laws
concerning rear seat belts however.
Children and seat belts Since the
beginning of September 1989 it has
been the driver's legal
responsibility to ensure that
children under the age of 14 use

seat belts or child restraints fitted in the rear of the car. Children under one year who travel in the front must use a child restraint.

A child travelling in the back does not have to be restrained if the only available restraints are being used by other children or by adults who are themselves belted in. **Adults and rear seat belts** Since the middle of 1991 adults have been obliged to wear seat belts, where available, when travelling in the back of cars and taxis.

Motoring offences and the endorsement system

Safe, conscientious drivers who know their Highway Code and keep their car and paperwork in good order should rarely fall foul of the law. For those who do, the box opposite shows just some of the offences they may come up against with their respective licence endorsement codes and penalty points.

What to do in an accident

There are three areas to consider if you have an accident.
Safety Ensure the safety of yourself and other road users by switching on hazard flashers, switching off your engine, putting out cigarettes and positioning a red warning triangle further back down the road. Arrange for the police and ambulance services to be called if necessary. Only move injured people if they are in immediate danger of further injury otherwise you may aggravate an existing unseen injury. Give first aid.
Legal You must stop after an

Offence code points

Failing to stop after an accident AC10 8-10
Failing to report an accident AC20 8-10
Driving without due care and attention CD10 3-9
Using a vehicle with defective brakes CU10 3
Using a vehicle with defective tyre(s) CU30 3
Reckless driving DD30 10
Using a vehicle uninsured against third party risks IN10 6-8
Driving without a licence LC10 2
Various speeding offences SP10-SP60 3
Failing to follow various traffic directions, signs and signals TS10-TS50 3

Under the points system, a driver is liable to disqualification when his or her total reaches 12 points within three years. Drink/drug related offences normally carry a minimum one year ban as well as any fine imposed.

---

accident and give your details to anyone who requests them. If someone was injured but the police not called at the time, report the accident to the police within 24 hours.
Insurance Get the name, address and, if possible, insurance details of any other driver. Also make a note of their car's registration number. Give your details too to anyone else involved in the accident. Ask for the names and addresses of any witnesses and make a quick sketch of the position of all the cars involved and the position of any

junctions, bends and so on. Contact your insurance company as soon as possible afterwards.

The golden rule as far as insurance is concerned is not to apologise or admit liability for the accident nor to give any money to any injured person.

The Highway Code

The Highway Code is an invaluable book for all road users but one that

Motoring finances

Setting a motoring budget serves two purposes – firstly it lets you know if you can really afford the car you want and secondly tells you whether you are actually getting value for money per mile travelled. In other words, would you be better off using public transport and maybe hiring a car for special occasions?

(a)

(b)

(c)

Do you know the Highway Code?
(1) Can you identify these road signs?
(2) What is the maximum national speed limit for cars and motorbikes on single carriageway roads?
(3) What are the shortest stopping distances at 30, 50 and 70 mph?

is frequently neglected once the driving test is passed. Surprisingly to many drivers, it is updated regularly – to take account of car phones (hand-held phones should not be used while your car is moving except in an emergency – Rule 54) for example, or some other development in road use, such as Red Routes.

If you fail to answer just one of the questions or wrongly identify one of the signs (the answers are shown on the opposite page), it is time you read the latest copy of the Highway Code.

Calculating your car's fuel consumption rate

You can work out your car's fuel consumption rate very accurately using the following method.

1. At your regular service station, fill your car with fuel until the pump cuts out. Your fuel tank is then completely full. Remember to set your car's trip meter to zero before driving off.

2. Keep a note of how much fuel exactly you put in your car over the next 700 miles or so.

3. When you are ready to work out the consumption rate, once again

fill your car with fuel until the pump cuts out. Make a note of the mileage you have covered to this point and total the fuel you have put into the car up to and including Step 3 but ignoring the quantity of fuel you put in at Step 1 to originally fill the tank.
4. Divide the mileage covered by the exact quantity of fuel used to give the consumption rate.

Note: 700 miles will normally be plenty to guarantee that you have driven in mixed conditions and on different types of road to get a fair reflection of your car's average consumption rate. You can also use this method during bouts of intensive urban driving, or when cruising to go on holiday, to get a picture of the consumption rates then too. Using the same fuel pump each time you add fuel, but particularly at Steps 1 and 3, will give greater accuracy. Repeating this exercise regularly will enable you to spot faults with your car that may otherwise have gone unnoticed as fuel consumption often rises when a car is not performing properly.

Insurance groupings and costs

Insurance companies classify cars into seven or eight groups which are closely related to their performance. The higher the grouping, the more you will pay for the policy you choose.

Against this basic policy price, companies set a range of other factors which may reduce or add to the overall cost. Drivers under 25 are considered a greater accident risk and their premiums are loaded

To prepare your own budget of your annual motoring costs fill in the following:

Fixed costs (those that remain the same however little or often you use your car):
Insurance £___
Road tax (per year) £___
MOT £___
Depreciation £___
AA/RAC membership £___

Variable costs (those that rise the more you use your car):
Fuel (average annual mileage divided by consumption rate multiplied by price) £___
Servicing £___
Repairs £___
Parking (including fines) £___

Total of fixed and variable costs £___

Divide the total by 52 to give you a 'weekly running costs' figure or by your annual mileage to give you a 'pence per mile travelled' figure.

Depreciation is simply the difference between what you think your car will be worth in a year's time and now.

Answers to
Highway Code questions

(1) a = no stopping
b = change to opposite carriageway
c = priority over vehicles from opposite direction
(2) 60 mph
(3) 23m (75ft), 53m (175ft) and 96 m (315 ft) respectively

accordingly. On the other hand, as you reach certain age bands, such as 35 and 55, you may be able to achieve substantial discounts. Other factors which affect your premium are your driving record, whether the car is garaged, and most importantly your No Claims Bonus.

For each year that you do not make an insurance claim, companies offer a discount on the basic premium cost which builds up to 65 per cent after five years. You will also get a discount if you agree to a policy excess – that is agreeing to pay the first £50, for example, of any damage – restrict who can drive the car or use the car for what is termed Social, Domestic and Pleasure purposes only – in other words, not for business.

Going to a broker

Insurance brokers deal with a wide range of companies and know which will offer the lowest price to you. Some companies specialize in insurance for female drivers, those with high-performance cars or those who have a poor or disqualified driving record for example. Contact more than one broker to maximize your choice of policies and take advantage of the computerization that has greatly increased competition in the car insurance market.

Choosing your policy

Price is a major factor in most people's minds when choosing a policy but it is very important to determine exactly what the policy does and does not cover too. You may have asked for Comprehensive cover for example, gone for the lowest quote and accepted it only to find that your attractive low premium has been achieved at the expense of cover for personal possessions.

Care and maintenance

The first step in looking after your car, and so making sure it looks after you, is to understand something of how it works.

The engine

Turning the ignition key begins a process in which the pistons in the engine cylinders move up and down in cycle. Petrol and air drawn into one of the cylinders is ignited by a spark from that cylinder's spark plug and the engine 'starts'.

From now on each cylinder is working in a cycle of drawing air and petrol in (when the piston is on a down stroke – the induction stroke), compressing the mixture (when the piston moves up again – the compression stroke), igniting the mixture with a spark from the spark plug when it is fully compressed (the piston is now driven hard downwards under the power of the explosion – the power stroke), and expelling the gases from the explosion (the piston rises and pushes the gases out of a valve at the top of the cylinder – the exhaust stroke).

With the car just 'ticking over' at traffic lights for example, the engine may be going through this entire process – one revolution – at a rate of 1,250 times per minute, hence 1,250rpm (revolutions per minute). Under hard acceleration in the lower gears, this rate could increase to 5-6,000rpm.

The greater the rpm, the more the amount of fuel the car is using. The gears help keep the rpm figure down while the speed of the car increases. Fuel flow to the engine is controlled by the carburettor. Pressing the accelerator pedal simply makes the carburettor squirt more fuel into the cylinders thereby increasing the power of the ignition explosion, the speed of the engine and the speed of the car.

How your car's engine works

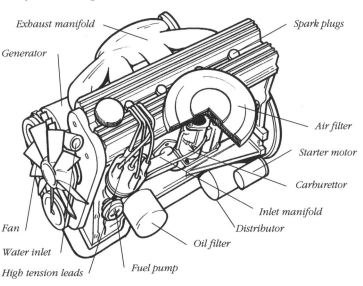

Exhaust manifold

Generator

Spark plugs

Air filter

Starter motor

Carburettor

Inlet manifold

Distributor

Oil filter

Fan

Water inlet

Fuel pump

High tension leads

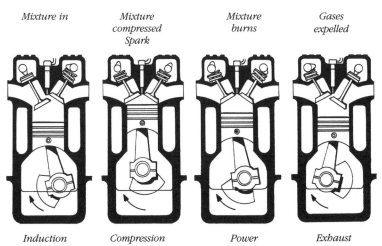

Mixture in	Mixture compressed Spark	Mixture burns	Gases expelled
Induction	Compression	Power	Exhaust

Maintenance schedules

Regular checks on your car will help avoid unexpected breakdowns.

Each time you use the car and before pulling away, check the following:
• that you have enough fuel for the journey
• that there is the usual brake pedal pressure
• that your instruments are working
• at night, that your lights work
• when raining, that your wipers and washers work

On a weekly basis check the following:
• windscreen washer bottle levels
• front and rear screen wiper condition
• tyre pressures and condition – including the spare

On a monthly basis add to your checks:
• the condition of the brake pads or discs
• the exhaust
• general condition of glass and bodywork
• engine oil level
• water level in the radiator
• brake fluid level in the reservoir
• clutch fluid level in the reservoir (some cars have a cable rather than hydraulic clutch. Check that the cable is properly secured).
• battery fluid levels, adding distilled water if necessary. Make sure leads are secure and terminals are clean.

Essential tools to carry

Everyone should carry a few basic tools in their car in case of an emergency. Remember, if you cannot use the tools you have got, a good Samaritan may find them very useful to help you on your way.

A small toolbox should comfortably hold the following:
• several screwdrivers – cross-head and Phillips – of different sizes
• several open-ended spanners
• pliers
• spare fuses
• tyre pressure gauge
• spare bulbs
• spare fan belt
• screen clean fluid
• insulating tape

Carrying a small torch, safety fuel can, warning triangle, water and a car fire extinguisher is also advisable. In winter, you may need jump leads (so that another car's battery can be used to start yours) too. It is also a good idea to have an ice scraper to clear the windows and windscreen.

Note the level of wear and tear varies with mileage and the make of car. Always follow the specific maintenance and service schedules given in your car's handbook. The monthly checks to the left are for guidance only. Most manufacturers recommend that their cars are serviced every 6,000 miles or six months for example.

Equipment to carry with you in your car

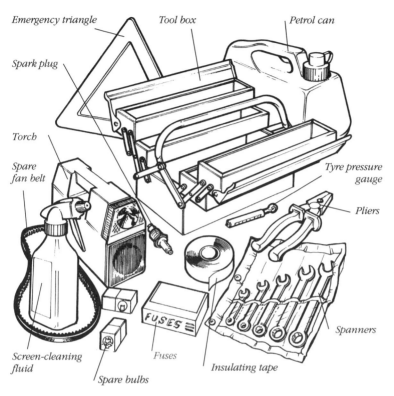

Emergency triangle

Tool box

Petrol can

Spark plug

Torch

Spare
fan belt

Tyre pressure
gauge

Pliers

Screen-cleaning
fluid

Fuses

Spare bulbs

Insulating tape

Spanners

Washing your car

Washing your car regularly will help keep the paintwork looking good and help you keep an eye on scratches that might call for repair. Follow the steps below for the best results:

• Wash the car in the shade after a shower of rain or sprinkle plenty of water over it first. This lifts much of the dirt without scratching the paint.

• Using a proprietary car shampoo, wash the bodywork from the roof downwards. Use more water than you think necessary and replenish your sponge constantly. Clean the windows separately.

• Work your way down and around the car. Wash the sills (the area beneath the doors), and front and rear under-bumper areas last.

• Wash the glass including lights.

• Thoroughly rinse everything with clear water.

• With a damp chamois leather or synthetic wash cloth, wipe the car over with a circular polishing motion. Rinse and wring the cloth constantly. Wipe up all water smears including dribbles that appear after you have finished an area.

• Clean the glass inside and out with a proprietary cleaner and finish with a chamois leather.

Winter preparations

Late autumn is a good time to check your car over so that the first cold spell doesn't leave you and your car stranded at the roadside. In addition to carrying out your weekly checks thoroughly, pay particular attention to the following:

• that there is sufficient anti-freeze in the coolant. To be sure, drain the system and refill with the recommended levels of water and anti-freeze for winter driving.

• that an adjustable air intake is set for winter. Usually this means that it is adjusted to take in heated air from around the exhaust system.

• according to the additive you use, you may need to double the amount of screen clean fluid in your washer bottle(s).

• that you carry an ice scraper in the car. Those combined with a wiper blade are good for clearing slush.

• that your rear screen heating element is working.

• that your car's heating system and fan are fully working.

• that all engine hosepipes are in good condition. Freezing water will force its way out of decaying hoses.

• that all your car's lights are clean. You may even need to wipe them over on a journey-by-journey basis (note how dirty your windscreen gets for example).

• that you keep a shovel, an old car mat or two and a blanket in the car particularly if you live in a rural area or are going on a long journey. The mats will help your tyres gain purchase on a particularly slippery patch – the blanket will keep you warm if you become stranded!

• At the winter's end, if you have not been doing so on a regular basis, have the underside of your car steam cleaned to wash away corrosive salt thrown up from gritted roads.

Summer preparations

The first fine weather of the year sees scores of cars overheating at the roadside. As winter passes check the following:

• that an adjustable air intake is set for summer. Move it away from the exhaust system so that it takes in cool air instead of warm.

• that the car's fan belt is in good condition. Where electric fans are fitted, check that they cut in and out properly.

• that your car's hosepipes are in good order. On a warm day in slow moving traffic your cooling system will be battling to cope. Boiling water will find the weak point in any hose.

• that your car's radiator is topped up to the recommended level. Do not drain the anti-freeze; it inhibits corrosion too.

Motoring organizations – are they worth it?

If you're a whizz at motoring DIY and the only one who drives the car, you may decide to spend your money on other things. For anyone uncertain about working on cars, who may travel frequently in their 'Sunday best' or who carries children with them, there can be little doubt that belonging to one of the motoring organizations is well worth while.

There are various levels of membership but for the best part of £100 per year you can have the peace of mind that comes with knowing that whenever you break down your car will be repaired for you or you will be taken on to your destination. You can usually add other family members to your membership for a nominal cost and you can use the service even if you are travelling in someone else's car.

In addition to the repair services, the organizations also give legal and technical assistance and offer route planning services for your longer journeys.

Repairs and servicing – dealing with the garage

Many people feel a hostage to fortune when dealing with garages but there are ways of ensuring you get a fair deal:

• If your car is still under warranty, use a franchised dealer for the make.

• For other cars, use members of a motor repairers' trade association, a garage approved by one of the motoring organizations or a repairer recommended by at least two friends.

• Get a written quote (legally binding) or estimate (not legally binding) for the price of the job including all that needs to be done and how long it will take. Where an estimate is concerned, tell the garage to get your approval before doing any other work not included on it.

• Find out what is guaranteed and for how long before you accept the estimate or quote.

• Get a written and fully itemized receipt.

If you are unhappy with the work done, talk to the manager as soon as possible. You may need to pay the garage to get your car back, in which case write a note saying that the payment is 'without prejudice'. You can then pursue your complaint in full. If the matter is not resolved straight away, contact the garage's trade association or your local consumer advice centre.

On the road

Even on today's congested roads, a car journey should be a safe and enjoyable experience. Frequently it is regarded as an inconvenient necessity to be rushed – often an attitude that leads to accidents. Help yourself steer clear of trouble by following some of the tips below.

Journey planning

Take a few minutes before a journey to study a map and work out your route. Remember that there are alternatives to the shortest route between two points. Choosing minor rather than major roads may help stimulate your interest in driving and your surroundings. At the least, it will relieve the monotony of making regular trips on the same route.

Particularly on motorways, know in advance at which junction you want to exit and the site of service stations you may want to use. Sticking a prominent note to your dashboard with the numbers of the roads you want to use can save searching for the right page on your map during your journey.

Before you set off, take advantage of radio traffic reports and retune your radio to the nearest lo al station (roadside signs give the frequency).

Driving abroad

Just the thought of driving on the right puts many people off driving abroad. But, with care, there is no reason why you should not drive safely and enjoy a foreign trip all the more for taking the car. Before you go:

• Check that your licence is valid. Pink British licences are valid in the European Community with occasional conditions. An International Driving Permit is required in many other countries. Consult your travel agent or motoring organization.

• Inform your insurance company of your planned trip. Give as much notice as you can.

Winter driving tips

• On wet, icy and snow covered roads, reduce speed. Whenever possible, brake only in a straight line. Avoid sudden steering movements.

• Leave a greater distance between you and the car in front.

• In fog, always make sure you can brake within the limit of your vision no matter how many cars overtake you. Use dipped headlights, switch your high intensity rear lights on when visibility is greatly restricted, use your demister and rear screen heater and switch your washers and wipers on regularly.

• On very cold days watch out for what look like dark damp patches on the road – this may be black ice. Be wary when driving where water may have gathered and frozen.

• Use your gears sensibly. Starting in second rather than first gear will help avoid wheelspin on snowy roads as will using one higher gear than normal once moving.

Summer driving tips

• Switch your headlights on as soon as dusk falls.

• After long dry spells, a sudden light shower can produce a slippery mixture of road dust and engine oil. Brake with care.

• Wear sunglasses to reduce glare. Remove them as the light fades.

• Summer is traditionally the time of long holiday journeys. Give yourself a break every two hours at least and rest if tired.

Driving on the right

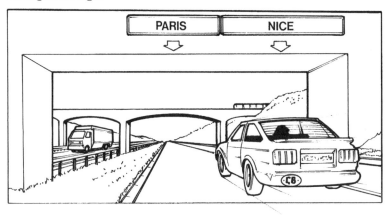

• Check with your travel agent or motoring organization specific requirements to carry in your car. Many countries insist on a warning triangle and spare bulb kits.

• From your motoring organization, local library or the tourist information office of the country you are visiting, obtain a guide to the local road signs and driving laws. On many roads in France for example, cars turning out of side roads on the right will have priority over you.

The advanced driving test

Each year, many motorists concerned to raise the standard of their driving take the Institute of Advanced Motorists (IAM) driving test. Over about 90 minutes with an ex-police advanced driver, this thoroughly examines a driver's control of his or her car. The IAM operates in all regions of the country and many people join after having attended one of the Better Driving courses run by their local authority's road safety team.

When you are abroad

• Give yourself plenty of time to adjust to driving on the right. There are numerous reminder signs in English at most ports but you will probably feel more at ease once you are out of town.

• Be particularly vigilant whenever you first get in the car. It is quite common to routinely stop for fuel and then drive off on the left!

• Do not rush turning, especially to the left where you are turning across traffic that would not be there in the UK.

• Remember that at roundabouts you will be travelling anticlockwise.

• Only overtake when you, the driver, can see it is safe. Trust in your passenger only to tell you when it is safe to ease out to look at whether it is safe to overtake, and to tell you when it is definitely not safe to overtake.

• Remember that fuel stations may close for a long period at lunchtime.

What to do if you break down

First ensure the safety of yourself and other road users by switching on hazard warning lights and moving your car off the road if possible. If you have a warning triangle, place it at least 50 metres away near the kerb. At night, switch your sidelights on and be careful not to stand in front of them while trying to repair the car.

To look under the bonnet it is best to stand at the side of the car away from the traffic. That way if something hits your car from the rear, you will be able to jump, or be knocked, clear.

On motorways, at the first sign that something is wrong use your mirrors, signal if necessary and drive your car on to the hard shoulder, preferably directly to an SOS telephone. Give yourself plenty of room to stop especially if there is another car already on the hard shoulder. Use only the nearside doors to get in and out of the car and use your hazard flashers and lights as necessary. If you have a warning triangle, place it at least 150 metres away on the hard shoulder. Do not let pets or children wander about. Either keep them all in the car or gather the children at the top of an embankment leaving the pets locked inside.

There has been much controversy over the best advice for lone women who break down on motorways. Circumstances vary but you should:
• inform the police via the emergency telephone that you are travelling alone.
• stay in or near enough to your car to get to it quickly. Once in it, lock the doors.
• remember that there is probably more chance of your car being hit by another car while on the hard shoulder than there is of molestation or attack.

STARTING A FAMILY

Planning for a new family can start long before your pregnancy. For many couples, planning for the birth seems unnecessary because it is such a long time away. But once you are pregnant, nine months speed past very quickly. If you are already pregnant, or even if you're hoping to get pregnant, now is the time to sit down and work things out carefully, to make sure that your pregnancy and the birth go as smoothly as possible.

Budgeting for the baby

The majority of mothers now return to work after having a child, so allowing for Maternity Benefit being paid, you will have to face loss of income for only a relatively short time. That is, provided you want to go back to work, and will be able to afford the necessary childcare.

Many mothers will defer the return to work for as long as possible, or may not be able to bring themselves to leave their baby in the care of someone else. If this is the case, it will have an effect on future family income, which you should consider right now.

Shopping for your baby

There are innumerable items to be collected together in preparation for your new baby. Some of these are obvious, such as clothes and cots, but many people overlook bedding, car seats and other ancilliary items, which can add up to a considerable total cost.

It is perfectly natural to want everything new for your baby, and to want the latest gadgets. But remember that young babies don't care what they wear, or how they look. If cost is a problem for you, don't hesitate to buy some major items secondhand. For example, prams do not wear out quickly; neither do cots. Classified advertisements for these items can produce bargains, and often all that is needed is to replace a mattress, or touch up the paintwork.

Even secondhand clothes can be useful, provided that they have been looked after, because for their first few months of life, babies are not active enough to wear out their clothes, which can be passed on to others.

Most new mothers make the mistake of buying lots of clothes in the first sizes, and these are also frequently given as gifts. But it is the larger sizes that you will need more of, once the baby becomes active and starts making clothes dirty or even wearing them out. Unfortunately, by this time, the thrill of your new baby may have worn off among your relatives and friends, and you are less likely to be given clothes in these more useful but more expensive sizes.

Of course, you will want many more items than shown on the list below, and you will also need to give consideration to more expensive pieces of equipment such as a combination carry cot/pram/buggy.

Buying these important items as a combination can save you money, and of course they are even more reasonably bought secondhand.

If you have a car, you will need a proper baby seat, with restraints. It is dangerous and illegal to dump a baby on the back seat in a carry cot, or to sit a baby or toddler on the front seat without proper safety restraints. Proper car seats fit on the passenger seat, with the baby reclining and facing towards the rear of the car. The seat is firmly held by the car's recoil seat belts. If you must use a carry cot, it has to be firmly and safely secured in the back seat by means of proper restraining straps.

Slings that hold your baby across your chest, leaving your hands free when shopping or working about the home, are very practical. The baby is comforted by the warmth, movement, and even the smell of the parent, and usually sleeps soundly, even though he is being bounced around. Make sure that the sling you buy includes a head support for use while the baby's neck is still weak. For older babies and toddlers, a back pack is more useful. It is more comfortable for carrying a heavier child, and the baby can see more from his position behind your shoulders.

The following is the absolute minimum of basic equipment you will need when you return from hospital – in practice, you will want to obtain many more items:

Clothes
3 stretch sleeping suits
All-in-one warm suit
2 pairs of scratch mittens
Hat
Mittens (for winter babies)

Linen
1 shawl
2 sheets
2 blankets
2 towels

Toiletry
24 disposable nappies (to start with)
Cotton wool
Muslin squares

Food
1 tin baby milk
2 feeding bottles
2 spare teats
Sterilizing equipment

Carry cot or baby basket

Bouncers of various types are enjoyed by all babies. A reclining bouncing chair is useful, because the baby can sit in it while being fed, and can still enjoy himself by kicking his legs. Never place a bouncing chair on a table or sofa as it can work its way over the edge as the baby bounces. Hanging bouncers, designed to be clamped in a doorway, should be used only for babies aged three months or more, once they can support their heads properly.

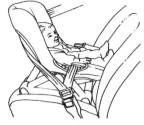

With a front car seat the driver can see (and be seen by) the baby.

A nursery

You will naturally want to have a proper nursery for your baby, but this is often impossible in modern homes with restricted space. Most babies share their parents' room for several months, so there is no rush to prepare a nursery, even if you do have sufficient space. You will find a spare room more useful at first for storing bulky items while you sort the house out after the birth. Then you can start to think about decorating it for your baby, once he is ready for his own room.

Fabric baby slings provide a comfortable 'seat' for the baby. You should always support the baby's head when you lean forward.

Don't forget that, just as with clothes, your baby won't have the slightest interest in the decoration of his room at first, so if cost is a consideration, don't overstretch yourself at this stage. The baby will be a few months old before he really begins to appreciate colours and decorations.

Your health

If you are planning to start a family, it makes sense to have a general checkup by your GP to make sure that you are thoroughly

Even a very young baby will soon learn to bounce in a bouncing cradle.

healthy. If you are on the contraceptive Pill, you will have to stop taking it for at least three months before you try to become pregnant. During this time you will need to use other contraceptive techniques such as the condom, as it is unwise to risk becoming pregnant while the powerful hormones contained in the Pill are still in your bloodstream. Similarly, if you are taking the Pill and you think its protection may have failed and you might be pregnant, you must stop taking it immediately, as if you really are pregnant, there is a chance that it could harm your unborn child.

If you are using the coil, you obviously need to have it removed if you want to become pregnant. If it has failed to prevent pregnancy, ask the doctor if it is wise to have it removed, or left in place to be expelled naturally.

One very important consideration is a check to see if you have had rubella, or have received vaccination. A blood test can show if you have antibodies against this disease. It is absolutely essential that this be done, as if you contract rubella during pregnancy, it can have a disastrous effect on the unborn baby, causing congenital defects. If you have to be vaccinated, you must take precautions against becoming pregnant for a further three months.

Age is an important factor to consider when planning a family. In older women, there is an increased risk of problems with the baby, and the doctor may advise you about this. There is usually no

reason to put off having the baby, but sometimes special tests are carried out to make sure that it is developing normally in the womb.

Clearly, the healthier you are when preparing for pregnancy, the more certain you can be of having a healthy, happy pregnancy and delivering a healthy baby. This means making sure that your body is in peak condition. If you are overweight, you should lose weight before becoming pregnant, as excess weight can be a health hazard. You should also make sure you are eating a healthy diet.

Follow the basic dietary recommendations laid down by the Health Education Authority (described in the Family Health section of this book), and you will not only lose weight, but will feel and be healthier, ready for the increased strain on the body that is caused by pregnancy.

If you smoke, stop now! There is absolutely no excuse any more for smoking during pregnancy, because it is firmly established that it harms the unborn baby. And if you are serious about getting pregnant, you should also know that smoking decreases fertility substantially. Subsequently, a baby born in a 'smoking family' runs an increased risk of breathing problems.

Keeping healthy through pregnancy

Your baby will obtain the food he needs from your own body, so it is important to make sure that you eat the correct diet during pregnancy. Eating a bad diet probably won't harm the baby, because he will take exactly what he needs from your system, but this in turn could mean that you experience health problems.

For most women, weight gain is the real problem. Some put on too much weight because they are 'eating for two', and then find it difficult to lose afterwards. It is generally recommended that you put on about 28lb during pregnancy; 10lb of this during the first 10 weeks. The baby will probably weigh only about 7lb, and the rest is made up of placenta, fluids around the baby, increased blood volume, heavier womb and breasts, and about 9lb of extra fat and body fluid!

The clinic or nurse will monitor your weight carefully. Although overweight can cause health problems, they will be just as concerned at low weight.

A healthy diet during pregnancy

This is much the same as the diet recommended for general healthy eating, with adequate amounts of protein and carbohydrates, and especially fibre, and a reduced intake of saturated fat and sugar. Vitamin supplements are usually unnecessary for good health, provided you eat plenty of fresh fruit and vegetables and a good mixed diet. However, sometimes supplements of folic acid are prescribed by the doctor, often combined with iron to help build healthy red blood cells. Do not take other vitamin supplements unless these are recommended by the doctor or clinic, as they could be harmful in excess.

Calcium is a vital constituent of the diet during pregnancy. It is important for bone and teeth formation, and the baby takes the calcium it needs from your own system. This can lead to your bones and teeth being weakened if your diet does not contain enough calcium. Drink lots of milk and eat plenty of dairy products during the later stages of pregnancy, and also eat leafy green vegetables, which also contain large amounts of calcium.

Exercise

Pregnancy and birth will be strenuous, and the fitter you are at the start, the better you will cope. You should make sure that you exercise regularly, and put the right amount of effort into it. Your clinic or nurse will be able to advise about specific types of exercise designed to help with the birth process, but it is very important to keep as active as possible right through pregnancy so your joints remain supple, and your muscles are strengthened. It has been found that women who are physically fit are 50 per cent less likely to have a Caesarian delivery than those who are unfit, and they also have fewer complications during pregnancy.

Obviously you should tailor your type of exercise to what you are capable of doing. Swimming is probably the best all round exercise, because it does not put excess strain on any part of the body, even when you are near full term. Walking is also good exercise, provided you are not overweight for your stage of pregnancy.

Ovum

Fertilization

Within a
few hours

After several
days

After 5
weeks

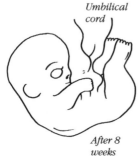

Umbilical
cord

After 8
weeks

Stages of pregnancy

After 8 weeks, the embryo is about 2.5 cm long and is
called a foetus. It has all its organs. At 12 weeks, the
placenta is about six times heavier than the foetus; by
16 weeks, the foetus weighs the same as the placenta.
The foetus begins to move its limbs about this time
and can be felt to kick. At this stage it is possible to
tell what sex the baby is. It can hear, tell light from
dark, swallow and suck its thumb. At 28 weeks, the
foetus can open its eyes, and by 36 weeks the baby is
ready to be born.

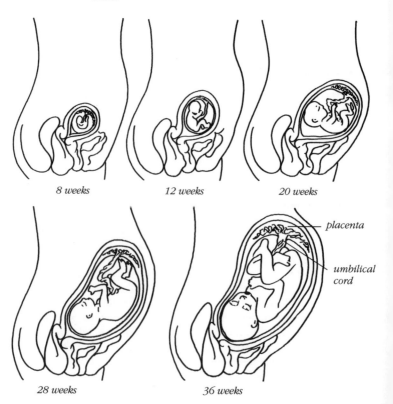

8 weeks

12 weeks

20 weeks

28 weeks

36 weeks

placenta

umbilical
cord

Follow some simple rules for keeping physically fit:

• Exercise regularly, for a set period of time.

• Ask the doctor or nurse for advice about the best form of exercise for you.

• Don't continue with exercise if it becomes uncomfortable or painful. You must build up your strength and stamina gradually.

• Practise breathing properly while you exercise. Breathe deeply and slowly – if you find you are panting, you are either very unfit or are pushing yourself too hard.

• Don't carry out exercise immediately after a meal, or you will risk heartburn or indigestion.

Ante-natal exercise

This exercise is one that you can practise during your pregnancy to help to control your breathing. This helps you provide your baby with an adequate supply of the oxygen it needs to develop.

Lie on the floor, supporting your head with a pillow, and with your hands resting on your lower ribs. Breathe in and out (breathe slowly to avoid becoming dizzy), feeling your ribs rise and fall as you do so.

Feel your abdomen rise as you breathe in through your nose. As you exhale pull your abdominal muscles inwards so pushing the air our of your mouth. Blow softly.

Common health problems during pregnancy

Because pregnancy places the whole body under a considerable strain, some health problems commonly occur. Many of these can be avoided with a little foresight and a good diet, and by becoming and staying fit right from the start.

Anaemia

A condition in which the body has too few red blood cells, or is low in red blood pigment (haemoglobin). Anaemia can be avoided by eating a sensible mixed diet with plenty of fresh food, and if recommended by the doctor, by taking iron supplements.

Backache

The increasing weight of your womb, and the change in centre of gravity of your abdomen as the baby grows, place an awkward and unaccustomed strain on your back. You can avoid backache by adopting a good posture and not slumping, and also by toning and strengthening your back muscles with plenty of exercise. Try to sit and stand with your back as straight as possible. Hot baths and back massage can help relieve back pain.

Constipation

This condition is usually caused by a bad diet, but in pregnancy it may be made worse when the growing baby presses against your internal organs. Do not take laxatives unless prescribed by the doctor. Eat plenty of fresh fruit and lots of food containing fibre, which will ease the problem.

Cramp

Cramp in the legs is very common, but the causes are not really understood. Try to keep your legs strong and supple with plenty of exercise, and if you do get cramp in your leg, straighten it out and point your toes. Massaging the affected part will also help.

Heartburn

This condition is related to constipation, because it is caused by pressure from the increasing size of the baby forcing gastric juices from the stomach back up the gullet. Gastric juices burn the gullet, and if they reach the throat, they cause an unpleasant sour burning sensation. Eat small amounts at frequent intervals to avoid overfilling the stomach, and sit up straight to take the pressure off your abdomen.

Morning sickness

Half of all pregnant women experience nausea, and this can be very worrying and unpleasant. There is no real treatment or cure, but the good news is that morning sickness usually clears up after three months. If you experience morning sickness, you probably won't feel very hungry, but eating a good diet may help.

Stretch marks

Stretch marks or striae are exactly what the name implies. The skin has become overstretched by the enlarged uterus or breasts and some of the underlying tissue tears.

Stretch marks start off an angry red, but eventually they fade to an inconspicuous silvery colour. There is no real evidence that oils, massage or any other treatments prevent stretch marks, but they may help.

Varicose veins
The pressure of the enlarging womb can interfere with the flow of blood through some of the veins in the abdomen. These return blood from the legs to the heart and if they are obstructed, the blood pools in the legs. The blood then finds its way back through smaller veins near the surface, enlarging them and making them painful. Regular exercise and loose clothing will help, as they encourage free circulation of the blood. If you develop varicose veins, it will help to rest with your feet supported above the level of your tummy, to help blood to flow back into the heart.

Birth and beyond

As the time for birth approaches, you will need to prepare the things you will take with you to hospital. Pack them in a bag at least two weeks before the birth is due, in case the baby does not wait. Make sure you have a minimum emergency kit (see opposite).

Choices in childbirth
In the UK, nearly all women give birth in hospital, because doctors feel that in these circumstances, they can better cope with any problems which might arise during the delivery. In fact, the risks of

any emergency are remote, but it is difficult to find medical assistance if you want to have a home delivery.

Normally, once your pregnancy is confirmed, you will be booked into a hospital antenatal clinic, where regular checkups will be made and the progress of your pregnancy carefully monitored. Unfortunately the health service is geared up to treating sick people, and pregnant women are still sometimes treated as patients, even though they are usually in glowing good health.

You will generally be given advice rather than treatment, so make sure you understand exactly what is going on, ask lots of questions, and don't be satisfied until you have the answers. Many women find the midwife more accessible than a doctor when they want advice and assistance.

You have a right to choose how your baby will be delivered, and the traditional delivery position of lying on your back with your feet in stirrups is not automatically the best for you. Many women choose

Your emergency kit
- Dressing gown or robe.
- Slippers.
- Two nightdresses, with front fastenings if you are going to breastfeed.
- Nursing bras and pads.
- Sanitary towels.
- Several pairs of pants.
- Salt for use in bath.
- Tissues.
- Personal toiletries.
- Money for the telephone.

to give birth squatting or kneeling, or even standing up – whichever position is the most comfortable. Similarly, you may choose to give birth without relying on the use of anaesthetics or other drugs. Discuss all these possibilities with the midwife before the birth process begins, so the hospital is fully prepared to meet your needs.

Labour

In the weeks and days before the birth, you will become conscious of odd contractions in your womb. These are not necessarily painful, but may be pulling sensations or cramps. Although you will probably think that this is the real thing, the true contractions are quite different, and are usually unmistakeable.

When labour starts, you will probably get occasional mild contractions, often with a backache. The contractions then gradually become rhythmic, and you may feel sick. The contractions become more frequent, and when they are coming at 10 to 15 minute intervals, it is time to call the hospital. They may ask you to come in right away, or to wait for a while until the contractions are even more closely spaced. In any case, once your contractions are less than 10 minutes apart, it's time to go in.

You may have a 'show', which is a discharge of sticky bloodstained mucus. This material normally seals off the cervix, and the show is a sign that the cervix is dilating, ready for the birth. Sometimes, your waters will break, producing a flow of the watery liquid that usually surrounds the baby. Either of these signs must be reported to the hospital right away, because birth could be imminent.

Once in the hospital you will be examined to see how the birth is proceeding. It will not take place until the cervix is fully dilated, ready for the baby to emerge. While waiting for this to happen, you may feel very restless. Some women like to rest, while many others walk about to try to get more comfortable. During this initial stage, you may be given a suppository to empty your bowels.

This first stage of labour usually lasts for from 6 to 12 hours with the first baby, although it can be longer. With subsequent babies, the first stage of labour is usually much shorter, and the whole birth can take place very quickly. It is important not to push to try and deliver the baby during this first stage, because this would only cause you pain and damage.

The second stage of labour is the actual birth process, when the womb contracts very strongly, forcing the baby out. This is when you will be able to put your breathing exercises to good use, to control the strength of the contractions so as to help the midwife. The hardest part is the delivery of the head. Once this has emerged, one or two more pushes cause the baby to emerge completely.

You should be given the baby immediately, without waiting to have him cleaned up. This is an important part of the process of bonding, when the baby and mother form powerful emotional attachments. If the father is present, it is also important for him to be close at this time.

The easiest part of labour is the third stage, which is the delivery of the placenta. This is usually quite painless, though you may need to be given an injection to help the womb contract and expel it.

Breast or bottle?

Views on the best way to feed a new baby vary, but the final decision must always be yours. For

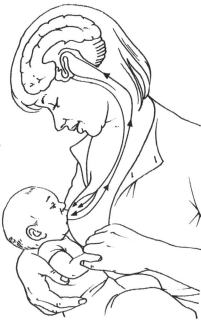

Breastfeeding
The 'let-down reflex' is an automatic response triggered by the baby sucking at the mother's breast. The pressure of his gums on her areola causes a signal to pass along nerves to the pituitary gland in the brain. This responds by releasing two hormones, oxytocin and prolactin. These cause the muscle cells in the breast to contract, thereby forcing milk out through the nipple.

Bottle feeding
When bottle feeding, raise your baby to a comfortable height by placing a cushion on your lap or by crossing your legs – don't strain your back by leaning forward. Make sure the bottle is tipped so that the baby is not taking in air as he sucks.

those women who like the idea of breastfeeding, it is a very rewarding experience. Mother's milk is perfect for the baby, and is precisely balanced for his needs. Apart from nutrition, it has another important function in protecting the new baby from infection, because it contains large amounts of vital antibodies. These protect the baby for the few weeks before his own immune system starts to function.

On the other hand, some women choose to bottle feed, or are unable to breastfeed. This is not a defeat, because modern milk formulas are very good nutritionally. Bottle feeding has another benefit, in that the father can also participate in what is otherwise exclusively the mother's job. This can mean a little more sleep in the first few weeks!

Good and bad aspects of breast feeding

Advantages

- Encourages close bonding between mother and baby
- Readily available, and free!
- Protects against infection
- Less risk of tummy upsets
- Stools are not as smelly as with bottle-fed babies
- Less risk of developing food allergies
- Nutritionally correct for your baby
- May help you recover your figure

Disadvantages

- Need for frequent feeds
- You have to do all the work
- Difficult to know if a full feed has been taken
- Reduced sexual interest in most women
- Almost complete dependence on mother for 24 hours a day
- Can be inconvenient or embarrassing when feeding in a public place
- Sore breasts
- Restrictions on alcohol and some foods that may enter breast milk

Bringing the baby home

Getting home with your baby can be a bit of a shock to the system. You will be understandably elated and proud, and you will be the centre of attraction for a while. But it's when everyone has left and you realize that you are responsible for the wellbeing of this tiny individual that the meaning of parenthood really strikes home.

Don't panic. Babies are really quite tough, and your baby will withstand baths and all the other obstacles you face, without coming to any harm at all. You must learn to organize the daily routine for yourself and your baby. You may find yourself resenting visitors for a while, because all your attention will be centred on the baby. But don't neglect your partner. He will have been kept out of things while you were pregnant, and he will expect to play a more active role again now. Make sure you allocate some of your time to resuming a normal loving relationship.

Handle your baby as much as possible, so both you and he gain

Picking up your newborn baby

1. Slide one hand underneath the baby's bottom to support his back and bottom. Support his head by slipping your other hand under his neck.

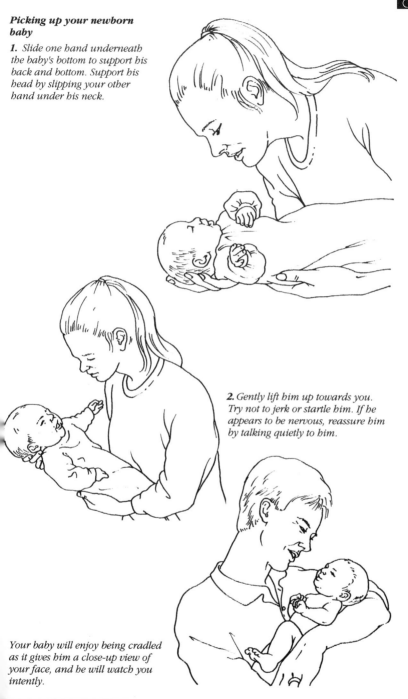

2. Gently lift him up towards you. Try not to jerk or startle him. If he appears to be nervous, reassure him by talking quietly to him.

Your baby will enjoy being cradled as it gives him a close-up view of your face, and he will watch you intently.

confidence. Ignore old wives' tales about the risks of 'spoiling' your baby by making too much fuss of him. They are complete nonsense: you can't love your baby too much.

Cry baby

The thing that upsets new mothers above all else is the crying. Remember that your baby can't communicate in any other way but crying. Especially in the early days, he is either asleep or nearly so for most of the time. When he wakes, he is hungry, upset, uncomfortable or frightened, and crying is his only way of telling you so.

Body contact, suckling at the breast or with a comforter, gently cuddling and rocking, and quietly talking to him are all ways to soothe a crying baby. If you have a car, you will probably find that the movement works like magic and soothes the most distressed baby, though it's an expensive way to get him to sleep.

Babies naturally swallow air as they suck, either at the breast or bottle, and this can produce tummy aches. You can wind your baby to prevent tummy pain by holding him upright against your shoulder, and gently rubbing or patting his back until he burps. Don't worry if he sicks up some his feed with his wind – all babies do this.

A few babies refuse to be comforted, and they are usually labelled as 'colicky' babies. There is no medical explanation for colic in babies, but some babies go through

To wind your baby, support him upright against your shoulder and gently pat his back.

If your baby has colic, try lying him across your lap on his tummy, and stroking his back.

A good night's sleep

There are several things you can do to help ensure a better night's sleep:
• Try to build up a regular routine. If your baby seems sleepy after his bath, put him down then.
• Give the late evening feed as late as possible, just before you go to bed yourself. Feeding makes babies sleepy, so you can get at least a few hours' sleep before he demands to be fed again.
• Don't let your baby become overtired and ratty before putting him down. This means that you may have to be firm with visitors who would like to keep him up playing later than usual.
• Don't tiptoe about the house with the tv or radio turned down to avoid waking him. Babies very quickly adjust to even the noisiest households, and by behaving normally, you will be forcing your baby to adapt to your routine, rather than having to adapt to his.
• Settle him down snugly in a warm bedroom. If he is too hot or too cold he will not sleep soundly.
• Make sure his room is dark. Small babies are not frightened of the dark, and he is less likely to stay awake if there is nothing interesting to look at. Use a dim night light when you come in to check on him.
• Some babies like to be securely wrapped and sleep better that way. Others hate the restriction, so try it carefully.
• Don't leave your baby to cry until he gets worked up, hot and sweaty. He will only take longer to go back to sleep.
• Keep night feeds as short as possible, making sure that everything you need is to hand. This way, he won't wake up completely. Don't wake him up too much by talking to him or playing in the middle of the night.

Getting your own rest

Babies are very tiring, and you will need to take special care to get plenty of rest yourself:
• Share the work with your partner, deciding in advance whose turn it is to get up to feed or change the baby.
• Seize every opportunity to have a rest during the day, in the odd quiet moments while your baby is asleep.
• Don't waste time after putting your baby to bed. Go straight to bed yourself.
• Get some privacy. As soon as you feel it is right, put your baby in another room. As long as you share a room with your baby, you won't relax properly, waking every time he stirs or whimpers.
• Don't put off the moment when you have to get out of bed to care for your baby when he wakes during the night. If you leave him to cry, he will wake up properly and become agitated, and so will you. Get it over with, and then you can both get back to sleep.

a period of acute stomach pain, often after feeds, causing them to bring their legs up to their stomach, and scream in real distress. The reasons for this are unknown, though it sometimes follows spicy meals in breastfeeding mothers. You should not give any soothing medicine to your baby unless this is advised by the doctor. The good news is that colic is usually temporary and clears up after a few weeks. Until then, you will have to grit your teeth and keep hoping!

Getting rested

Lack of rest is a problem for all new parents. Many small babies demand feeding at three-hour intervals, and with the time taken for changing nappies between this leaves hardly any time for sleep. If you are breastfeeding, it places the onus on you to do all the work. It may be worth letting your partner have his rest at night provided he makes up for it by looking after the baby for you during the evenings, while you try to get some sleep in. Learn to express breast milk so he can help with a bottle. If your baby is bottle-fed on formula, then you can take turns in getting up to give the feeds.

A role for father

Your body has been changing to accommodate the needs of your growing baby during pregnancy, but your partner does not have the advantage of the hormonal changes that made you feel pregnant; neither has he had the close physical presence of the unborn baby, feeling its every movement, as you have. So although most new

Here are some practical ways for your partner to help

- Participate in the pregnancy as much as possible. Attend the ultrasound scan, and go to antenatal classes where both partners are welcomed.
- Look around the hospital together before the birth, so you can give practical help and support during the birth.
- Make sure you are present at the birth (provided you think you can cope).
- Take time off work after the birth, when lots of help and support is essential.
- Help with practical jobs like ironing, washing, shopping and preparing meals, which all still need to be looked after.
- Share nights 'on call'.
- Learn to bottle feed your baby using expressed breast milk or formula feeds.
- Look after your baby while your partner goes out and about, to give her a little freedom.

fathers are thrilled to see and handle their new baby, they often take a while to adjust to the feeling of fatherhood.

Fatherhood is just as much a full time job as being a mother, and there are very many ways in which your partner can play his full role in caring for the baby. Apart from breastfeeding, your partner can do everything for the baby that you do yourself. In practice, he may often be at work while you carry out the routine baby care. But in the evenings and at weekends, he can take over much of the caring leaving you to rest or to catch up with other work.

Fitting into the family

Your new baby means an upheaval in your own life, but it also affects other children in your family. They will have been awaiting the new arrival with excitement, and sometimes with anxiety. They see your bump steadily growing bigger, and they know that something is going to happen, though not exactly what it will involve. Often they feel that they are being squeezed out of your life, as they see you becoming more preoccupied with your pregnancy. Even when you return home with your new baby, things don't revert to normal, because you are still preoccupied, and they think they no longer occupy the predominant place in your affections that they enjoyed before. You need to be very careful in these early days to avoid the development of rivalry, which can sour family relationships for years. Take positive steps to avoid this happening:

• Keep children fully informed about your baby, and what will be happening before, during and after the birth.

• Make sure you allocate lots of time and attention to your other children, not concentrating exclusively on your baby.

• Give your other children some special care and treats so they know you still love them.

• Though they will be excited about the new arrival, anticipate

some jealousy when the initial thrill begins to wear off.

• Make your other children feel important by encouraging them to help you care for the baby. Let them handle him under your or your partner's supervision.

• Don't let them see the whole family life changing to suit the demands of the new baby.

• Make sure they appreciate that the baby is an new addition to *their* family.

• Don't ever leave your baby unattended with a small child, because even the friendliest of children can be uncharacteristically spiteful on occasion.

Baby blues

Having a baby should be one of the happiest times of your life, but many mothers become tearful and feel that they cannot cope with the experience. Frequently the trouble is exhaustion, and the common reaction is to lash out at the nearest person you can blame for everything going wrong – your partner. After all, it was he who made you pregnant! Then you feel guilty, and this makes you feel worse, setting up a vicious cycle of blame and guilt, which can eventually lead to depression.

You probably won't feel like this at all, but if you recognize the possibility, you may be able to head off such problems. Your whole body is awash with hormones during your pregnancy and immediately after, and it is perfectly natural for these to affect your emotional state. Changing hormonal levels are probably responsible for the weepy feeling many women experience a few days after the birth, and these normally clear up quickly. A few women suffer true depression however, and this can be very distressing. There are some things you can do to help fight off post natal depression:

• Try to avoid making other drastic changes in your life, such as moving house, until you are properly settled with your new baby. Similarly, your partner should avoid making drastic changes such as a career move, which could make you feel insecure.

• Don't be afraid to lean on others for help. Relatives and friends would probably love to help, but may not want to interfere.

• Talk to other mothers who have experienced post natal depression, and find out how they coped.

• Tell the doctor and nurse how you feel. They will have heard it all before, and can offer help and advice.

• Try to resume some of your former leisure interests, so the baby is not the only thing on your mind.

• Don't squeeze your partner out of your emotional and physical life. He may be just as miserable as you are. Try to set aside some time to be together.

• Don't fight a losing battle to keep your house as tidy as it was before the baby – it never will be. Don't worry about mess. There will be plenty of time to clear up when you feel better, and meanwhile, ask your partner to help.

Top names for babies

Boys' names

Adam	Biblical: the first man, from the Hebrew for 'red', possibly because God is said to have fashioned man from clay and then breathed life into him.
Alan	Either from the Old English for 'harmony', or from the Celtic for 'rock'.
Alexander	From the Greek, meaning 'defender of men'.
Andrew	From the Greek for 'warrior'.
Angus	From the Gaelic for 'unique choice'.
Anthony	This is a Roman family name, as in Mark Anthony.
Ashley	A transferred use of the surname meaning 'ash wood'.
Barnaby	A modern version of Barnabas, from the Hebrew for 'son of consolation'.
Barry	From the Irish, meaning 'spear'.
Benedict	From the Latin, 'blessed'.
Benjamin	Biblical: the youngest of Jacob's 12 sons.

Bernard	From the Old German words for 'bear' and 'strong', the name implies 'brave'.
Blair	A Scottish name, meaning 'flat land', it has been transferred from use as a surname.
Blake	Originally meaning 'black' or 'of dark complexion' in Old English.
Brendan	From the Celtic: 'prince'.
Brian	Old Celtic for 'hill', 'high', or 'strength'.
Carl/Charles	From the Old German, 'man'.
Christopher	From the Greek, 'bearing Christ'.
Clifford	From the place name, meaning 'a ford at a slope'.
Clive	From a place name, meaning 'cliff'.
Craig	The transferred use of a Scottish surname, from the Gaelic, 'crag'.
Dale	Transferred use of the surname, meaning 'valley'.
Damian	From the Greek, meaning 'to tame or subdue'.
Daniel	From the Hebrew for 'God is my judge'.
Darren	Of uncertain origin.
Darryl	From the Old English 'darling'.
David	Biblical. The boy David slew the giant Goliath, became King of Israel, and fathered Solomon.
Duncan	From the Gaelic, 'brown warrior'.
Edward	From the Old English, 'guardian of riches'.
Felix	From the Latin, 'happy'.
Fraser	Transferred use of the Highland surname, originally meaning 'curly haired'.
Geoffrey	Old German in origin, this name could mean 'peace of God' or 'peace in the district'.
George	From the Greek, 'tiller of the soil'.
Gerald	From the Old German, meaning 'rule by the spear'.
Graham	Transferred use of the Scottish surname.
Gregory	From the Greek, 'watchful'.
Guy	From the Old German, 'wood' or 'wide'.
Henry	From the Old German, 'home ruler'.
Ian	Scottish version of John.
Jack	Originally a pet form of John.
James	The name of two of Jesus's disciples.

Jason	In ancient Greek legend, Jason was the leader of the Argonauts, who went in search of the Golden Fleece.
John	From the Hebrew, 'God is gracious'.
Justin	From the Latin, 'just'.
Kevin	From the Irish, 'handsome at birth'.
Luke	From the Greek, 'man from Leucania'.
Matthew	From the Hebrew, 'gift of God'.
Stephen	From the Greek, 'crown' or 'wreath'.
Thomas	From the Aramaic, 'twin'.
William	From the Old German for 'resolution' and 'helmet'.

Girls' names

Alice	From the Old German for 'nobility'.
Amanda	From the Latin for 'loveable'.
Beatrice	From the Latin, 'bringer of joy'.
Briony	From the plant of the same name.
Camilla	An old Roman name, given by Virgil to one of his heroines.
Celia	Originally from the Latin, 'heavenly'.
Diana	Latin name of the moon goddess.
Donna	From the Italian, 'lady'.
Elizabeth	From the Hebrew, 'oath of god'.
Emma	From the Old German, 'universal'.
Fay	From the Old English, 'fairy'.
Fiona	From the Gaelic, 'white' or 'fair'.
Gemma	From the Italian, 'precious stone'.
Glenda	From the Welsh, 'holy good'.
Harriet	The feminine form of Henry or Harry.
Helen	Greek, from the word for the sun.
Isabel	From the Spanish form of Elizabeth.
Jane	The feminine form of John.
Jasmine	From the flower name.
Jessica	From the Hebrew, 'God beholds'.
Karen	A Scandinavian form of Katharine.

Kylie	An Australian girls' name meaning 'boomerang'.
Laura	Derives from the Latin for 'laurel'.
Lucy	From the Latin for 'light', this name was originally given to girls born at dawn.
Maria	Like Mary, this name is thought to mean 'wished-for child'.
Melissa	From the Greek, 'bee'.
Natalie	From the Russian, Natalya.
Natasha	From the Russian, a pet form of Natalya.
Olivia	From the Latin, olive.
Ophelia	From the Greek, 'help'.
Priscilla	From the Latin word, 'ancient'.
Rachel	From the Hebrew, 'ewe', an animal associated with gentleness and innocence.
Rebecca	Biblical. Rebecca married Isaac and bore Esau and Jacob.
Rosemary	The name of the plant. This has the Latin meaning, 'dew of the sea'.
Sally	Originally a pet name for Sarah.
Sarah	From the Hebrew, 'princess'.
Sian	A Welsh form of Jane.
Sophie	A pet form of Sophia, from the Greek, meaning 'wisdom'.
Stephanie	The feminine form of Stephen.
Susan/Susanna	From the Hebrew for 'lily'.
Tanya	The short form of Tatiana.
Thea	The short form of Dorothea and Theodora.
Tiffany	From the Greek, 'epiphany', which means 'appearance of God'.
Tracy	Formerly a masculine name, and before that, a place name.
Ursula	From the Latin, 'little bear'.
Vanessa	A name coined by Jonathan Swift for his friend Esther Vanhomrigh.
Victoria	From the Latin, 'victory'.
Wendy	Coined by J.M. Barrie for Peter Pan.
Yvonne	From the same root as the French boys' name, Yves, meaning 'yew'.
Zoe	From the Greek, 'life'.

Your healthy baby

Your new baby will be examined several times during your brief stay in hospital by the doctor and midwife. The first examination takes place in the labour ward, immediately after the birth, when the midwife will check for any obvious defects. Usually a paediatrician will also examine the baby, making certain tests which demonstrate that he is properly developed:

• The doctor will check the shape of the baby's head, and the 'soft spot' on top of the skull, where the bones are incompletely fused together.

• The baby's hands and feet are checked carefully. Conditions such as Down's syndrome can be suggested by certain patterns on the baby's hands.

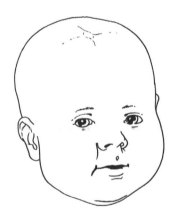

A newborn baby will have a soft spot, called the fontanelle, at the top of his head. This enables the bones of his skull to overlap as the head passes through the birth canal. The bones will not fuse together until he is about 18 months to two years old.

• The heart and breathing will be checked with a stethoscope.

• The umbilicus is checked to make sure there is no sign of a hernia or other abnormality.

• The genitals are carefully examined, and the hips checked to make sure that there has been no dislocation during birth.

• Inborn reflexes are also checked, because these show that the nervous system is properly developed.

Early development

The size of your baby is measured in terms of both height (length) and weight. Just as with adults, the build of a baby can vary, and what the clinic will be interested in is the rate of increase in weight and length, rather than the size of your baby at any one stage. This shows that he is feeding properly and making full use of all the nutrients in the feed.

If you are small yourself, or smoke during pregnancy, your baby is likely to be born small. Premature babies are small, as are small-for-date babies, who for some reason did not receive sufficient food while in the womb. These babies usually grow very fast in the first few weeks and soon catch up with normal birthweight babies, while premature babies take a lot longer to catch up. Fat bouncing babies used to be something to be proud of, but now overweight babies are frowned upon, because they have a tendency to remain overweight throughout life.

The charts on the right and on the next page show the usual range of heights and weights for baby boys and girls. The centre line is the average, while the lines above and below show the 'normal' range. These charts are only a guide, and you should not worry unduly if your baby does not seem to fit the categories shown. Within the normal range it is the rate of increase in weight and length that is important, not the actual weight at any one time. The most important use for such charts is to monitor the baby's progress, and to alert the doctor if the growth rate alters unexpectedly, as this could indicate some underlying problem. The baby may lose weight as a result of even minor health problems, such as a cold. Diarrhoea usually causes rapid weight loss, and this is one of the reasons why diarrhoea always needs medical treatment in young babies. Babies who are a little underweight are usually healthy, so there is no need to worry.

Illnesses of the early years

You will soon know your baby very well, and you are the best judge as to whether he needs medical attention if he is ill or off-colour. Small babies can become seriously ill quite quickly, so you should know the key symptoms that could mean urgent medical attention is required. Don't let yourself be put off by the doctor's receptionist if you are convinced that there is something seriously wrong – you must insist on seeing the doctor even if you have to wait.

Children are prone to many infections, most of which are quite

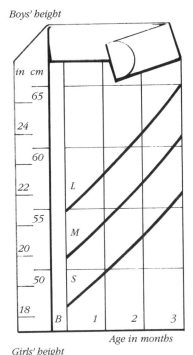

Boys' height

Age in months

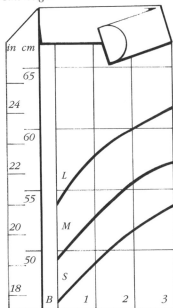

Girls' height

Age in months

Boys' weight

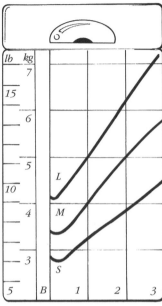

Age in months

Girls' weight

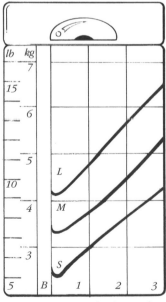

Age in months

minor. Some are more serious, and require medical treatment. The most common problems are :

Colds

Uncommon in babies under six months, who are still protected by the mother's antibodies. After that, they catch cold after cold. There is no real treatment other than giving paracetamol syrup to keep the temperature down, and giving plenty of drinks. Small babies become distressed when their breathing passages are blocked with mucus, and you must clear this away regularly.

Fevers

Most infections result in a raised temperature, and this makes children feel ratty and restless. Sometimes their temperature shoots up and needs to be controlled by sponging the body with lukewarm water. A damp cloth applied to the head will also help. Rarely the temperature rises so high that it causes a convulsion or fit. If this happens, sponge the baby to bring the temperature down then call the doctor immediately.

Chickenpox

This is a very contagious condition, caught by most children. By the time the spots appear, it is too late to isolate the infectious child from others. It does not make a child feel particularly ill, but the itching is infuriating and when the child scratches the spots, it may cause scarring. Calamine may relieve the itching.

Warning

Do not give aspirin to small children to control temperature. It can be very dangerous. Use paracetamol syrup to relieve a fever.

Rubella

Rubella or German measles starts with a fever, followed by a rash and flat red spots which first appear behind the ears, then spread over the body. The glands in the neck may also swell. It does not make the child feel very ill, but its real significance is the risk it poses to pregnant women who have not had the disease, or been vaccinated. Rubella can cause devastating damage to their unborn child. It is essential for all women to be checked to see if they are immune to rubella if there is the faintest chance of becoming pregnant.

Measles

Measles is a more serious infection, which is highly contagious and can have dangerous after-effects on a child. It starts like a cold, then continues with a cough and a high fever. There are clusters of small red spots spreading over the body. There are continued efforts to eradicate measles, which remains one of the more serious threats to child health.

Mumps

This infection causes the familiar swelling of cheeks and neck, as it attacks the glands in these regions. Infected children are feverish, thirsty and uncomfortable because of the swelling. The main risk is of the condition spreading to infect adults, who can become seriously ill. Mumps in adult women and men may result in infertility.

Immunization

Children can be protected against most of the common childhood diseases as well as some more serious infections (see Family Health section). As with any medical treatment, there is a slight risk of reactions or side effects, but this is far outweighed by the benefits of protection from the misery of preventable disease.

Boosters will be given at a later date, and your child may also be offered immunization against tuberculosis (TB) or meningitis.

Your doctor or health visitor will recommend the time for immunizations, but the following is the usual immunization schedule:

Age	Immunization
3 months	Whooping cough Diphtheria Tetanus Polio (by mouth)
4-5 months	Whooping cough Diphtheria Tetanus Polio (by mouth)
8-11 months	Whooping cough Diphtheria Tetanus Polio (by mouth)
About 15 months	Measles Mumps Rubella

Landmarks in growth and development

Remember that every child is an individual, and there is no such thing as the 'average' child. Each baby will develop at a different rate, and in a different way, according to his physical abilities and his personality. It is true to say that there are some milestones which are commonly reached at a particular age, but you should not be alarmed if your child does not seem to develop quickly enough. The clinic or health visitor will be keeping a check on his progress and will alert you if necessary.

Physical development

Most children:
• Can raise their heads by three months.

• Reach out and try to grab objects between three and five months.

• Grip an object and put it in their mouths at five to eight months.
• May try to crawl around at six months. They do not usually perfect this art until nine months, or may miss out crawling and go straight to walking.

• Sit up without support between six and eight months.
• Stand up and 'cruise' round the furniture between six to ten months.

• Start to try feeding themselves (messily) at about 10 months.
• Begin to walk without support between 10 and 16 months.
• Try to feed themselves with a spoon around 14 months.
• Are dry during the day between two and three years.

Language and hearing

Most children :
• **Are scared by loud noises, immediately from birth.**
• **Start to experiment with noises other than crying around three months.**
• **Recognize their parents' voices around three months.**
• **Make speech-like sounds at six months.**
• **Can say 'Mama' and 'Dada' from about six months. After ten months they will say these words appropriately to their parents.**
• **Have a vocabulary of up to 20 words by 18 months, but understand many more words.**
• **Start to string words together at age two.**
• **By age three they should be talking quite clearly, though with disregard for pronunciation and grammar.**

Problem children?

Remember that whatever problem your child may have, someone else has shared it, and has overcome it. Although some of the most common childcare problems are listed here, don't go looking for them, because most children sail through childhood without causing great problems.

Picky eaters

• Don't worry if your child isn't very interested in food. He will probably eat when he is hungry enough. As long as he gains weight and is healthy, there is nothing to worry about.

• Give small portions, which pose less of a challenge to his appetite.

• Don't make an issue out of mealtimes. You can't force him to eat if he doesn't want to.

• Encourage him to eat with other children whom you know have a good appetite.

• Cut out snacks and sweets between meals.

• Remember that children do not get bored with eating their favourite meal day after day. You may not like eating baked beans every day, but a toddler will accept this as normal.

• It could be that your child doesn't like the food you are giving him – not everyone likes spinach. Your child's diet will probably be much more nutritious than he really needs, and it is highly unlikely that he will suffer any deficiencies by refusing to eat one or two types of food.

Sleep disturbance

• Don't be too rigid about bedtimes. Make sure your child is really tired before putting him to bed, and relax him with a warm bath and a snack if he is reluctant to settle.

• Leave a night light on if your toddler seems fearful of the dark. A radio quietly playing may help him to sleep.

• If he won't settle, leave him playing quietly in bed with his favourite toys. You can tuck him in when he drops off to sleep.

• If all else fails, take him into your bed for a while, but make sure he goes back to his own bed once he is relaxed and sleepy.

• Be prepared to grit your teeth and put up with crying if you are sure there is nothing really wrong, and he simply wants to grab your attention. Some children will try this gambit for a few nights running before they realize it won't work and settle down quietly.

Tantrums

• Many children go through a period of temper tantrums around age two. They may be a symptom of frustration, because the child cannot express himself properly, or can be part of a trial of strength between the parent and a child who is demonstrating that he has a mind of his own.

• Don't react strongly to a public tantrum, even though it is embarrassing and annoying. A child who sees he has succeeded in upsetting you has proved to himself that he can influence you when he wants.

• Try distracting a child in the throes of a tantrum.

• If this does not work, you will have to sweat it out. You should never smack or punish him. Instead, pretend to ignore the tantrum. If you can, walk away into another room and busy yourself with normal household activities. If it happens while you are out, abandon the shopping trip and return home without comment. Never give in, and especially never bribe the child with sweets, or you will simply be rewarding his bad behaviour.

Working mothers

Deciding when or if to go back to work depends largely on your family circumstances and your personal inclinations. Some women in a stable relationship are perfectly happy to stay at home raising their family, while others are forced to go back to work for financial reasons. There may also be social pressures, with friends and acquaintances suggesting that you ought to resume your career, or that you run the risk of becoming a boring housewife if you stay at home with your family. Try to ignore all the pressures and comments, and reach a conclusion that suits yourself.

• If you are returning to work for financial reasons, consider how much you will earn once you have paid for childcare.
• Will your child accept being away from you? How can you prepare him for it? For example, could you gradually build up the time he is away from you?
• Do you feel guilty about the idea of returning to work?
• Are you being pressured into returning to work?
• How does your partner feel about your returning to work?
• Will your job allow you to take time off if your child is sick?
• Do you have any back-up if childcare breaks down, even for one day?
• It may be difficult to combine work and motherhood – can you cope without exhausting yourself?

If you have both thought things through and you think you can manage, fine, go back to work and enjoy it. You may be able to start part-time, which gets you and your child used to the new situation.

Child minders

Child minders are people who are (or should be) registered with the local authority as being suitable people to care for children, and who have the facilities to provide proper care. Registered child minders are checked out by the local authority, so they are your best bet, even though they may charge more than unofficial (and technically illegal) child minders.

The following guidelines may help you in selecting a child minder:
• Are the children they care for happy? Make a point of visiting a potential child minder when there are actually children there, not just in the evening. Does she/he really seem to like children?
• How many children does the minder care for? Can she cope?
• Are there adequate play facilities? Is there plenty of space?
• Do you know exactly what you will be getting for your money? What about hours, holidays and illness?
• Does your child have any special problems or requirements that the child minder should know about?
• Do your instincts tell you that this is a person that your child will get on with?
• Is this a registered child minder? Has she been personally recommended?

Personal recommendation from

friends and neighbours should satisfy you that your child will be happy as well as safe.

Organizing your home life

Going back to work will not be easy. You will be exchanging a full-time childcare job for a full-time paid job, and you will still have another half-day of childcare to face when you get home, as well as all the housework. But on the positive side, your child may be more happy than you could imagine, because he is enjoying meeting lots of new children, and participating in the group games from which adults are excluded.

You can make the transition from full-time mum into a full- or part-time employee easier by straightening out your home life:

• Plan your daily routine so you and your partner can allocate time for housework, shopping and caring for your child.

• Expect some tears and tantrums at first, once your child realizes that you have some other interests in life apart from looking after him. Don't let this panic you into thinking that working is not such a good idea after all. Your child will soon get used to it.

• Give him lots of love and affection when you are with him.

• Get plenty of rest (if you can)! The extra work will prove a strain, but don't let household chores assume too much importance in your changing lifestyle.

• Make contingency plans. Make sure the child minder, nursery or school knows how to get in touch with you if things go wrong, and tell them how to contact another responsible person if you cannot be reached.

• If you can afford it, use some of your new earnings to buy yourself labour-saving items such as a microwave cooker, washing machine or tumble dryer. These will all help save you precious time to be with your family.

EDUCATION

Education is a topic of central importance to the whole nation. The crucial significance we place on it is reflected in the attention the subject receives nationally and domestically. Ever since the 1944 Education Act made schooling the right of every individual and legally enforceable, it has been one of the means by which successive governments have been seen to succeed or fail. At no time in the past however has education been so scrutinized, criticized, homogenized and revitalized. Although these are hard times for teachers and education authorities, whose jobs can be here today and gone tomorrow, there is a potential, regardless of party politics, for the education system that is currently evolving to offer the babies of today the opportunities of knowledge and skills for a full and meaningful life in tomorrow's world.

'It takes 20 years to educate a child.'
Shirley Williams

We tend to think of education as that which takes place within the boundaries of the many and various schools provided by the state or independent institutions. But it is not. It is a process that takes place between willing partners and the most important of these partners is the person who is learning – be she baby, child, teenager or mature student.

Babies cannot resist the drive to learn. They start the moment they are born and learn to suck on breast or bottle. Most babies have loving parents, willing and able to provide for them and protect them from cold, hunger and danger. Within this cocoon, the drive to learn pushes young children on at breakneck speed to acquire a language; learn to walk, run, and jump; learn manipulative skills; begin to have some social skills such as cooperation in play; and to understand some of the physical dangers they need to avoid.

The heartbreaking pictures of children in orphanages in Eastern European countries reveal the importance of the parents' role in these early years. Without our care and protection our young will fail to thrive, physically and mentally. As time goes on, parents and children are helped by external agencies such as playgroups, schools, churches, social services and an abundance of charities, so that the drive to learn is not lost through lack of opportunity but can be stimulated and helped.

Education begins at home, therefore. It begins with a two-way partnership of parent and child, and develops into a three-way relationship of parent, child and educational establishment.

Education is not something that is done to children. It cannot take place if the child's drive and willingness to take part are not present. Channelling this willingness and drive into appropriate directions is the task of all educators, be they parents or teachers. Deciding what directions are appropriate is the task of parents, teachers, governments, churches, and all those who offer the sources of learning, whether for intellectual, moral or practical skills. Conflict at any point confuses and inhibits children – they have to feel confident that their parents value education in general and their children's learning in particular.

Maintained and grant-maintained schools

In 1990 there were 27,385 schools in England alone, of which 25,019 were provided or 'maintained' by the state. Maintained schools are state schools, run by their governors and supported by local education authorites under the rules and regulations set out under Local Management of Schools (LMS).

Grant-maintained (GMS) or 'opted-out' schools are funded directly by the state through the Department of Education and Science. They do not have a slice of their income retained by the local education authorities for the advisory and welfare services that LEAs provide.

Entrance to maintained schools

Although it may be necessary to put your child's name down at birth for certain schools in the independent sector, this is not the case yet in the state sector. Recent legislation has made it possible for parents and children to have some choice in the matter of which secondary school to attend. There are some limitations, however.

Open enrolment means that parents must be given a place for their child in the school of their choice, unless of course the school is full. Admissions criteria must be made public by the schools.

For detailed information about entry contact the schools concerned. If you are refused a place at the school of your choice you can appeal against this decision if you wish.

Making an appeal against a decision refusing your child a place in the school of your choice is a tricky business. Get full information and guidance from the Advisory Centre for Education in London.

Ask for the leaflet 'School Choice and Appeals' for initial background information and advice.

Nursery provision

Successive governments have accepted the idea that children can benefit from attending a nursery school or class. However, LEAs are not obliged to provide nursery places and there is only patchy provision for children under the age of five years. Depending on where you live, you might find a state nursery school, or nursery class as part of a large primary school. Enquire about these through the Education Authority in the borough or county where you live. If you would like your child to have a place in a state nursery then you will need to make an application as soon as possible as places are often made available on a first-come-first-served basis.

Nursery provision tends to be concentrated in urban areas, but if there is no state nursery in your locality, private creches, nursery schools, kindergartens and charities such as the Pre-School Playgroup Association go a long way to fill the gap. The cost of these can vary from about £1.50 per session for a playgroup place to quite large sums for private nurseries that provide mainly for children of working parents.

Primary school nursery classes

Your child could attend a nursery class of a primary school for half a day every weekday. She might be offered a morning or afternoon place, and each session will last for

about two-and-a-half-hours.

Well equipped and staffed by professional teachers and nursery nurse assistants, these classes can be a joy to be in. It is unlikely that there will be any formal teaching of numbers or letters, but play will be constructive and development will be observed and recorded. Skills such as cooperation with others over a task and extended concentration will be encouraged. Opportunities to play with a wide range of educationally sound toys are available. Painting and modelling, sand and water play, singing and dancing, speaking and listening to stories are just some of the activities in which your child could take part.

There is a legal obligation on parents to send their children to school from the age of five years, unless you make it clear to your education authority that you wish to educate your child at home and offer evidence of your ability to provide structured formal learning (see page 202). Visit the schools in your area about a year before your child is five, and give the selection some careful thought.

Schooling structure

Depending on where you live, you will find schooling between the ages of five and 18 years organized in a variety of ways. First, middle and upper school is one kind of division. Primary (comprising infant and junior) school and secondary (or high) school is another. Some counties retain a few grammar schools, but comprehensive secondary schools are the norm in today's system.

The ages at which children go from one to the other can also vary. Typically, infants are aged 5-7 years, juniors 7-11 years, and secondary 11-18 years (although small secondary schools may take children only until they are 16). In Scotland, children transfer from primary to secondary school at 12 years of age. First schools typically take children between the ages of five and nine. Middle schools cater for 9 to 12/13 year-olds. Upper schools offer places for 12/13 to 18 year-olds.

School age

Primary schools usually take in new children every term, and will take a child at the beginning of the term during which she is five years old. Therefore, if your child is five in November, she could be invited to take up a place in the preceding September. Again, this is common practice, but you should enquire about individual entry policy when you begin to investigate local schools.

It is possible to find that you live on a boundary between two areas that are organized differently, which gives greater choice. You can then select between the first, middle and upper school structure, and the primary and high school structure.

The independent sector

Independent is the umbrella word that describes the 2,500 schools that are funded by fees paid by parents or other private monies. This includes all so-called 'public'

and private schools, from pre-preparatory through to senior and sixth-form levels. About 600,000 children are being educated in independent schools in Britain at present.

Although funded privately, many of these schools are charities and are not run for private profit – any surplus income is ploughed back into the school budget. The schools are managed by a Board of Governors, which looks after the finances. The Head is responsible to the Governors, although the day-to-day running of the school and the appointment of staff are the Head's responsibilities.

How to apply

Some independent schools are selective while others have open entry. There are boarding and day schools; some large and some small; mixed or single sex; urban or rural. Many are very academic. The Independent Schools Information Service provides a nationwide guide to 1,400 independent schools, the kind of education they provide, the fees and how to pay them, the subjects for study offered by each of the schools included, and the sports and other extra-mural activities available.

Entrance qualifications

Most independent schools require some form of test to be undertaken before accepting a child. This test can vary from a written report about the child through to the Common Entrance Examination. The child may need to attend an interview as well.

Ages of pupils at different sorts of independent schools

England and Wales

Age	Type of School	Curriculum
2/5-16/18	ALL-THROUGH	Some independent schools take pupils from the early ages right through to 16 or even 18.
2-7	PRE-PREPARATORY (Pre-prep) also called nursery schools or kindergartens	Corresponds to nursery and infants stages in local authority schools. Reading, writing, numbers, learning to play. Attached to junior schools.
7-11+ or 13+	JUNIOR SCHOOLS often called preparatory schools or prep schools	General subjects leading to admission to senior schools at 11+ or through the Common Entrance Examination.
11-18	SENIOR SCHOOLS sometimes called secondary schools	Schools which admit pupils at 11+ sometimes have a lower school for children ages 11-13. There may be a special entrance examination to the upper school at 13.
13-18	SENIOR SCHOOLS	Some boys' senior schools still have the traditional age of entry at 13. One year of general studies followed by 2 years of GCSE and 2 years for A-level.
16+	SIXTH FORM (VI Form)	Many senior schools admit students at 16+ into the top of their schools usually for the 2-year A-level courses or occasionally to re-take GCSE

Scotland

Age	Type of School	Curriculum
4-13	PREPARATORY	Largely boys' schools, many of which have a number of girls, preparing for the Common Entrance Examination and for entry to senior schools.
8-13 10/13-18	JUNIOR SENIOR	A variety of boys' schools, girls' schools, some of which have small junior departments. The senior schools prepare pupils for Scottish examinations and in many cases also for A-levels.
4-18	ALL-THROUGH boys, girls and co-educational	Many of the senior schools in Scotland have their own junior departments so pupils can progress through the various stages of education whilst remaining at the same school.

This table is kindly supplied by ISIS from their book 'Choosing Your Independent School'.

Common Entrance Examination

These examinations are devised by the Common Entrance Board. Your child will sit the examination during the academic year preceding the year of entry for the senior school to which you are applying. This could be at 11, 12 or 13.

The examination aims to test intelligence and learning. At 11 your child will be expected to answer questions on English and maths, and there will be a test of verbal reasoning. At 12 and 13 the examination includes more subjects such as French at 12, and at 13 there are optional papers in Latin and Greek, for example.

The school to which you are applying marks the examination according to criteria deemed important by that school. Contact your chosen school or the Common Entrance Board for details.

Fees

Fees range from about £900 a year for a nursery or pre-prep school place through to around £11,000 a year for a place at a senior school. There are many ways of meeting these costs and advice and help is available through ISIS and through insurance companies offering suitable policies.

The schools themselves may help through bursaries and scholarships. The Government has an assisted places scheme whereby bright children offered a place at an independent school may receive help with fees depending on the income of the parents.

The school will advise you if it takes part in the assisted places scheme and provide application details. Because of the direct relationship between payment and the service offered, independent schools are quick to respond to consumer demands.

Independent schools do not have to follow the National Curriculum but they tend to group together in associations of schools with a similar ethos in order to set standards and maintain high levels of achievement. Two of these associations are the Headmasters' Conference and the Governing Bodies of Girls' Schools' Associations. Some independent schools provide for special requirements, such as music and religious needs. ISIS can help.

Parents as educators 1: Informal learning at home

Education is not something that is done to our children at school. It is a lifelong process starting at birth. Not valuing formal education is like not appreciating those magic moments when a child says her first word or takes a first step. Formal education is going to be more diverse and go on longer as our world becomes more complex. But there is a great deal more to learning than that which is delivered during school hours.

Hobbies

From stamp-collecting to train-spotting, model building to cookery, gardening to rambling, bird- or badger-watching to wild flower spotting, the possibilities for hobbies are endless and all offer a good potential for learning as well as plenty of enjoyment.

Keep a globe nearby or an atlas open when sorting stamps into their different countries of origin. Trains and stations offer possibilities for engineering and commercial knowledge. Cookery creates opportunities for measuring and adding as well as manipulative skills. From modelmaking in plaster or balsa wood children absorb ideas about form, volume, areas and balance. Through the garden or on country walks a great deal of natural history can be experienced.

Children pick up enthusiasms for hobbies or learn craft skills from parents or friends for little or no cost. They need encouragement and help and the opportunity to do things for themselves, but very few will maintain an interest if left to get on with it on their own. Parents or friends need to be involved and offers of help and company need to be maintained.

Sport

Schools provide opportunities for team games, gymnastics and athletics, but perhaps your child would like to do more. Find out through other parents or by telephoning the local sports hall what opportunities there are for children in your locality. Public swimming pools run courses of lessons for children. Babies can be taken to swim as soon as they have had their first inoculations. Children's football clubs abound and tennis facilities are improving. Perhaps you can use the school's facilities out of school hours if you are prepared to start a club with

other parents' help. Clubs for adult players of various sports often have a junior section that will, after all, provide the senior members of the future.

Youth clubs

Brownies, Guides, Cubs, Scouts and Woodcraft Folk provide opportunities for learning and pure enjoyment. Going away on camp is usually the highlight of the year and this experience will help your child along the road to independence in a very enjoyable way. Group leaders can always use help from parents and friends.

Youth Clubs provide opportunities for young teenagers to be independent (and to listen to loud music elsewhere). Youth leaders generally arrange activities that vary from helping old people with gardening and other nature conservation activities, through to visits to cinemas and theatres.

Family activities

Whether visiting a museum or going on a foreign holiday together, your family outing gives children valuable learning experiences. Museums and art galleries often mount special exhibitions, but you do not need to wait for these. A group of infant children on a visit to The Tate Gallery in London were spellbound by the large, colourful shapes in the paintings and enjoyed remembering one of their choice to paint for themselves at home. Holidays abroad open young minds to different languages and cultures. Shopping in a French market for food is a pleasure for all.

Music

Music is a foundation subject of the National Currriculum and so wherever your child goes to school some music will be offered. Build on the skills taught at school by encouraging practice at home. Young violinists and pianists can start to play at the age of three or four. Encourage your child to play in a recorder group at an early stage. Find out if you have a children's orchestra nearby.

Coping with fees

If your child is particularly talented in one of these pursuits and would benefit from professional coaching, it is possible that there is a grant-aiding body that will help with fees. Your local Citizens' Advice Bureau or library will have a guide to such organizations.

Information can be gathered from other parents, health visitors, local libraries and sports facilities, and of course by referring to the telephone directory.

Parents as educators 2: Educating children at home

Some parents want even greater involvement in their children's learning and choose to educate their young at home. This can be a most wonderful experience for children and parents alike, but it should not be undertaken without a great deal of careful forethought and consideration. Discuss the difficulties and the advantages with others who are 'home educating' their children. Spend a few hours or even better a few days with the families, talk to the parents and children separately.

If you would like to know other people in your geographical area who are following this form of schooling, contact Education Otherwise (Tel: 0926 886828). The Children's Home-Based Education Association (Tel: 0302 833596) supports home-educators and parents wishing to supplement their children's schooling.

Home education and the law

Education Otherwise is a support organization that gets its name from the 1944 Education Act, which states, in Section 36, that the parent(s) of children of compulsory school age must 'cause their children to receive efficient, full-time education suitable to age, ability and aptititude (and any special needs), either by regular attendance at school or otherwise'.

There are some differences in the law for those people who take children out of school, and for those living in Scotland and Ireland. Check on the legalities of your own situation with either Education Otherwise or The Children's Home-Based Education Association (above). Parents have the right to choose which form of education they prefer for their children.

Qualifications for home education

You do not need to be a qualified teacher, but you do need confidence and commitment. Research the subject well if you think you would like to keep your children with you allowing them to learn to a curriculum and timetable of your joint choosing. Booklists and resources guidance are available from both of the support groups. Although you do not have to follow the National Curriculum, you can buy all National Curriculum documents from Her Majesty's Stationery Offices and follow all or as much as you and your children find appropriate.

Aren't home-educated children lonely?

With a little research you can build up a neighbourhood network or community of home educators. This means that the children get to meet each other for play or for visits to museums, galleries, theatres, sports and other outings.

Differentiation by age or sex does not occur to the extent that it does in schools. Some home educators pool their skills, and those more able in one subject help children of other parents and vice versa, so there is some group learning, although the children are likely to be of a variety of ages, often cooperating with and helping each other.

The advantages of home education

Children are learning at their own pace and in a way that takes in their enthusiasms and talents. They don't have to stand in a queue to wait for a spelling to be checked or while 29 other children have their shoelaces tied. Lunch can occur at the most appropriate moment. If a child wants to finish a book in a day, there is no artificial timetable

to tell him to go out to play. If a child becomes spellbound with a new discovery in maths or science, he can go on practising and developing the skill to the extent of which he is capable without interruption. Music lessons do not have to be squashed into teatime hours when children are more tired. Some of the less desirable aspects of school, such as bullying and having a whole class disturbed by one or two badly behaved children, do not occur.

Fitting in with traditional schooling

If you have been home educating your children and you wish, for one reason or another, to start sending them to school, then you need to apply in the normal way to the school of your choice. It is quite common for parents who have educated at home up to the age of 11 years to place their children in maintained or independent secondary schools. Or you can slot in at most times during either primary or secondary years. However, you do need to think about it carefully. The years 14-16 are particularly sensitive as the children are involved in GCSE syllabus work in all subjects.

General Certificate of Secondary Education

GCSE and the National Curriculum

Key Stage 4 of the National Curriculum covers the ages 14 to 16, or Years 10 and 11, and coincides with GCSE courses. GCSE syllabuses need to complement the demands of the National Curriculum so that in studying for GCSEs students are also receiving the curriculum to which they are entitled. It is not yet clear how Key Stage 4 will be tested, since it is not reasonable to ask students to do two sets of external examinations at the end of Year 11.

England, Wales and Northern Ireland

During Years 10 and 11 schools provide GCSE courses, and students opt for the subjects they wish to be examined in. This selection process begins at the end of Year 9 (age 13/14), and it can be fraught with problems. All the core and foundation subjects (except art) of the National Curriculum will need to be studied once they have been introduced, although a student may not wish to take GCSE examinations in all of them. Teachers will want to give recommendations about which exams students should concentrate on, parents will have views, and students will have their own ideas on what they want to do.

Most students would prefer not to sit any examinations at all and find it difficult to study and cope with all the other tensions that the teenage years bring. Being available, willing to talk to your child and the school, being patient, positive and understanding, even when this means having to give up some of your own ambitions for your child, are essential at this phase of her development.

The General Certificate of Secondary Education replaced GCE O-level and CSE national examinations in the summer of 1988. It removes the necessity of having to choose between the two styles of examination that GCE and CSE represented.

GCE O-level/GCSE/CSE Grades Comparison

O-level GCE	GCSE	CSE
A	A	
B	B	1
C	C	
D	D	2
E	E	3
	F	4
	G	5

Differentiated assessment

The examination assessments differentiate in one way or another in most subjects to enable all students to demonstrate what they 'know, understand and can do'. Differentiation means that, according to the paper the students take or the questions they answer, they may be able to get a grade A, B or C, equivalent to an O-level grade, or they may get a maximum D grade. This enables less academic children also to get positive results.

Examining boards

Although aimed at students aged 16+, anyone can sit GCSE examinations through schools or colleges of further education. The syllabuses and examinations are designed by groups of regional examining boards. MEG is the Midlands Examining Group and ULEAG is the University of London and East Anglia Group, and so on. These groups comprise both the GCE and CSE examining boards. The syllabuses are designed using nationally agreed criteria.

Coursework

A considerable amount of work undertaken over Years 10 and 11 was eligible for assessment as coursework elements of GCSE examinations, but coursework is being drastically reduced. The Government feels that coursework was not a good test of students' abilities, whereas the teaching profession feels it is a great bonus, particularly for students who are very nervous of timed written examinations or who simply do not work particularly quickly but who are capable of very good work. Students maintain good levels of effort and commitment throughout the GCSE two-year course when they know that this work will contribute to their final mark.

Scotland

In Scotland too examinations have changed to give all children an opportunity to succeed. At 16 or at the end of year S4, their fourth year in secondary school, students take examinations that lead to the Standard Grade of the Scottish Certificate of Education. Again, differentiation in the tasks or the outcome of the exams will offer students the opportunity to get a Credit (grade 1 or 2), a General

(grade 3 or 4) or a Foundation (grade 5 or 6) award at Standard Grade. Those who complete the course, but who show very little achievement, might get a grade 7.

Scottish Certificate of Education 'Higher' Grade is taken during the two academic years following the Standard Grade. When the students take it depends on their award at Standard Grade. Those who wish to go on studying in further or higher education need to take 'Highers'.

Independent or maintained?

Although your demands will change slightly over the years during which your child is in school, if you are clear about what you expect in the first place the essentials will alter very little. Do not assume that you are unable to choose an independent school because you do not have the means to pay the fees. The Government has an assisted places scheme which allows parents of bright children to choose an independent school, usually at secondary level, and have some or all of the fees paid by the Government. The schools will tell you whether or not they operate the scheme and how to apply. If your income is over £20,000 a year you will not receive much help. If the family income is less than £8,714 a year, your child could win a free place if she passes the entrance tests.

The factors that cause some parents who struggle on low incomes to send their children miles every day to the nearest independent school and other well-off families to choose the local maintained school depend on the parents' own schooling experiences, their impressions of the available schools, their political and/or religious beliefs, their expectations both of the school and of the child, and, most importantly, what they know of their children. A school selected for one child may not be the right choice for her brothers or sisters, but choosing a school that will go some way to meeting the needs of all the children in your family is going to make the organization of your daily life much easier. The only situation where this may not apply is where you have a child with special needs.

How to choose

The most important element in all of this is your child or children. Talk to grandparents, friends and relations who know your children well and get their opinions about whether or not you need to look for some special characteristics in a school. Although you may not always be able to choose according to the child's own preferences, it is a very good start either to school life in general or particularly at secondary level if you can go along with the choice your child makes.

Contact your local education authority for the names of the maintained and grant maintained schools in your area. The local office of the Independent Schools Information Service (ISIS) can provide a list of independent schools nearby. If you are choosing a boarding school, the official ISIS guide contains details of these nationwide. It also contains a guide on how to apply and what to look for. In rural areas your choice of day school will be limited, whichever sector you choose. The local Citizens' Advice Bureau and Social Services department might have a list of private nurseries and kindergartens.

Maintained schools

Your local County or Borough Education Authority will send you lists of maintained and grant maintained schools in your area.

Other parents are another source of information about schools. Ask people you meet through playgroup or other activity groups. They may have older children already at primary or high schools and are usually quite happy to describe their own experiences of the establishment they know. It is necessary, however, to keep a sense of proportion about this kind of advice. Do not generalize from one person's experience. Just keep it in mind when visiting the various schools.

The school prospectus

Telephone the schools in your area and ask for a prospectus. All schools use the preparation of the prospectus as a first 'selling tool'. Every additional child through the doors of the school, whether maintained or independent, means cash. Filling all the places available means more money for teachers' salaries, books and equipment. The prospectus therefore will paint a glowing picture. Independent schools have always had to sell their places to parents, but it is relatively recently that this cash concern has affected maintained schools whose brochures are becoming very informative, although they are probably not quite so glossy. As well as reading what the school has to say about itself, read between the lines.

Questions to ask when choosing a school for your child

• Can you assess what the general character of the school is?
• Do academic concerns receive the most emphasis, or do the pastoral aspects of education get equal billing?
• A 'broad and balanced' curriculum has to be delivered in all maintained schools, but what else is on offer?
• What does the prospectus say about discipline?
• What clubs or societies could your child join?
• Do you detect that music, sport and drama are important?
• Does the school have a uniform?
• Do you want your child to wear school uniform?
• What arrangements are made for the delivery of religious knowledge and personal and social education (education for life skills)?
• What arrangements are made for parents to talk to teachers once a child has started in the school?
• And last but not least, give detailed consideration to the examination results.

Results tables have to be read in conjunction with some consideration of the school's 'catchment area'. A school nestling in the centre of a well-to-do suburb will expect considerable parental involvement in the children's education and financial contributions to School Funds and Parent/Teacher Association events. A school for children in a decaying inner city area may face greater social difficulties. The examination results of the school in such an inner city area may reflect these social difficulties, or they may not. If they do not, then the school is doing exceptionally well for its children.

Arrange a visit

From the prospectuses and what you have heard about schools you should be able to tell which ones you want to visit. Telephone the head teacher and make an appointment. Secondary or upper schools hold annual open evenings to demonstrate how the school runs and what it has to offer. Current students show groups of parents around the school and you are free to ask them questions. You will meet the teachers working in all departments, and you should get a chance to speak to the Special Needs teachers should you want to. Sports facilities can be inspected, as can music suites, technology departments and school kitchens. This can be no more than a superficial glance at a school, and for a more detailed, personal visit make an appointment through the school office. However, on the open evenings you will get an impression that will confirm that you want to know more, or have seen enough.

How to choose a maintained primary school

Primary schools are usually divided into infant and junior schools. These correspond with Key Stage 1 (infants) and Key Stage 2 (junior) of the National Curriculum. In Scotland transfer from primary to secondary school takes place at 12 rather than 11 years of age (Year 7). In those areas of the country where there is a first, middle and upper school system, children transfer from first to middle usually at the age of 9, or after completing Year 4, and from middle to upper at 12 or 13 (Year 8 or Year 9).

School visits

If there is more than one primary school nearby, telephone and ask for prospectuses from all of them. Read them carefully, particularly trying to discover how caring each one is, how the National Curriculum is being introduced, and how broadly based all sports, music, and other activities are. You will need to make judgements about disciplinary policies, and multicultural and equal opportunities policies. Does the school make any arrangements for the gentle introduction of children entering their first school? Can parents stay with children, all day if necessary?

The first full-time school that you select is the school that sets your child on the path to literacy and numeracy. Are the school's facilities, resources and techniques for achieving a happy and positive introduction to the joys and excitement of books and numberwork up to scratch, and how do you judge?

Reading

How is reading taught? Is there a school reading scheme, or more than one scheme? Since children themselves vary, it is wise to look for a school that employs more than one scheme. Are there plenty of attractive books accessible to the children? Is there a 'book corner' where they can sit on cushions and look at books independently of the teachers?

Numberwork

Many fun ways have been devised for learning to do maths. Make sure you take a look at the materials available and find out if the school employs any particular maths schemes that the children progress with through the school. If there is a scheme take a look at the later stages as well as the early books. Find out how the children learn tables, and when. Find out if the teachers take the children out to do measuring and research in the local area for information for graph work, for example.

Information technology

Reception and early years classrooms need their information technology as every other classroom does. Find out about the software available in the classrooms. Is it appropriate for early readers?

A rich and positive environment

When you look at the reception and early years classrooms or teaching areas ask yourself, does this appear to be a rich and positive environment for learning to take place? This does not mean that the facilities and buildings need to be palatial or luxuriously furnished. You should find the children's work decorating the walls, which will disguise the fact that the walls probably need a coat of paint. Look in at the classrooms of the older children. Look at the work displayed to get some idea of the children's achievements as they rise through the school.

A caring environment is achieved not only through the staff, but in the way in which children are encouraged to care about and for each other and their environment. What system of rewards encourages good work, and caring and sharing? Is there litter to be seen? Check out the cloakrooms and toilets.

Early and middle years teachers

The best appointed buildings can never make up for poor teaching, and it is therefore very important to meet the teachers. This is a very special group of people. They are the front line in our children's education. They need all of the qualities of saints – patience, warmth, a high degree of organization, and an ability to think of everything and watch everyone – as well as know how to teach reading, writing, maths, technology, science, history and geography,
music and PE, run assemblies and deal with the personal and social aspects of our children's lives.

Discipline

When young children in particular are absorbed in their work and are finding their activities intrinsically interesting and the atmosphere positive and rewarding, the problems of discipline are very greatly reduced. Repressive methods cause some children a degree of difficulty that then rebounds on the staff and the rest of the children. Good teachers will have ways of bringing out the quiet and reserved child and involving that child in all the learning activities, as well as strategies for employing the extra energy and high spirits of the noisier, bouncy child who could disrupt the others.

Special needs

There are children everywhere who have difficulties and some present problems. The pastoral work that takes place in and through schools with the help of people like outreach teachers, school nurses, educational psychologists, and educational welfare officers, is considerable. These services are there not to deal with high spirits but to look after and care for children who have special needs of an educational or social kind. Ask the head teacher of the schools you visit about what arrangements are made for children with special needs. If a child is having difficulty with reading and writing, how soon is this likely to be picked up and what special teaching can that child expect?

Results

The national curriculum tests for Key Stage 1 and 2 (Standard Assessment Tests or SATs) are set by outside bodies and schools will have results that you should discuss with the head teacher. Ask to see an example of the reports or continuous assessments provided for parents to be able to follow their children's progress.

Choosing a maintained secondary school

Whether or not you have a choice, try to see the school or schools during working hours to get a detailed picture. Take your child with you and encourage her to take an objective view. Her opinions and choice are of paramount importance. No matter how rationally you attempt to choose, going to a new school is a nerve-racking experience and your child will probably want to go where her friends are going.

Academic success

You will get an overall impression of how highly the school rates academic success. Is your child going to be happy put under a lot of academic pressure? Is she likely to succeed in an atmosphere of academic pressure or will she wilt and fade away? Encouraging each child to succeed within their own skills and abilities is the hallmark of a caring establishment, but there is a growing need for young people to emerge with qualifications that will equip them for employment or further study.

What to look for when visiting a school

• It may seem obvious, but is the school tidy? The orderliness of rooms and corridors not only affects your impressions of the place but the students' own sense of status.

• Are you given a warm and efficient welcome at reception?

• Are the classrooms and corridors brightly decorated with students' work?

• Is the library well-stocked? Are there books to interest your child? Is it a comfortable place to be in?

• Do the English and drama teachers encourage play performances with the children involved in wardrobe and design?

• Is there a school orchestra, or other group musical activity such as choir or recorder group, pop music or jazz band? Will your child get the opportunity to learn an unusual musical instrument, such as the trombone or trumpet?

• How many foreign languages can your child experience?

• What technology is available to modern language teachers? Is there a language laboratory?

• Do any of them speak the language that they teach as a mother tongue?

• Is there adequate provision of information technology throughout the school?

• How is the National Curriculum in information technology delivered? This is a cross-curricular activity. Maths teachers use spreadsheets. Typically the science departments use databases. Wordprocessing is frequently used in English.

- Can students pick up IT credits as they go from subject to subject to give them a sense of continuity?
- Are children taught keyboarding skills at an early stage?
- Do the History and Geography rooms have interesting wall displays?
- Are there opportunities for students to take part in fieldwork in these subjects?
- Are the science laboratories well organized and lively?
- What sort of science equipment and facilities are available?
- Craft, design and technology workshops and art studios should have visible examples of the students' work to amaze and impress you.
- How is religious education delivered? Is there a chance to learn about the religions of other races?
- Ask about the school's multi-cultural and equal opportunities policies.
- What are the school sports facilities like?
- Are students involved in inter-school sports fixtures? Are girls allowed to play football and cricket, or do some old-fashioned ideas about sport and gender prevail? (They don't have to play together in mixed teams.)
- How many children go on to sixth-form studies?
- Does the sixth form provide vocational education as well as A-level studies?
- What provision is made for careers advice? What sort of careers have recent school leavers opted for?
- At what age are students encouraged to think about their careers?
- Is there a whole-school policy and syllabus for personal and social education?
- How is sex education dealt with? Some extremely interesting trials have been carried out in the teaching of AIDS awareness, whereby sixth form girls and boys have been trained by their local education authority to run student group discussions on AIDS. They have returned to their schools and, with teacher support, have helped their peers in discussion groups that are inevitably freer than if a teacher was present.
- Would your child have the same tutor throughout the school or do tutors change with every academic year? Both systems have their advantages and disadvantages.
- What attitudes does the school encourage in matters such as politeness and thoughtfulness?
- Are the students encouraged to do community work?
- Find out about the school's disciplinary procedures.
- How does the school organize each yearly intake?
- Do they 'band' students into broad bands of ability?
- Are children put into streams based on ability from the outset?
- Are the classes in some or all subjects broken up into 'sets' of children of similar ability, and at what point and how are the sets created?
- Is it possible for children to go from one set to a higher set (or vice versa)?
- Or are all children taught in mixed ability classes?

Family support

How well each child is known and understood could be a function of the size of the school, but more than anything family support and involvement throughout a child's school life give a child security and confidence and pay dividends in the long term.

Transferring to the big school

When the time comes to move from a middle to an upper school, or from a primary to a high school, whether at Year 7, 8 or 9, there will be some excitement and some fear involved for most children. The excitement is due to the increase in the scope of activities and friendships that will be available and to the fact that the move is an obvious sign of maturing. The fears, whether real or imagined, range widely and include anxiety about having many teachers instead of just one or two, and how strict they will be; doubts about ability to do the new work; having homework in possibly two subjects every night; concerns about new subjects, such as French; fear of bullies and a much bigger school; worry about uniforms, and the greater expectations that are placed on children at this stage.

Bridging the gap

Secondary schools have strong links with 'feeder' primary schools. In some cases, secondary teachers visit and teach the children in the top classes of primary schools to remove some of the fear of the unknown. In exceptional cases, children who are transferring are invited to meet each other socially at the new school and sometimes even go on a camping holiday together at the end of the term before they move.

Loss of status

From being top of the pile, these children become the youngest again. From being given responsibilities and special tasks, they are treated even by the most caring staff as the least competent. From having their own classroom and special teacher, they now have to organize their books and move from one room to another, and from one teacher to another. If you are 11 and in Year 7, the boys and girls in Years 12 and 13 will be very big and possibly at times rough and loud. The lunch queue can be overwhelming.

A helping hand

Preparation for secondary school life is just as critical as preparation for the first term at primary. By talking about what to expect and visiting the school before the first term starts whenever opportunities are offered you can help your child cope with the first few weeks.

Have a copy of her timetable at home so that you can check each day that all the books needed are in the schoolbag. Make sure there is a table somewhere quiet for homework. It is not advisable to do homework for children, but never turn down a request for help and advice. You will soon find out if your child is completely lost in the new regime if you involve yourself in the homework routine initially.

Form tutor and tutor groups

New pupils will be organized into forms or tutor groups and will get to know their form tutor straight away. Form tutors are teachers with subject specializations, who take on the tutor role as a part of the pastoral care system offered by the school.

The tutor is the main point of contact between parents and the school. The tutor sees her group every day for registration and will often teach personal and social education during her tutor time. She will help new children to be well organized and to follow their timetables. She is the person to listen to problems. She may remain with that tutor group all the way through the lower school, or even throughout the group's secondary school years. Students and tutors get to know each other very well, and tutors can be a very positive influence on children's school careers. Get to know your child's tutor and make it clear that you want to support your child in whatever way you can, and that you want to be informed if there are any problems.

Beyond year eleven

There are some very interesting developments taking place in education beyond the age of 16. Young people who formerly found there was nothing for them beyond the fifth form in school will find real stimulus and relevance in the host of subjects to be studied in Sixth Form Centres and Colleges, and Colleges of Further Education.

A- and AS-levels

A-levels continue to be offered. The AS-level available in most subjects is an excellent course that fills the gap between GCSE and A-level. It offers those who do not want to continue in sixth forms after one year a qualification which they would not otherwise have had. Discussions with teachers in Year 11 should help you and your children to decide on the most suitable courses to follow.

Advising students on their next step after GCSE is for parents, teachers and careers advisers to discuss together. Students need to consider what to do next at the time that they are studying for GCSE examinations. It may be impossible for them to focus on the future for a while. Some will be so stressed that all they will want to do is stop studying, regardless of subject or outcome.

Careers advice

The Careers Service is going to be greatly improved through funds provided by the Training and Education Council (TEC). All young people between the ages of 16 and 18, who are not in full-time education, will be eligible for Training Credits with which they will be able to 'purchase' further education and training in Sixth Form Colleges and Colleges of Further Education, which will be independent and funded through central government. At the same time, some sixth forms will become Sixth Form Centres, offering a wider selection of vocational and academic courses and serving a much wider geographical area.

Education and Training for the 21st century

The title of the Government white paper suggests the real concerns being voiced at present about post-16 education. All UK counties are looking at what is needed to rationalize the vocational training at present available and give it a boost. A-levels and 'Highers' are a 'gold standard' for entry to higher education in academic subjects, and the Government, through the City and Guilds of London Institute, wishes to create a structure of awards for vocational studies and training that will have equal esteem with A-levels.

National Vocational Qualifications (NVQs) exist and are rapidly spreading through the work skills courses so that they either are already or will be attainable at levels 1 to 4 for most skills studied. The awards structure has been created by the National Council for Vocational Qualifications, which body is working with the C&G in order to fit NVQs into the new Diploma of Vocational Education.

In some schools, students study one-year courses in sixth forms for a Certificate of Pre-Vocational Education, or CPVE. Foundation courses for CPVE qualifications are sometimes offered in Years 10 and 11. These will be replaced by the Diploma of Vocational Education, Foundation level. Courses leading to the Intermediate and Advanced levels of the Diploma will be available in the near future. The Advanced Diploma will have equal esteem with A-levels and will lead students to places in higher education if that is what is desired.

Parent governors

Being on the Board of Governors of your child's school is an excellent way of being involved in your child's education whether at primary or secondary level. The governors have responsibility for the school as a whole and for the school's budget. Governors, and particularly the Chairmen of the Governors, are no longer figureheads to be wheeled out at prize-giving ceremonies wearing flowery hats and broad smiles. It is

A brief guide to governors' responsibilities

- The forming of policies that describe the character of the school.
- The employment of staff.
- To decide, within the prescriptions of the National Curriculum, the school curriculum, particularly in such areas as personal and social education.
- To oversee the school's budget, and decide on spending.
- To make decisions such as whether or not a certain child should be excluded from school.
- To produce an Annual Report and hold a Parents' Meeting.

Education is a business unlike any other, and it takes some time before new governors fully understand everything that is going on.

an important role and considerable expectations are placed on these volunteers.

How to be elected

There must be at least one parent-governor on the board of every school (or occasionally group of schools). Elections take place every three years, and local education authorities set down the procedures that elections should follow in order to be fair. Some schools have three parent-governors or more and elections are staggered so that only one parent retires each year and there are at least one or two experienced parent-governors remaining.

The school will notify every parent of a forthcoming election. If you wish to stand for election you need to get other parents to nominate you and second the nomination. Your name will then go forward as a candidate. A meeting of interested parents should take place. At this meeting you could describe your reasons for wanting to be a governor, and what special interests you have in the school that you would wish to pursue as a governor.

The parents of every child in the school have one vote each. A date for the election will be announced, and the results made public. If you are elected, you should attend school events, perhaps wearing a badge showing your name and position, in order to get to know other parents and so that parents know who you are and can contact you if they have relevant school business to discuss with you.

You will be the parents'

representative on the governing body and they need to know how to contact you.

Once on the board you would do well to get to know the other parent-governors so that you can support one another. Local education authorities produce guidelines and information for parent-governors in their schools and once you have been elected you will receive all the necessary papers. There are books published on how to perform well as a governor, and the Open University sells a special governors' course which your school may have purchased. Spend time learning the procedures and you will be able to function well in this position of responsibility.

The National Curriculum

The Education Reform Act of 1988 established the National Curriculum Council whose responsibilities include devising a curriculum for most subjects taught to all children, be they under five, compulsory school age or in the 16-19 age group in maintained schools in England and Wales. Scottish schools have taught their own national curriculum for many years. Northern Ireland maintains some grammar schools, as do some counties in Britain. Similar provisions for a national curriculum and its assessment are made through the Education Reform (NI) Order 1989 as are in place in England and Wales.

The 1988 Act says that the school curriculum must 'promote the spiritual, moral, cultural, mental and physical development of pupils' and must 'prepare pupils for the opportunities, responsibilities and experiences of adult life'. In order to ensure that this takes place a complex legal Order is written for each subject and the Secretary of State for Education is obliged to ensure that these documents are followed in all maintained schools.

Year groups

In order to make it easy to describe all children, whatever kind of school they are in, the NCC introduced the numbering of year groups and this is now in common use in most schools. It brings order to the otherwise confusing array of names given to classes of students in their different schools. No matter whether a 12-year-old child is in a secondary school that takes 11-16 year olds or a middle school that takes children of 9-13 years of age he will be in Year 7. The expectations of the NCC for that child and of his teachers are described in the Orders for the National Curriculum subjects for children in Key Stage 3 which begins with that year group.

The Key Stages

The Act provides for subjects to be taught in stages, called Key Stages, rather than within year groups.

Each subject will have its own set of Orders, which can be purchased at HMSO or read in public libraries. A copy of all of the Orders should be held available for parents in every school.

Schools are also expected to teach religious education, although it is not one of the ten standard National Curriculum subjects, and the syllabus is agreed between schools and the local education authorities.

Attainment targets

All ten subjects have their own sets of attainment targets. For example, in English, initially, there are five attainment targets. AT1 is 'Speaking and Listening'; AT2 is 'Reading'; AT3 is 'Writing'; AT4 is 'Spelling'; and AT5 is 'Handwriting'. AT4 and AT5 combine after a certain amount of learning has taken place to become AT4/5 'Presentation'. Again after further learning has taken place AT4/5 becomes part of AT3 'Writing'. Attainment targets are the goals set for what students should know, understand and be able to do within the specialist subject areas.

Levels 1 – 10

Each attainment target is divided into ten levels of attainment or achievement. Level 1 in any attainment target is the easiest and

Key Stages	Year groups	Ages
Key Stage 1	Years 1 and 2	5-7
Key Stage 2	Year 3 - 6	8-11
Key Stage 3	Year 7 - 9	12-14
Key Stage 4	Years 10 and 11	15 and 16

EDUCATION

The ten National Curriculum subjects

The National Curriculum provides for all children a broad and balanced diet of subjects. The NCC has laid down which ten subjects must be taught.

Core subjects
English (Welsh in Wales)
mathematics
science

Foundation subjects
geography
history
a modern language
technology
art
music
physical education

---

is aimed at children just starting primary school who are working within Key Stage 1. Level 10 will not be achieved by all children even by the end of compulsory schooling.

Statements of attainment

Within each level there are a number of expectations of students and teachers and these are called statements of attainment. There may be only one statement of attainment, as in level 1 of English AT3: Writing, which states: 'Pupils should be able to use pictures, symbols or isolated letters, words or phrases to communicate meaning.' This applies to children in Key Stage 1. Level 10 in English AT3 has four statements of attainment. The fourth reads: 'Pupils should be able to demonstrate in discussion and in writing, knowledge of criteria by which different types of written language can be judged.' This applies to students working within Key Stage 4 who are taking GCSE examinations.

What to expect

The essence of the intentions behind the National Curriculum is that all children, wherever they live, are entitled to the same standard of education. It had been felt that some children did better than others, not because they were necessarily brighter, but because they happened to live near a better school. The Act places the responsibility for the delivery of the National Curriculum to all children, regardless of race, gender or creed, on the shoulders of teachers and, therefore, those who train teachers. As a result, children are tested and schools and teachers are inspected and assessed to ensure that the law is being carried out and that standards are being maintained or improved.

Assessment and reports

Children will be assessed continuously by their teachers. By assessment against the objectives set out in the National Curriculum, a profile of each student's achievements is maintained.

Standard Assessment Tests (or

Levels of attainment that are expected of children within each Key Stage will vary slightly from subject to subject. For example:

Key Stage	English	mathematics
1 (5-7 years)	levels 1 - 3	levels 1 - 3
2 (8-11 years)	levels 2 - 5	levels 2 - 6
3 (12-14 years)	levels 3 - 8	levels 3 - 8
4 (15-16 years)	levels 3 - 10	levels 4 - 10

From this chart you can see that levels of ability are reflected in what is expected of children. The range of achievements grows wider as the children grow older. For example, a 14- or 15-year-old may manage only level 3 in English or he may achieve the complex literary skills that are demanded at level 10. However fairly and evenly education is delivered, it cannot make up for the fact that we vary in our natural abilities.

SATs as they have become known) were initially designed to show not only how well a child was doing but where the child had difficulties that could be remedied. The difficulties encountered with the SATs at Key Stage 1 were such that simplified pencil and paper tests are being suggested as an alternative. These will give less information about each child, but can be done in considerably less time. Whether or not it is wise to subject all children to tests of this sort is a problem that has not been resolved.

It is not yet clear how Key Stage 4 will be tested as students completing Key Stage 4 will coincidentally be studying for and sitting GCSE examinations.

Annual reports must go to all parents, with parents and students contributing to the overall picture that is created. A Record of Achievement showing all achievements such as sport, charitable work, and other non-academic work is prepared by students and teachers together before the student leaves school. It can be used to show potential employers a rounded picture that includes a great deal more than just grades for examinations taken.

Implementing the National Curriculum

As Orders are written and become law, so the range of subjects taught according to the National Curriculum increases. The chart opposite shows subjects already being taught and the suggested timetable for those remaining.

Pre-school educational choices

In March 1991, the Pre-School Playgroups Association had about 628,000 children attending sessions run by member playgroups. Although the figures cannot be compared directly, 577,000 under-fives were in maintained nursery and primary schools in England in January 1990. The provision of maintained nursery and primary places caters for less than half the population of three- and four-year-olds.

The PPA is a non-profit-making charity. It attempts to fill the gap between provision for under-fives through the local authorities and the demand for nursery places. The PPA is not the only resource for the under-fives. The independent sector is increasing the supply of places in pre-preparatory schools. Some independent schools can offer a child a place from the age of two through to 18 years.

Particularly where the supply of maintained school nursery places is patchy or even non-existent, private nurseries are a growth industry. They have to comply with stringent rules and be approved by the local authority, and the owners prefer to make a profit.

With over a million under-fives in playgroups, nurseries or schools of one sort or another, and a growth in the number of places

available in the independent section, the message is clear. Parents of these young children believe that their children will benefit from the various kinds of experience they are receiving.

The experience is indeed very varied. The two-year-old in a mother and toddler group will be being encouraged to play with other children – to wait in line for his turn on the slide and not hit littler ones with his plastic hammer.

Children in playgroups that are associated with the PPA benefit from the training in under-fives' development and skills that the playgroup leaders all have to undergo. You will not find children sitting with pencil in fist attempting to write their names (unless they really feel like it), but you will find organized play, specially designed craft activities, paints (and overalls), singing, storytime, dressing-up box, and other parents who help on a rota basis.

The three- and four-year-olds in

The National Curriculum timetable

Subject	School term	KS1	KS2	KS3	KS4
Mathematics	Autumn	1989	1990	1989	1992
Science	Autumn	1989	1990	1989	1992
English	Autumn	1989	1990	1990	1992
Technology	Autumn	1990	1990	1990	1993
History	Autumn	1991	1991	1991	1994
Geography	Autumn	1991	1991	1991	1994
Art	Autumn	1992	1992	1992	1995
Physical Education	Autumn	1992	1992	1992	1995
Modern Foreign Languages	Autumn			1992	1995

a maintained school nursery class will have the benefits of a trained nursery teacher, usually assisted by an equally trained nursery nurse. A child will not be expected to know or learn how to write but will be helped with his manipulative skills in painting and drawing, modelling and building. He will be encouraged to learn how to tie his shoelaces, learn primary colours, sit quietly while listening to a story, and to cooperate with the other children. In fact, he will learn all the skills that make transfer to a primary class in the term in which he is five an enjoyable experience that presents few problems either for him or his teacher. He is likely to be ready to start learning to read, write and cope with numbers.

Some private nurseries and pre-prep schools encourage reading, writing and counting at an earlier stage, because they feel that this is what parents want. A child's readiness for formal learning will distinctly affect the benefit he receives from early attempts to learn. Too much too soon can be as damaging, particularly in the short term, as too little too late. It can cause unnecessary distress, unwillingness to attend and even, in extremes, schoolphobia.

If you choose early formal learning for your child make sure you choose a nursery class with trained nursery teachers who are sensitive to a child's state of readiness for formal learning. Other Europeans do not send their children off to full-time school until they are six or even seven. There is so much to be learned, about the world and themselves, and there is

plenty of time for formal schooling. However, other European countries provide much better for their pre-school children and their working parents. A huge improvement is needed in this area of our state provision.

The costs

Nursery classes attached to maintained primary schools do not cost parents anything. Attendance may be restricted (half a day every day for instance) or could be full time. If there is a class in a school near you, you are expected to notify the school of your wish to send your child to that school and that you would like a place in the nursery class. You will be notified if a place becomes available in the nursery class. Otherwise you may have to wait until your child is 'rising-five' before you are allocated a place in the reception class.

There are places available in local authority nurseries, but these are few and far between and are often allocated on the basis of need. They are not necessarily free, but again need plays a part in the calculation of charges.

The average fee per session for under-fives groups associated with the PPA was £1.26 in 1991. All groups have to raise funds and many receive grants from town and parish councils, social services, and some from the PPA Branch or County. Charities such as the BBC Children in Need Appeal and the Telethon Trust also provide funds. The fees for private nurseries and pre-prep school nursery classes vary from school to school.

FAMILY HEALTH

Keeping healthy does not just mean an absence of disease – it means feeling good as well. And if you want to feel good, and be sure that your family feels just as good as you do yourself, you have to work at it. To keep your body working well, you need to understand a little about how it functions, and be aware of some of the potential problems that you could avoid by changing your behaviour or seeking medical help promptly.

When to call the doctor

The list of signs and symptoms that could indicate a potential health problem is immense, but your commonsense should tell you when the doctor needs to be called. Any change in normal body patterns may indicate that something is going wrong. Such things as unexplained bleeding, pains or high temperatures are obvious causes for concern. If you become feverish and achy, while there is a flu epidemic around, then you probably won't need any medical treatment, while the same symptoms appearing after travelling in a hot country could suggest a dangerous condition like malaria.

You will need to use your own judgement, but if in doubt, ask for professional medical help from your GP, or in emergency, from the hospital. Remember that a baby is much more at risk from fevers and diarrhoea than a healthy adult.

Elderly people suffer from their own characteristic health problems, and because these come on slowly, they may not realize that there is anything wrong. You should never be afraid to contact the doctor.

Talking to your doctor

When you visit your GP, write down any key points so they don't get overlooked. Never be self-conscious or embarrassed about describing what's wrong. The doctor will get a much better picture if you are clear and direct, even if it means talking about things you would prefer to leave unsaid. Make sure you understand exactly what the doctor tells you, especially about any drug treatment he may prescribe. Follow dosage instructions exactly, and if you are still not entirely clear about them, ask the pharmacist when you collect your prescription. The pharmacist can also be very useful for minor problems, as he will be able to recommend a number of non-prescription drugs, if these are what is required.

More and more, doctors will not give prescriptions for minor problems that can be self-treated (with aspirin, for example), or which clear up on their own after a few days (as happens with most colds and many other virus infections). The doctor may refer you for tests, or for other treatment by a specialist or a therapist. For many people, the greatest benefit from attending the surgery is reassurance, gained from talking about a problem that has been niggling away in the back of the mind for some time.

Checkups

Health checkups are now regarded as an important part of the NHS, and many people also choose to use private clinics for the same purposes. Well Woman clinics are now very common, and GPs and local health clinics usually operate these services. They concentrate on identifying women's diseases in the early stages, and advise women on how to maintain their health. Such clinics will advise on weight control, take smear tests which will detect the first signs of cervical cancer, make routine breast examinations, and teach women how to check for breast lumps themselves.

Similarly, Well Man clinics are available at many doctors' surgeries. These concentrate on such things as blood pressure and the state of the heart and circulation, as the risk of heart attacks and other circulatory disorders is greater in men. They also advise on how to check for testicular cancer.

Drugwatch

All drugs supplied by the chemist, either prescribed or bought over the counter, carry instructions for use which should be followed precisely, as otherwise they will be ineffective, or could cause side effects. All drugs are capable of causing side effects, even the mildest remedy that you may have been using for years.

Herbal remedies bought in health food shops are not subject to the strict analysis and quality control of drugs you can buy in a chemist's. Some contain powerful plant drugs, and the quantities present can vary widely. If in any doubt, take them to the chemist, and ask the pharmacist for his advice about using them.

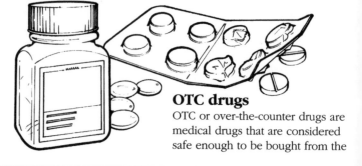

OTC drugs
OTC or over-the-counter drugs are medical drugs that are considered safe enough to be bought from the

chemist without prescription. It is usually best to ask the pharmacist for his advice when buying such drugs, as their properties do vary considerably. They are very useful for treating minor medical problems, such as headaches, stomach upsets, skin problems and diarrhoea, but if they do not provide relief, see your doctor. Among the most useful OTC drugs are:

Aspirin Relieves pain, reduces inflammation, reduces temperature. Useful to relieve symptoms of colds and flu. Do not give to children. May cause stomach upsets or gastric bleeding if taken regularly.

Paracetamol Similar drug to aspirin, which can be given to children (follow dosage instructions exactly). Does not cause stomach upsets. Dangerous in overdosage.

Ibuprofen Powerful aspirin-like drug that is very effective in relieving severe pain.

Antacids Various medicines and tablets that neutralize stomach acid, and so can be useful in indigestion, heartburn, and some similar conditions.

Hydrocortisone cream A steroid cream that is very effective in relieving inflammation and rashes. It must be used exactly as recommended, as over-use can cause permanent skin damage.

Antihistamines Tablets or creams that relieve allergic effects. Antihistamine tablets are used in treating hay fever, but many of

them are strong sedatives, and can be dangerous if driving or using machinery.

Decongestants Shrink the lining of the nose and reduce the secretion of mucus. They are useful in treating cold symptoms.

Laxatives Various drugs that speed up the passage of food and waste through the gut. They must never be taken regularly without medical advice. True constipation is uncommon, and it is not necessary to empty the bowels every day.

Anti-diarrhoeals Always ask the pharmacist for advice before taking these. Medical treatment may be necessary; alternatively, use a rehydrating mixture and the condition will usually clear up within a day.

Vitamin supplements Very seldom necessary, because our diets contain many more vitamins than we actually need. Generally harmless, if they are taken in the recommended amounts. Don't try 'megavitamin therapy' without proper medical advice, as some of these substances can be poisonous in large amounts.

Prescription medicines

The doctor can prescribe literally thousands of drugs. Basically these fall into a number of main categories, which define the conditions they are used to treat:

Analgesics For the treatment of pain. Some analgesics resemble aspirin in their effects, others are more like morphine and pethidine, used for severe pain.

Antacids Drugs that neutralize excess stomach acid and are taken for indigestion.

Anti-arrhythmics For controlling irregular heartbeat.

Antibiotics Effective against infections caused by bacteria, but not against viral infections.

Anticoagulants Commonly given after a heart attack, to prevent the formation of blood clots.

Antidepressants Widely used drugs to treat depression. Have unpleasant side effects like dry mouth and sedation.

Antihistamines Drugs that relieve the symptoms of hay fever and other allergies. Many are strong sedatives.

Antihypertensives Reduce raised blood pressure.

Anxiolytics Also known as tranquillizers, these drugs are not now commonly prescribed, because of their side effects and the risk of addiction if they are used for a long time. Withdrawal symptoms may be severe.

Beta-blockers Stabilize the beating of the heart, and reduce high blood pressure.

Bronchodilators Open up the air passages, making it easier to breathe with bronchitis.

Corticosteroids Commonly known as steroids, these drugs reduce inflammation. They have very severe side effects if used for too long at high doses.

Diuretics Increase the flow of urine from the body. Used to relieve waterlogged tissues, and to reduce blood pressure.

Hormones Used to replace substances produced naturally by glands in the body. HRT or hormone replacement therapy is sometimes given during the menopause.

Insulin Given by injection to diabetics, to help the body control the breakdown of sugar.

Sedatives Drugs that produce sleep. Not commonly given now, because they resemble tranquillizers in having a risk of addiction.

Tranquillizers Drugs that have calming effects.

Vasodilators Drugs that widen blood vessels, improving the blood flow.

Hospitals – what to expect and how to cope

In an obvious emergency, you will go directly to a hospital Emergency Department for instant treatment. Sometimes, the GP will refer you directly to hospital, and will call an ambulance for you if this appears necessary. Usually, however, your doctor will write to a consultant in

FAMILY HEALTH

the local hospital, explaining your condition and asking for you to be examined and treated.

Life-threatening conditions are treated without delay, and so are those which will deteriorate quickly. But most people are referred for chronic conditions such as arthritis or bronchitis, which although extremely unpleasant, can be kept under control by treatment prescribed by the GP, until a hospital appointment can be made.

The hospital's primary objective is to bring under control or treat your immediate problem, so your GP can take over your case again. The specialized services offered by the hospital are too expensive and thinly stretched to allow continuous treatment in all but a few very serious conditions, although many patients will be treated for a period in outpatient clinics.

When your treatment is deemed complete, you will be referred back to your GP, who will have been informed about your progress so he can continue the treatment along the lines established by the hospital specialist. In most cases, your GP will have known you and been familiar with your medical records for a long time, so he is the best person to oversee your routine healthcare.

Understanding your medical rights

The National Health Service in the UK provides medical services to everyone, on the basis of clinical need. This service is provided irrespective of the ability to pay, although charges are made for certain services such as prescriptions, dental treatment, and eye tests (these may be provided free for some patients).

You have a statutory right to have any proposed treatment explained to you, together with any alternatives, before you agree to the treatment being started, so you need never feel pressurized into agreeing to surgery, for example, without exploring all the viable alternatives. If you are treated in a teaching hospital, you do not have to take part in medical student training if you do not want to. Neither do you have to take part in any clinical trials.

Your medical records are always completely confidential, but if you are unsatisfied about any aspect of your treatment, you can insist upon your right to see them. You are also entitled to receive detailed information on the standards and performance of local health services, in order that you and your doctor can exercise a degree of choice about any service to which you may be referred. In addition, you have a right to full investigation of any complaint you may make about the treatment you receive.

First aid

The aim of first aid is to help someone who is sick or injured, without making the problem any worse. To do this, you will have to be able to assess the situation and decide if it is something you can safely deal with, or whether you need to call professional medical assistance.

Most minor problems like cuts, splinters and bruises can be safely

dealt with at home, but serious injuries or illness mean getting help quickly. If you are trained in first aid techniques you may be able to give practical assistance, but you must be aware that doing the wrong thing could make matters worse or even threaten life. Why not sign up for a course on first aid? It might save the life of a member of your own family, or help others.

Minor emergencies

To cope with everyday emergencies, your first aid and medicine cupboard (kept locked) should contain:
1 Adhesive dressings
2 Sterile eye pads
3 Triangular and roller bandages in various sizes
4 Assorted plasters
5 Surgical tape
6 Sterile cotton wool
7 Eye ointment
8 Tweezers
9 Scissors
10 Safety pins
11 Gauze
12 Aspirin or paracetamol
13 Antihistamine cream for treating stings, sunburn and rashes
14 Calamine lotion
15 Antacids for indigestion and heartburn
16 Hydrocortisone cream for skin inflammation (short-term use only)

Most minor household accidents and emergencies can be dealt with yourself, using this simple basic first aid and emergency kit, but you should never hesitate to seek medical advice if you suspect that it is necessary.

Dealing with serious emergencies

Your first priority in an emergency is to save life, then to minimize any further damage until medical assistance can be obtained. If someone is unconscious, there are three essential components to the first aid ABC:

A is for airway. Your first move must be to make sure that the air passages are not blocked.

B is for breathing. If the casualty is not breathing, you must immediately start mounth-to-mouth resuscitation.

C is for circulation. If the casualty's heart is stopped, you will need to begin external chest compression. Any serious bleeding must also be dealt with promptly.

Clear the airway

Falls, immersion in water, electric shock and various other accidents can cause unconsciousness. When faced with an unconscious casualty, you must make sure nothing is blocking the air passages, such as vomit, the tongue, or dentures. Place one hand on the forehead, and the other beneath the neck, and tilt the casualty's head right back (1). Now push the chin up, so the tongue is lifted out of the throat (2). If breathing does not start, sweep your fingers round inside the mouth to clear any debris (3).

> You should attempt resuscitation even if you think the casualty cannot be revived. Continue until breathing and heartbeat have returned or until medical help arrives.

1

2

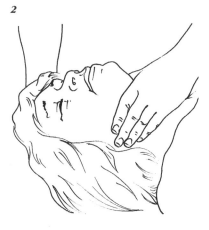

3

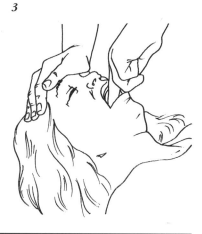

Getting the casualty breathing

If the casualty does not start breathing immediately after you have cleared the airways, you must carry out mouth-to-mouth resuscitation. For adults, this means pinching the nostrils shut (1), sealing your lips round the casualty's mouth, and blowing steadily to inflate his lungs (2).Watch carefully to see if the chest rises (3). If not, the airways are still blocked and you must check them at once. Small children are resuscitated by sealing the lips over their nose and mouth. Don't blow too hard, or you could cause serious damage.

Inflate the lungs every 3 or 4 seconds, and once the casualty begins to breathe again, turn him into the recovery position. If his heart has stopped, you must carry out external heart compression too.

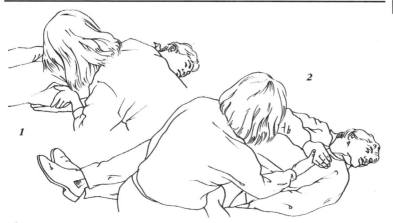

The recovery position

Once the casualty is breathing, he must be put into a safe position for recovery, so he cannot choke on his vomit, or have his throat blocked by his tongue.

Kneel alongside the casualty, and tilt his head back (1). Lay the nearest arm alongside his body, with the hand tucked beneath the buttocks. Lay the other arm over the chest, and cross the far leg over the nearest leg (2). Now you can turn the casualty.

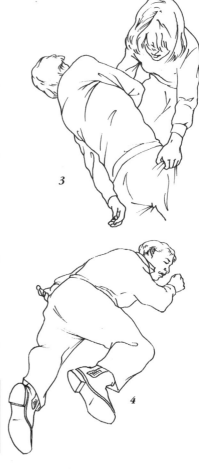

Grip the clothes over the farthest hip, and support his head, then roll him towards you, on to his side (3). Make sure the head stays tilted well back. Raise the uppermost arm and then bend the upper leg so the casualty does not roll right over on his face. Extend the lower arm behind him, so he won't roll backwards (4). Now you can treat any minor injuries while waiting for medical assistance.

Remember

Do not move the casualty if you suspect a fracture of the spine.

Restarting the heart

You can check if the casualty's heart is beating by feeling gently alongside the larynx or voicebox for the pulse in the neck. Never use external heart massage if the heart is still beating. To restart the heart, lay the casualty flat on his back and lift the chin to clear the airways. Now lace your fingers together, and locate the lower part of the breastbone, in the centre of the chest.

Hold your arms straight, and using your clasped hands, press the breastbone down about 5 cm (2 in). Release the pressure, then repeat, timing yourself by counting 'one and two' under your breath every time you press. After each 15 compressions, pause to give two breaths of mouth-to-mouth resuscitation until the heart starts. Then stop the compressions immediately and continue with the mouth-to-mouth resuscitation. Once the casualty is breathing steadily, turn him into the recovery position.

External heart massage

Choking fits

Choking happens when food or some other object lodges in the air passages and obstructs breathing. Coughing is the body's way of dislodging this, but when this does not work, several hard slaps on the back will usually expel the obstruction. Small children can be laid over the thigh or along the arm, and slapped lightly on the back up to four times.

If this does not work, do not delay. Check to see if you can hook out the obstruction with your finger. If not, you will need to carry out a life-saving procedure called the Heimlich method. In an adult, stand behind them, wrap your arms round their middle just below the ribs, and clasp one clenched fist in the other hand. Now pull inwards

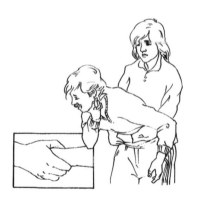

Heimlich method

and upwards sharply, and the obstruction will usually be shot free from their throat.

The same process can be carried out in a child, who is sat on your lap, and the pressure is applied with only one hand, to avoid damage.

If this does not work, begin mouth-to-mouth resuscitation, which will probably force air past the obstruction until help can be obtained.

Dealing with shock

After any medical emergency, shock can cause the blood supply to fail. The signs of shock are that the casualty becomes cold and sweaty, with a fast but shallow pulse and breathing rate. He may become unconscious and could die.

Treat shock by keeping the casualty warmly wrapped up, with his feet raised a little to help blood drain from the legs back into the body. Treat to stop any bleeding. Loosen any tight clothing and turn the casualty's head to one side. Don't give any food or drink, and send for medical assistance.

Stopping bleeding

Blood loss after an accident must be stopped as soon as possible, as it can quickly lead to dangerous shock. Don't delay, but put pressure on the wound, using a pad of cloth, or your fingers. Press down firmly until the bleeding slows and stops, and keep up the pressure for from 5 to 10 minutes. Injured arms or legs can be raised to help reduce the blood flow. Don't try to remove any foreign bodies from the wound, as this may make the bleeding worse. Once bleeding has stopped, cover the wound and get medical assistance.

Sprains, fractures and dislocations

In an ordinary sprain, a joint is bent too far so the tough ligaments that hold it together are torn. This causes painful swelling, which can be minimized if a bag of ice can be applied immediately, or the joint held under cold running water. If the joint is rested, it will normally heal quickly. Dislocations are very severe damage caused when a joint is levered apart, and like a fracture, you cannot treat it except by immobilizing the joint in the position in which you find it. Do not attempt to straighten the damaged limb, but keep it still by tying it loosely to a stick. Legs can be loosely tied together, and arms should be bound loosely against the side of the body. Keep the casualty warm, and watch out for signs of shock.

Burns

For all burns, the first principle of first aid is to cool down the damaged area as fast as possible, then to protect the wound from infection. Cool the damaged area by holding under cold running water for up to 20 minutes. Never try to remove fire-damaged clothing, as this would cause further damage to the skin, but in chemical burns, clothing should be carefully cut away. Cover the burn with a clean dressing, and treat for shock if the burn is serious. You should seek medical attention for all but the most minor types of burn.

Protecting the eyes

Eyes can be permanently damaged if they are not treated properly after an accident. When foreign bodies such as grit get into the eye, they are normally washed out by tears. If they have lodged beneath the eyelid, they must be removed. Get the casualty to look down, then pull the lower eyelid down. If the object is visible on the eyeball, you may be able to remove it by gently dabbing with the corner of a clean handkerchief. If the object is under the upper eyelid, get the casualty to look down, then pull the upper eyelid down over the lower eyelid. Should this not work, try getting him to blink several times under the water flow from a cool tap. If all of this fails, get medical help. Frequently a small scratch will remain for a few hours, and the eye may still be painful for a while.

Positive health

There is a growing awareness that positive health is not just the absence of disease, but means actually feeling good, and this is something that the individual can take responsibility for.

There is no doubt at all that following some simple guidelines for healthier living can extend your life, and will make some common diseases much less of a threat. Switching to a healthier lifestyle can take place at any time of life, even in the elderly, although exercise programmes need to be started with some caution in those who are unused to engaging in physical exertion.

The following basic rules for a healthier lifestyle will make you feel good, and help to keep you feeling healthy:

1. Take exercise at least twice a week, and make sure it is sufficient to make you out of breath.
2. Eat a sensible diet. Reduce your intake of fat, sugar and salt, and eat more fibre, fruit and vegetables.
3. Make sure you are not overweight.
4. Reduce your alcohol intake, and cut out smoking completely.

Healthy children

You owe it to your children to be as concerned about their health as you are with your own. Overweight

Simple tips to keep your child healthy

• Get her eating a healthy diet right from the start. Cut down on sugar, fat and salt in the diet of the whole family.
• Get her used to exercise as a family pursuit, and match the type of exercise you do to a child's interests.
• Make a positive effort to find healthy snacks that your children will enjoy, so they don't feel deprived when they are with friends.
• Don't expect your children to eat healthily and take proper exercise if you don't do these things yourself. Children learn by example, and will usually follow their parents without question if you start early enough.

children often become overweight adults, so it is important to watch your child's weight carefully, right from the early days. Discuss her weight with the doctor or clinic if it does not seem right; note that this applies equally to over- or underweight children.

Cutting out smoking

Smoking is responsible for, or makes a great contribution to, many serious diseases, and these are not just confined to the lungs and respiratory system. Smoking causes damage in several important ways, which are associated with its main constituents:

Nicotine
This substance is a powerful poison, and a stimulant. It is nicotine which people claim gives them a 'lift' when they smoke, and a burst of nicotine reaches the brain within only seven seconds of the first draw on a cigarette. Because it is a stimulant, nicotine speeds up the heart, putting extra strain on the whole circulatory system. It is a very powerful addictive drug, causing unpleasant withdrawal effects and cravings when you try to stop smoking.

Carbon monoxide
This is a poisonous gas which enters the red pigment in blood cells, changing it so that oxygen cannot be released into the tissues. Therefore, oxygen is no longer distributed properly around the body, and this can be particularly serious in people whose circulation is already damaged. It is especially harmful to the heart muscle, which needs a very efficient oxygen supply.

Tar and other solids
Tar, soot and other substances are also deposited in the lungs from tobacco smoke. Many of these substances cause cancer when they are in contact with living tissue. They also paralyse the tiny beating hairs that normally remove dirt from the lungs, so mucus and other materials accumulate, contributing to many lung diseases.

The dangers of smoking
People who smoke 20 cigarettes a day are twice as likely as non-smokers to die before age 65, but the risks are greater still for some groups. Pregnant women double their risks of a miscarriage, and are likely to have a premature baby. Their babies will also be very vulnerable to other diseases.

• Passive smoking, or being exposed to other people's smoke, is now recognized to be a serious hazard to health. Children whose parents smoke grow less rapidly and are more prone to respiratory diseases than the children of non-smokers. It is also believed that passive smoking can cause lung cancer in people forced to live or work with smokers.

The following conditions are either caused by or associated with smoking:

- Cancer of mouth and throat
- Heart attacks
- Cancer of the gullet
- Hardening of the arteries
- Lung cancer
- Formation of blood clots, and artery blockage
- Emphysema (when the lung tissue breaks down)
- Strokes
- Chronic bronchitis
- Bladder cancer
- Chest infections
- Gastric ulcer

Giving up smoking

The medical risks reduce as soon as you give up smoking, but it may be several years until you run no more risk than a lifelong non-smoker. The way you choose to give up depends a lot on your personality. Some people simply stop, and fight off the craving with coffee and willpower. This actually seems to be the most effective way of giving up. Others switch to slightly less harmful filter cigarettes or low tar cigarettes. However, they often need to smoke more of these to obtain the same 'lift' as with their original cigarettes, so there may be no real advantage. Cutting down gradually can work, but any stressful event is likely to make you reach for the cigarettes again.

If you want to give up, you will need to find the method that suits you best. If it seems too difficult, ask your doctor for advice, because there are medical aids such as nicotine chewing gum and nicotine 'plasters' that are simply stuck on the skin, which can help you through the worst stages of withdrawal. There are also many smoker support groups which provide reassurance and information on smoking cessation. You may be able to get in contact with these through your doctor, or find them through your local library or social services department.

The psychological addiction to smoking is most difficult to break, and some people obtain relief from acupuncture or from hypnosis, which can help to relieve the feeling of needing a cigarette to cope with minor stressful events throughout the day.

The healthy diet

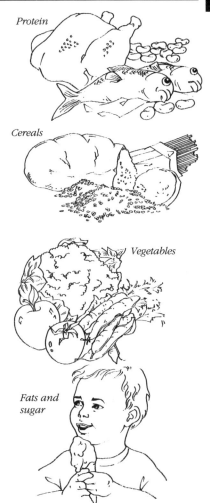

Protein

Cereals

Vegetables

Fats and sugar

Most nutritional authorities agree on ways in which our usual diet can be improved. These important recommendations are:

• Reduce your total daily intake of fats, and especially reduce the amount of saturated fat you eat.

• Reduce your intake of salt, because it is thought to be a risk factor in developing high blood pressure. Many foods already contain plenty of salt.

• Reduce your intake of sugar by 50 per cent. We all eat far more sugar than we need, and it is present in large amounts in some packaged and prepared foods.

• Increase your dietary fibre intake by 50 per cent. This may reduce the risk of diseases of the heart and circulation, and also helps to prevent constipation.

There are several different types of nutrient in the food you eat, and it is very important that your diet contains the right proportions of these nutrients. Most prepared or packaged foods carry labels listing these constituents in detail.

Fats

These are a concentrated source of energy, so to control your weight you should not eat too much of any food containing lots of fat. Oils count too: they are only a form of fat which is liquid at normal room temperatures, and are used by the body in the same way.

Vegetable oils are often hardened or saturated to make margarine and other cooking ingredients, and this makes them similar to saturated fats obtained from animal sources in their effects on the body. Saturated fats in the diet are now believed to increase the risk of heart disease in later life, and to contribute to the blocking of blood vessels with sticky deposits, leading to the hardening of the arteries, strokes and other diseases of the heart and circulation.

Health experts recommend that we decrease our intake of saturated fats and substitute polyunsaturated or monounsaturated fats where possible, although in smaller amounts to cut down the total energy intake. Fried food obviously contains a lot of fat, and you should switch to grilled food wherever possible. Sometimes fat is hidden in prepared foods. Biscuits and bread, for example, contain a lot of fat. Foods which are low in saturated fats, but high in mono- or polyunsaturated fats are better for you, but you will have to read food labels carefully to decide which types are in the food.

Common sources of fat

• Saturated fats: red meat, hydrogenated vegetable oils, dairy products, margarine, coconut and palm oil, nuts.

• Polyunsaturated fats: cooking oils such as corn, sunflower and groundnut oils. Specially formulated margarine. Oily fish such as mackerel, herring, salmon and sardines. Avocados.

• Monounsaturated fats: olive oil, oily fish, free range poultry (but don't eat the skin).

Carbohydrates

This major group of food substances can be divided into three different subsidiary groups.

Sugars are present in many foods. Their only function, apart from tasting sweet, is to provide energy, but because they are such an excellent energy source, a diet containing too much sugar will result in the excess being converted to stored fat, as well as contributing to tooth decay.

Starchy carbohydrates are better for you, because they take longer to break down into sugar and release energy. This helps to give you a more constant energy supply. Starches are present in cereals and root vegetables.

Fibre is a very important part of the diet. Fibre is a form of carbohydrate found in unrefined foods such as wholemeal bread and other whole grains, as well as fruit and vegetables and pulses. These wholesome unrefined foods also contain large amounts of starchy carbohydrates, making them a useful part of the diet.

Fibre cannot be digested, and is therefore not a nutrient, but it plays an important part in keeping the gut healthy. Some types of fibre bulk up the food, and help to prevent constipation and several other diseases of the digestive system. Other soluble types of fibre are sticky, and work by slowing the absorption of sugar into the blood.

Bran is particularly rich in fibre, but it should not be necessary to add bran to your diet if you already eat plenty of wholemeal bread and flour, which are rich in fibre.

In moderation fibre is very good for you, but don't overdo it, as in excess it can prevent the absorption of some important minerals. This won't happen if you stick to eating foods that are naturally rich in fibre, and don't smother everything with bran.

Common sources of carbohydrates

• Sugars: table sugar, sweets, biscuits, cake, syrup, ice cream; large amounts present in many ketchups, sauces and tinned foods.
• Starchy carbohydrates: potatoes and other root vegetables, flour, bread, pasta, pulses.
• Fibre: natural unrefined grains, wholemeal, bran, brown rice, breakfast cereals such as muesli, fruit, vegetables, pulses, nuts.

The recommended daily amount of protein for women is 54g (or a little more for very active women), and for men, it varies from 60g to 84g per day, the larger amount being needed by very active men aged from 35 to 64 years.

Common sources of protein

• Animal proteins: meat, milk, cheese, eggs, fish.
• Vegetable protein: wholegrains, soya, beans and other pulses, nuts.

Proteins

These essential nutrients are obtained from food by the process of digestion, and are used to build new cells in the body. Meat consists very largely of protein, together with fat, and there are also many vegetable sources of protein, such as lentils. People eating an average diet obtain about two-thirds of their protein from meat, and the rest from vegetable sources.

Vitamins

These substances play a part in many important body processes, even though some are needed only in tiny amounts. If you eat a good mixed diet, with plenty of fresh fruit and vegetables, you are unlikely to need to take vitamin supplements. The chart below shows vitamin sources and uses.

Some common vitamins, their uses and sources

Vitamin	Use	Source
Vitamin A (retinol)	Needed for body membranes, healthy eyes, and many other organ systems of the body	Liver and dairy products, fruit and vegetables
B vitamins (riboflavin, thiamine, niacin)	Release of energy in the body	Wholemeal bread, cereals, pulses, dairy products
Vitamin C	Healthy bones and teeth, and tissue repair	Fresh fruit, vegetables and potatoes
Vitamin D	Maintenance of blood calcium levels, needed for healthy bones	Made in the skin on exposure to sunlight; present in fortified margarines, cereals, eggs, oily fish, liver
Vitamin K	Blood clotting	Made in the bowel by bacteria. Also in leafy vegetables.

Minerals

Like vitamins, minerals are important to many body processes. Some are required in large quantities, while others, called trace elements, are needed only in tiny amounts. Minerals are present in the food we eat, and are especially abundant in vegetables. Because minerals dissolve easily in water, they will be washed out of food that is over-boiled. You should cook vegetables lightly (this will also conserve vitamins), use the

Tips for healthier eating

- Switch to wholemeal bread, pasta and flour, to keep up your fibre intake.
- Use less meat, and more vegetables in your main course. Try meat and three veg.
- Use mature cheese in cooking. It costs more, but because it tastes stronger, you need to use less.
- Eat fish once or twice a week, instead of meat.
- Use plenty of pulses as an alternative source of protein that is very high in fibre.
- Used skimmed or semi-skimmed milk instead of full-fat milk, and cut down on butter and rich sauces.
- Reduce the amount of sugar, fat and salt in recipes – you probably won't even notice the difference.
- Switch to yoghurt instead of cream, and use low-fat cheeses where possible.
- Eat more potatoes, especially potatoes in their jackets. When you peel them, you throw away the most nutritious part.

Food safety guidelines

- Take chilled or frozen food home as quickly as possible.
- Keep your fridge/freezer at the correct temperature – buy a fridge thermometer.
- Cook food thoroughly.
- Do not eat raw eggs.
- Observe microwave standing times.
- Store raw and cooked foods separately.
- Check dates on goods, and use food within the recommended period.
- Do not reheat food more than once.
- Keep pets out of the kitchen. Wash hands after handling them.
- Keep your kitchen clean and dry – wash and dry utensils between preparation stages.
- Always wash your hands with warm soapy water before preparing food.

cooking water in food preparation, or steam vegetables.

Food and hygiene

There have been several recent scares about food poisoning, and more than 44,000 cases are reported each year. These have made most people aware of the need for better food hygiene.

The official guidelines on food hygiene above are based on recommendations from the Health Education Authority. They were produced because of increasing concern about food contamination, and can make an important contribution towards health.

Some people such as the very old, the very young, pregnant women and people on certain powerful drugs (usually after an organ transplant or cancer therapy) are very susceptible to infection. It is recommended that these susceptible groups should avoid eating blue or unpasteurized cheeses, and make sure that eggs are thoroughly hard-boiled before being eaten. This also means avoiding foods that contain raw egg like freshly made mayonnaise. In addition, they should be careful to reheat cook-chilled ready meals and ready-to-eat poultry until they are piping hot, to eliminate the risk of infection with bacteria, which can thrive even in refrigerated conditions.

Exercise and fitness

Physical fitness is as important as proper diet in maintaining and improving health. There is increasing evidence that taking the right kind of exercise regularly can protect against diseases such as heart attacks and strokes, by improving the efficiency of the circulatory system. And there is no doubt at all that taking exercise makes you feel good.

During exercise, the muscles need greatly increased supplies of oxygen, and this is provided from the blood circulating around the body. To cope with the increased demands for oxygen, the heart has to work harder in order to pump more oxygen-laden blood around the tissues. At the same time, the blood vessels widen to allow extra blood to flow through.

Sensible exercise

It makes no sense to rush into an exercise schedule without proper preparation. Your body will soon tell you that you are overdoing things, and you will be stiff and achy the next morning. You should build up gradually, starting off with only a short session of not-too-strenuous exercise, and gradually increasing the pace. Your breathing rate and pulse rate will tell you if you are exercising the right amount – if you have to stop because you are too out of breath to continue, or you can feel your heart pounding violently, back off a bit and be more patient. Your strength and fitness will take a while to build up.

What regular exercise could do for you

- You will have better stamina, allowing you to work and play harder.
- More energy will let you cope with occasional hard exertion like DIY or gardening without getting tired and achy.
- The health of your circulatory system will be improved, and this will keep you healthier for longer.
- There is some evidence that your sex life can be improved.
- You will help control your weight, by burning off some excess calories.
- You will sleep better.
- Menstrual pain can be reduced by exercise before and during periods.
- Dependence on smoking may be reduced.

Exercise can be a family pursuit, and activities such as swimming, cycling and walking can be enjoyed by people of any age. By mixing different forms of exercise, you will ensure a good mix of the three key elements of strength, suppleness and stamina.

Strength is exercising the muscles. The muscles respond to exercise by becoming larger and stronger, just as they waste away when under-used, for example when someone is bedridden.

Suppleness is the ability to bend and turn freely, without the risk of damaging muscles or joints. Under-used muscles shorten and restrict movement, and some forms of exercise such as swimming, dancing and yoga can give great improvements in mobility.

Stamina is very important to health, allowing you to carry out exercise for a long time without getting tired. When vigorous regular exercise such as jogging leads to better stamina, your heart and circulation will work more efficiently to pump blood around your body, and your muscles will use oxygen more efficiently.

Dental hygiene

Care of the teeth and gums is an elementary form of hygiene. Bacteria swarm in the mouth, feeding on the material we eat, and thriving particularly on sugar in the diet. The bacteria live in a sticky layer called plaque. As they break down this sugar, the bacteria produce acid which eats into the teeth, causing cavities and allowing the teeth to decay. In addition, hard stony tartar is deposited round the base of the teeth, and as this accumulates, it damages the gums and allows bacteria to cause infections which can result in tooth loss. Gum infections and decayed teeth cause halitosis; a condition in which the breath smells foul.

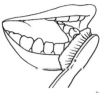

1. Brush up and down to remove plaque and debris between the teeth.

2. Clean the back of the teeth carefully.

3. Clean the biting surfaces of the back teeth.

4. Clean between the teeth with dental floss, with an up-and-down motion.

Regular cleaning of the teeth with toothpaste containing fluoride strengthens the teeth against bacterial attack. Fluoride hardens the tooth enamel so that it can resist acid attack and is less liable to the consequent bacterial decay. The use of fluoride toothpaste and the addition of fluoride to the water supply in some areas has led to a dramatic drop in tooth decay among children, and it is not uncommon to find children with no dental decay at all – unlike their parents, who probably had several fillings by the time they reached their teens.

Tooth damage can also be substantially reduced by cutting down on the sweetened foods and drinks that encourage bacterial growth and acid production, and reducing the amount of acidy soft drinks consumed, as the acid they contain can also cause serious tooth damage.

Both children and adults should take particular care to clean the teeth properly. This means using a toothbrush with a small head which can get right in between the teeth, with soft bristles which will not damage the gums and make them bleed. Teeth must be cleaned with an up-and-down movement which allows the bristles to penetrate between the teeth, removing sticky plaque and particles of trapped food. It is essential to clean between the teeth, as well as front and back, with particular care for the large teeth at the back of the jaw.

Even more plaque and debris can be removed with the proper use of dental floss. This is special thread that can be worked gently between the teeth to remove inaccessible material. Medicated toothpicks can also be used for the same purpose. Both floss and toothpicks must be used carefully to avoid damaging the gums.

Regular checkups will detect any developing tooth damage, so it can be treated at an early stage. In addition, a visit to the hygienist will allow removal of the unsightly tartar that builds up around the teeth, usually at the back where it is most difficult to clean.

Vaccinations

Vaccination causes the body to become immune to an infection in the same way as it would after actually having had the disease. Immunity is produced by introducing into the body either live but harmless disease causing organisms, killed bacteria, or parts of the organisms. The body reacts against these in the same way as it would to a normal infection, producing antibodies and 'learning' how to cope with the disease organisms the next time they are encountered. Sometimes this immunity is lifelong; in other cases it lasts for a short time, and the vaccination then needs to be repeated. Vaccination was first developed as prevention for the killer disease smallpox, and it has proved so effective that the disease is now extinct.

Vaccination means that many other formerly feared diseases are now rare, and seldom cause problems. Diphtheria, for example, is now extremely rare.

Vaccination of children

Childhood vaccinations provide protection against tuberculosis (TB), polio, diphtheria, whooping cough or pertussis, rubella, measles and tetanus. In addition, mumps vaccination is sometimes offered, but as this disease is quite mild, mumps is often regarded as an acceptable minor hazard of children, to which they will be completely immune after an attack.

Mumps can be quite serious in adults, however, because it may sometimes attack the testicles in men, and the ovaries in women. These conditions are very painful, and can result in sterility.

Special vaccination can also be provided to give protection when there are local epidemics of rare conditions like meningitis.

Vaccinations are safe and easy, and even though there may be an extremely small risk of reactions in some children, this risk is far outweighed by the very serious complications that can follow many of these common diseases. Because vaccination is so straightforward, there is no reason why any child should have to suffer measles, or why girls should risk their children being born with rubella damage. Rubella is particularly dangerous because it attacks the unborn child, causing deafness and sometimes deformity or death.

The only children significantly at risk from vaccination are those known to be prone to convulsions, or with a proven family history of convulsions, and you should always discuss this with the doctor beforehand. You should also tell the doctor if the child has a cold or other infection, before vaccinations are given.

It is very important that your child receives immunizations at the proper time, and they can start when a baby is only a few weeks old. Vaccinations are usually carried out at intervals, starting in the first few weeks of life, and continuing right through into the teenage years. The vaccination schedules change periodically, and your doctor will be able to give you a leaflet explaining the current recommendations.

Vaccinations in adults

You should have received all routine vaccinations during

childhood and adolescence, but it is advisable to check with your doctor about having boosters for polio and tetanus, as the immunity produced by vaccination is not permanent.

If you are planning a foreign holiday or travelling abroad on business, you may encounter infections that could cause serious illness, and because you have probably never been exposed to them before, you will have no immunity. Check with your doctor to see which vaccinations are required. The recommendations vary from time to time, as the pattern of diseases changes.

Vaccinations are available against Hepatitis A and B, Yellow fever, cholera, polio, typhoid and paratyphoid and tetanus. Influenza vaccination is also available in the autumn, when epidemics are most likely to occur. It is not completely effective, because the type of influenza virus varies each year, so immunity may not be complete. Flu vaccination is advisable for the very old, or those at special risk because of breathing problems.

Holiday health

Commonsense eating will avoid most tummy bugs. These minor infections, causing diarrhoea and vomiting, are often carried on food or in water in countries where the levels of hygiene are not what we are used to. You will already be immune to many common bacteria at home, but when you travel, you will encounter slightly different forms, to which you have not yet built up immunity.

To protect yourself, peel fruit, avoid eating salads, and drink bottled water if the local supply is suspect. And of course, don't swim in areas where there is any chance of sewage contamination. If you are unlucky enough to get an infection, just drink plenty of fluids, and don't eat anything for a day or so, until you feel better. If a child is infected and has serious diarrhoea, make sure she drinks a lot to replace lost fluids, and give her drinks containing rehydrating salts, which can be bought at a chemist's. Do not give antibiotics, which can sometimes be bought over the counter in some overseas holiday destinations.

Over-exposure to the sun can cause problems too. Avoid sunburn by using sun screen creams, oils or lotions containing a high filter factor. Sunbathing before you have built up a proper tan can cause severe blistering after only an hour or so. If you do get sunburned, use soothing creams to relieve the itching. Antihistamine creams often help. Sunstroke is more serious, and happens when the body becomes seriously overheated, causing sickness and fainting. The person affected must be cooled down immediately by sponging with cool water, and given plenty of fluids to drink, and must then receive expert medical attention without further delay.

Alternative health

Many people seek medical treatment outside the normal health services. This may be because they have not received adequate relief

Health insurance

Health insurance is designed to provide an income if you have to be hospitalized or are unable to work for some time through ill-health, and to provide access to medical assistance whenever it is needed. It can be very expensive, and the actual costs depend upon your age when taking out the insurance, your state of health, and the type of care you can be expected to receive.

In practice, the type of treatment provided by private health insurance is no different from that available on the NHS, and in fact, private patients are often treated at NHS hospitals.

The real benefit is the possibility of short-circuiting the long waiting lists which are a problem for some sufferers with chronic conditions. The NHS provides immediate care of serious and life-threatening illness, but if you have a less serious complaint, it can take many months before you are treated.

from their problems from their doctor or hospital, or because they do not wish to be treated by orthodox means or by prescribed drugs. This has led to the development of a whole range of alternative treatments. These are forms of treatment which cannot be explained or justified by orthodox medicine, but in many cases, appear to satisfy patients' needs.

Many people are extremely happy with the results of

alternative therapies. They form part of a broader pattern of holistic medicine, in which the whole body is treated, rather than just an affected organ. Consideration of the whole body includes the influence of the mind or spirit on health, and some forms of alternative therapy are spiritually based, or may have a religious basis, such as spiritual healing. Other forms of alternative therapy concentrate on positive aspects of health such as improved or specialized diets, meditation to avoid stress, exercises, massage or other different forms of personal development.

Alternative medicine can certainly contribute to a feeling of wellbeing, although direct physical benefits may be somewhat harder to demonstrate. Many people go to alternative therapists because they wish to avoid powerful drugs or surgery. Alternative therapies do generally offer a 'safer' alternative, and one where a close relationship of trust can be built up with the practitioner, providing counselling and a generally more sympathetic approach than the conveyor-belt system of the NHS.

Some forms of alternative medicine have been around so long that they have almost become conventional forms of treatment, and doctors sometimes recommend them when other forms of orthodox treatment have been unsuccessful, and patients are desperate for relief from their condition.

Osteopathy is an alternative therapy in which manipulation of the spine, muscles and other bones and joints is carried out to relieve pain. It appears to provide quick relief of some forms of chronic pain, although the theory underlying the manipulation is unconventional. It is based on the idea that misalignment of the bones causes disease. Chiropracters carry out a similar form of manipulation, but their system is based on the theory that disease results from faulty working of the nervous system. Unlike osteopaths they concentrate on treating a small area of the body such as a joint.

Acupuncture is an ancient Chinese form of medicine in which long needles are inserted into various

Acupuncture points

parts of the body and twirled or manipulated. This is said to produce beneficial effects by influencing a series of channels through which spiritual energy flows around the body. Acupuncture was not taken seriously in Western countries until comparatively recently, when it was medically proven to relieve certain types of pain, and was shown to have a direct effect on the nervous system. Acupuncture is now widely used to give temporary pain relief, though some of the other claims made for it are less well proven.

Homeopathy is a system of medicine based on the theory that the unpleasant symptoms of disease are caused by the body's attempts to cure itself. It uses various medicines, some in doses so small as to be unmeasureable. Treatments are based on giving drugs which, in larger quantities, would produce the sort of symptoms affecting the patient. There are many medically qualified homeopathic doctors who can be consulted and homeopathic treatment is sometimes available on the NHS.

Hypnosis is used by some doctors and by many other therapists to control pain, and to treat conditions such as withdrawal from the effects of smoking addiction, anxiety and phobias. The exact mechanism by which it works is not understood, but there is little doubt that it can be effective for some people. It seems to work best in certain personality types, and many people find hypnosis can relieve the anxiety they experience about their medical problems.

The beneficial effects of these forms of alternative therapy can be at least partly explained by conventional medicine. But there are a whole lot of more recent therapies that cannot be scientifically explained. Such treatments as spiritual healing, aromatherapy, reflexology, EST, colour therapy and others often become briefly fashionable, and a few will inevitably become established, as has happened with homeopathy and osteopathy.

How can you know if an alternative therapy is a 'quack' treatment, or one that could actually cause harm? For an alternative therapy to work, you must have faith in it, and in the therapist. Very few alternative therapies are capable of causing any direct harm, even if they do not work. The main drawback could be that too much reliance upon them could prevent you from going to the doctor for treatment that could have provided faster relief. In a few cases, life could be threatened by delay in seeking conventional treatment.

If you are considering alternative medicine to keep you healthy or to help with an existing health problem, it is best to regard it as 'complementary' therapy rather than 'alternative' therapy. In other words, use it as an addition to the medical treatment you receive from the doctor rather than an alternative. And be sure to let your doctor know what alternative therapy you are undertaking, in case it conflicts with the treatment he provides and complicates your condition.

The types of qualifications held by alternative therapists vary very widely, and not all disciplines have a rigorous training programme. If you want to choose an alternative therapist, the best method is to follow personal recommendations.

YOU & YOUR JOB

It can seem very difficult deciding what kind of career you want when you first stand on the edge of the world of work. And sometimes, if unemployment is rising, it can seem difficult to get any kind of job. But, whether times are bad or good, there are always more and better job opportunities if you know what you want and what you don't want. The first and most important thing to realize is that nowadays hardly anyone will have exactly the same job all their lives. This means more variety in the types of jobs people take up in their working lifetimes, and it also means no-one has to be stuck forever in a job they really hate. People move house more often and they move jobs more frequently than ever before.

Two golden rules for choosing a new job
- Do something you're interested in.
- Do something you're good at.

Whatever level or type of career you're aiming at – and whether you're just starting full-time work or you're already at work and trying to decide what your next job should be – following simple guidelines is the best way to start making plans.

If you hate driving, it won't do either you or your employer any good at all if you try to work as a taxi driver. The stress caused by your dislike of the job will probably wear you down and at the very least cause you to be less efficient and safety-conscious than you would be in a job you actually like doing.

Similarly, if you like children, you'll obviously get on better in a job in a nursery or school, than someone who can't stand people under the age of 18.

The plus and minus test
The best way to start making any kind of basic career choices is to get a page of blank paper and draw a line down the middle so you have two columns.

Head the left hand column PLUS and the right hand column MINUS.

In the PLUS column put down your achievements so far.

PLUS

Your individual achievements

For example, all exams passed – this means not only qualifications like GCSE, A-level, BTEC, HND, City and Guilds, RSA and other formal exams taken at school, college, or university, but also exams or tests passed at work such as NVQs (see later in the chapter if you're not sure what these are). Also exams passed in sport, music, dance, ballet, martial arts etc.

Put down other skills you haven't necessarily passed exams in, but which are still valuable, e.g. I can swim, ski, make clothes, repair cars, do basic First Aid, etc.

Personal skills e.g. I am good with my hands. I am a good talker and listener etc.

Languages I can speak some French, German, Spanish, etc.

Travel I like travelling and I have been to the following countries: Spain, France, USA, etc.

Transport Put down any driving tests passed. Do you have a car, a motorbike, a scooter or a pedal bike?

Hobbies If you haven't covered these already, do you have any hobbies that may help you to decide what type of work you really want to go for?

Team achievements Put down any school sports teams or school societies you were a member of, also groups like Guides, Scouts, Boys or Girls Brigade etc.

If you're older put down any military experience like the Territorial Army or experience in the Armed Forces if you have it.

Also include any committee experience, such as helping to run a playgroup, a parent-teacher organization, or a Neighbourhood Watch Scheme for example.

Employers like to see that people are capable of working in a team and group activities show that you're willing to work with others towards common aims.

What you enjoy doing

Write down which of these pluses you enjoy most.

What you'd like to do

Write down any jobs you'd really like to do that fit in with your own personal choices and skills. Pick three jobs at the most and concentrate on finding out about them in detail.

MINUS

Most people won't write down as much in this column as in the Plus column, but it is important to write down the things you really do NOT like doing or are absolutely hopeless at. For example:

I have not passed any exam in Biology/Maths/French/Physics/Chemistry etc.

I don't like cats/dogs/animals/hospitals/working at night/meeting a lot of people/working on my own all day/being inside/being outside/travelling away from home/being under pressure every day etc.

I don't want to be a traffic warden/teacher/nurse/bank clerk/shop assistant/long distance lorry driver etc.

You don't want to concentrate for long on the minuses, but it is important to take note of things you're not good at, or that you feel really strongly about, and work out some of the reasons why. Also you can work out areas where you could improve with more training or experience, and use that knowledge to influence your career choices as well.

If you're interviewed for a job that really doesn't suit you, even if you convince the interviewer, and get the job, within a few weeks or months you won't convince anyone, because your heart won't be in that job. And if you really deeply dislike a job, you're more likely to get the sack for not turning up or not coming up to the required standards. And that doesn't look good on your work record at all.

The main sources of information about jobs are

- Talking to other people in detail about their work.
- Books – most local public libraries have a wide selection of general careers advice books and books on specific careers.
- Job advertisements – libraries also have local newspapers plus daily and Sunday newspapers, and trade magazines.
- Advice from school – careers officers and/or careers teachers.
- Advice from your local Jobcentre.
- Advice from your local Youth Training Office or your local TEC, which stands for Training and Enterprise Council. Local addresses and phone numbers for both YT and TECs are available from your local Jobcentre.
- Advice for students is available from university or college libraries and from Student Careers Officers.
- Agencies for temporary or permanent posts can offer a very wide range of jobs, not just office work, but catering, nursing, security, computer programming and a range of other jobs. Fees are usually paid by employers.

Getting career information

Now you've made some decisions about your likes and dislikes, and your strengths and weaknesses, you need to find out as much as possible about the jobs you want to concentrate on.

If you are unemployed

You should register at your local Jobcentre where you can get free advice from your New Client Advisor to help you decide what to aim for. All teenagers aged 16 or 17, who are not either in work or studying at school or college, are guaranteed a Youth Training place, and some can get extra cash to help with travel, lodgings and other expenses.

If you are over 18 and unemployed for more than three months, you are entitled to attend a Job Search Seminar or a Job Review Workshop, which each last two days and are completely free. If you are unemployed for more than six months, you can join a Jobclub or a Restart programme or a JIG, which stands for the Job Interview Guarantee programme. JIG may include work experience or new training, but, in common with all the other schemes listed here, it does not affect the payment of your state benefits.

Getting a job – basic guidelines

It's important always to prepare yourself so that you can present your case for getting a job in the best possible way to potential employers. One of the most useful first steps you can take is to prepare your CV.

On the next page you will find all the information your CV should contain.

What is a CV and how do you write one?

CV stands for the Latin words Curriculum Vitae, which, translated literally, mean 'the course of a life'. In business it means an outline of a person's educational and professional experience clearly set out with dates and qualifications.

The best CVs, however long or short the career they are covering, should be short. One typed page is certainly enough for most people. Never send a handwritten CV. Be positive and sell yourself without exaggerating.

Your first rough draft of your CV will probably be longer than one page, but don't worry about this, as you will almost certainly need to

shorten it, and you may want to change your description of your skills as you remember more things you've done in the past that are not now at the forefront of your mind.

Why you should always have a CV

It's a very good idea to keep updating your CV even when you're not looking for a job, because you never know when you might need it. Also, if you keep your CV up to date by looking at it every six months, you'll find it easier to keep your own career in perspective.

Either you'll be cheered up to see how well you're doing, or you'll start thinking about your next promotion, or you might start wondering why you're going nowhere in a particular job.

Guide to application forms

Many people find their heart sinks when they see an application form. The questions worry them, and so does the whole business of filling in the form neatly. But if you take it step by step you can take away some of the strain.

Get a copy of the form

Get the form copied at a local photocopying shop. This is useful not only because you can fill in the copy of the form first and decide what to say and change it before you fill in the original form neatly, but also because it's sensible to have a copy of the form anyway. If you do get an interview for a job, you need to know exactly what

What to put in your CV

Your name – Your home address – Your home telephone number

Profile
This is a description of yourself in a work context in one or two sentences.
For example:
• An enthusiastic and reliable school leaver with experience in catering.
• A trainee motor mechanic with experience of many different makes of vehicle.
• A bilingual secretary with extensive word processing and supervisory experience.
• A trainee manager with specialized knowledge of fashion retailing.
• An HGV driver with experience of delivery throughout Britain and the EC.

Skills
Another two sentences will do, outlining your main skills. For example:
• Reliable, trustworthy and with a good attendance record.
• Accurate typing with RSA qualifications, currently responsible for word processing, correspondence, ordering office supplies, and liaising with customers.
• Self-starter with daily sales and marketing experience.
• Ability to work effectively under pressure.
• Good communicator with both written and verbal skills.

Career
Always start with your current work and go backwards through your career.
Keep dates simple by putting years only, not the exact months when you changed your job.
For example:

Sky Television, camera operator	1990-present
BBC Television, trainee technician	1989-90

Education and qualifications
Work backwards again. Start with your last university, college or school and give the qualifications you gained.
If you didn't get a lot out of school, but have since gained a number of practical qualifications, put these down here as well as the years you gained them. Put any driving licences here.

Interests and hobbies
Many people feel they are too busy to have hobbies, but everyone has interests, for instance, football, swimming, martial arts, sewing, travelling, music etc. If you are a school leaver, try hard to put something else besides pop music! Whatever you put, don't put anything unless you're prepared to talk about it at an interview.

you've answered in response to the particular questions on that form. If you can look at your copy just before the interview, you'll feel more confident and you're more likely to make a better impression.

References

Application forms sometimes ask for the names of two or even three people who can give you a good reference and say you're both honest and wonderfully suited for this particular post. These people may be current or former employers or professional people who know you: for instance, a lawyer, a doctor or a minister of religion. Do not put down members of your family. Most forms specify that family members are not appropriate, but, even if they do not say this, it hardly looks very experienced to put down someone you are related to. Thinking of the names of referees can sometimes be difficult if you haven't applied for a job for a few years, so this is another reason for keeping your CV plus referees always up to date.

To type or not to type

If you have access to a typewriter and you are used to typing or keyboard work, it is a good idea to type your answers on an application form, as this is easier for employers to read, and it does look more professional.

However, if you are not used to typing, you'll only send your blood pressure up by trying to type something very important very neatly. It's better in that case to write everything out in capitals on

your photocopy and then copy it out neatly on to the original form. Remember, it's better to use capital letters as they are clearer and easier to read than ordinary handwriting. Your application may be one of many, and if the people who receive it can't read it easily, you're not very likely to be called for an interview.

Applying by phone

Using the phone means you can apply for jobs as soon as you see them advertised. It's a very good idea to phone up quickly as, if you wait and worry for a few days about whether to apply, other people can go ahead and get the job that would have suited you.

Many job applications nowadays are dealt with almost entirely on the phone. You may be asked to bring your CV to an interview within a day or two of ringing up about a job, instead of waiting for letters to go back and forth. If you go to an employment agency, you may be sent for a job interview on the same day you first walk in their door. And if your first interview doesn't bring a job offer, you'll be telephoned by the agency for more interviews.

Further information

For more details on applying for jobs you can buy The Employment Pack, price £3.99. This is written by the Institute of Personnel Management, and available only from branches of W.H. Smith.

Telephone manners matter

When you're on the phone people obviously concentrate on your voice and form an impression about you from the way you speak. Small things matter.

If you never say 'Please' when asking for information, or 'Thank you' when receiving it, you can easily unintentionally give the impression of rudeness and spoil your chances of getting considered for a job.

Applying by letter

It's important to type letters when you apply for jobs. Only a school leaver can get away with something handwritten and that must be written very neatly. You should also try to write clear sentences that are not too long, and, as with your CV (which should always be typed) be positive and sell yourself.

Before the interview

• Try to find out some facts about the company or organization, for instance how many people it employs, and what its main products or services are, so you don't appear completely ignorant. You can ring the company itself, and, if it's a large company, you can look for more information at your local library.
• Find out as much as you can about the job you're applying for.

For instance, if you are sent a job description, make sure you read it properly.
• Look at your application form and prepare the most important points you want to make about yourself.
• Decide what you want to say if you're asked: 'So why do you think *you* should get this job?'
• Prepare an answer to those tricky questions: 'And what would you like to be doing in five years time?' or 'Where would you like your career to go in this company?'
• Prepare something to ask the interviewers in case they say at the end of the whole thing: 'Now is there anything *you'd* like to ask *us*?'
• Always work out your route before the day you have to set off to the interview.
• If your shoes need polishing, polish them the night before the interview. Shoe polish can go everywhere when you're nervous and in a hurry.
• Wash your hair and have a bath or shower, so you know you'll be at your cleanest and best.

On the day of the interview

Sometimes a first interview will be carried out on the phone, so it's a good idea to be well prepared with your answers about yourself, the job, and the company, as soon as you've sent off the application form.

Most people feel nervous when they first come face to face with a

• ALWAYS CHECK AND DOUBLE-CHECK FOR SPELLING MISTAKES.
• ALWAYS SEND YOUR JOB APPLICATIONS BY FIRST CLASS POST.

SPECIMEN APPLICATION LETTER

Your full home address with
your postcode

The organization and
address you are applying to

The date

Dear Sir or Madam

The job as described in the advertisement
(e.g. Trainee Security Officer/ Junior Clerk etc.)

Your advertisement for the above post in the *Enfield Gazette/The Times* etc.
interests me very much and I enclose my CV (substitute 'my application form'
if this is what is asked for). As you will see, I have current experience as (put
your experience relevant to the post. If you are a school leaver, emphasize
your enthusiasm, reliability and responsibilities at school and/or in
organizations outside school).

I am keen to work for you because (put a positive reason such as 'I want to
work for a market leader', or 'I want a career with a leading and established
company' or 'I am keen to work with a larger company' etc.)

My skills and background are particularly relevant to this post because (put
the reasons why you think you can do this job well). (Next mention any words
from the advertisement. If it says 'must have office experience', put yours
here. If it says 'must have a driving licence', put 'I have a clean driving
licence'. If it says 'must be a good timekeeper', put 'I am punctual and
reliable' etc.)

I would be pleased to attend an interview and can be contacted on my home
number during the evening (put telephone number).

Yours sincerely

(your signature handwritten)

Your name typed

potential employer, so on the next page are a few tips.

Your first job

Getting on at work, whatever type of work you do, and whatever level you want to reach, does take some effort. It takes some of us quite a time to realize that work is not like school where a certain amount of progress is built in automatically every year. Work is much more like the school playground, where there aren't many rules and things are not always fair or kind.

In addition, the hours are longer than school and people expect more of you. They will not usually be impressed if you don't do things as soon as you are asked, if you forget to do things, refuse to take on tasks without good reason, or if you are late.

You must make your own way at work, though, of course, that doesn't rule out making friends with people who know the organization better than you.

Your rights at work

Your work and duties should be defined in writing. If this is not written in a formal contract, you are entitled to a written statement giving the main terms and conditions of your employment.

This must be given to you within 13 weeks of starting a job. If your employer has more than 20 workers, you must also receive an additional note stating disciplinary rules and grievance procedures (except on health and safety) and the name of someone to contact on these issues.

What is a written statement?

Details that should be included in a written statement are:

• Your name and your employer's name;
• Your job title;
• The date your employment began;
• Your rate of pay and how it is calculated;
• How often you are paid, for instance, weekly or monthly;
• Your holiday entitlement, including public holidays;
• Rules about absence due to injury or sickness and details of sick pay;
• Your pension arrangements;
• The period of notice for both you and your employer.

If your employer does not give some of these details, omissions must be mentioned in the written statement. Also, any changes to the terms referred to in the statement must be given to you in writing within a month of changes being made to work arrangements.

How to cope with interviews

The most important advice to help you cope with job interviews is:

ALWAYS TAKE TIME TO PREPARE YOURSELF BEFOREHAND

DOs and DON'Ts for your interview

DO

• Set off early. Make an effort not to be late.
• Wear something smart but comfortable. Before you set off, give yourself time for a thorough check for problems like hairs on shoulders, ladders in tights or stains on ties.
• Take the application form with you and also any certificates and qualifications directly relevant to the job.
• Try to walk into the room confidently however nervous you really feel. First impressions are very important.
• If you smoke, use a mouth wash or spray beforehand to freshen up.
• Try to keep your hands still in your lap as much as possible.
• Try to work out the main things the interviewer or interviewers are looking for so that you have your answers well prepared.
• Try to be yourself. It's best not to pretend to be something you are not.

DON'T

• Don't wear tight skirts or trousers.
• Don't be late.
• Don't eat a sandwich, have a drink, or smoke a cigarette directly before an interview. Crumbs and cigarette ash, smudges on faces, and bad breath are all guaranteed not to impress your interviewers.
• Try not to take accessories like umbrellas, newspapers, or street maps with you unless you can put them all into one bag or briefcase before you walk into the interview room.
• Don't sit down until you are invited to. This is a formal situation and you will look bad mannered if you march in and take a seat without being asked.
• It's natural to be nervous about a job interview. Try not to say too much or too little just because of nerves.
• It's best not to smoke during the interview, even if you're asked if you want to. Smoking always creates a bad impression and may betray nerves.
• Unless specifically asked, it's best not to mention your family, if you have one, as many employers may see this as unprofessional.
• It's a good idea not to accept a cup of tea or coffee because if you're nervous you're likely to choke, rattle things or even drop them.

Why haven't I got a written statement?

If you are self-employed, or work fewer than eight hours a week, you do not have the right to a written statement. Some trainees, and some contractors, plus most people working outside Britain, and most people who work between eight and sixteen hours a week and have not yet completed five years of continuous service, are also not covered by this right.

If you are dissatisfied with your written statement or terms of employment, you can take your case to an industrial tribunal. You can find further information on the tribunal system in the Employment Department booklet ITL1: Industrial Tribunals Procedure, which is available from any local office of the Employment Service (this is the new name for offices of the Department of Employment).

Safety in the workplace

Safety is an issue affecting everyone at work. Every year around 700 people are killed at work in Britain. A further 900 die from industrial diseases, and more than a quarter of a million people are injured in accidents at work. Factory, restaurant, building and shop workers are often lifting heavy loads or working with dangerous substances or processes, but there are health hazards too for office workers, particularly those working with new technology. They may be prone to Repetitive Strain Injury, known as RSI, and other permanent health problems. (See below, Working with screens and keyboards.)

Your right to be safe at work

Enforcing laws and regulations on safety at work is the responsibility of the Health and Safety Commission, and under the Health and Safety at Work Act 1974, and the Regulations on Safety Committees, employees can appoint Safety Representatives and form committees to investigate safety and talk to their employers and to the HSE.

Tips for the top

- **CONFIDENCE** If you decide you want to get on in your present organization, you must have the confidence to get yourself noticed by taking on responsibilities, and then delivering results reliably.
- **RELIABILITY** A reputation for reliability is worth its weight in gold. If you do make a mistake, people are more likely to give you the benefit of the doubt if you have never let anyone down before.
- **NETWORKS** Networking is a very useful way of getting on, both inside and outside your organization. If a colleague surprises you by knowing about something new at work before everyone else, you'll often find that there's a connection via sport or social activities where they've met someone from another department, or another company, and found out some useful information. Networks can be formal, involving specific clubs or groups, or informal involving people you know socially via your children's school, a religious group or a hobby. If you write down all the different types of people you know, you'll see how many networks you're already in, and you can work out what other groups you could join.
- **KEEP FIT** By taking exercise or doing sport on a regular basis you will keep up your energy levels, stamina, and capacity for hard work. This is a better policy for success in your career than frequent late nights, pub crawls, all-night parties or discos.

If you have a recognized trade union at work, the union, not the employer, has a legal right to appoint safety representives and the employer must recognize them and allow them to set up a safety committee if they so wish. This means people can, hopefully, deal with worries about safety before they become dangers.

You can be appointed a safety representative if you have more than two years' work experience.

The Trades Union Congress, Congress House, Great Russell Street, London WC1B 3LS, has leaflets on Health and Safety at Work. 'Know Your Rights – TUC Guidelines on Safety Representatives and Safety Committees' costs 80p from TUC publications at the above address.

Written statement of health and safety policy

If your employer employs more than five workers, he or she is required by the Health and Safety Act to provide you with a written statement detailing the firm's health and safety policy.

Working with screens and keyboards

Millions of people nowadays spend their working days chained to a computer keyboard, and while new technology has brought great benefits in the speed and efficiency of data processing in many walks of life, it has also brought new health hazards. However, back problems and constant muscular pains like RSI and WRULDS (Work Related Upper Limb Disorders) may be avoided if basic ergonomic

guidelines are followed.

Ergonomics is the study of the relationship between workers and their environment. It acknowledges that workplaces and their furniture and equipment should be designed to avoid the new physical strains modern technology has brought into many people's working lives – strains that could be avoided if people did not try to use new equipment with old-fashioned desks and chairs.

New European rules

You may have seen the words 'ergonomically designed' creeping into advertisements and brochures for office equipment. The European Commission has issued a directive ordering all member states to pass laws setting good ergonomic standards by the end of 1992.

After that employers have four years to bring existing equipment up to the new legal minimum standards, while all new equipment must meet the requirements of the EC rules. Anything ordered now but not put into service before 1993 will be required to comply immediately with the new rules.

These rules set standards not only for display screens and keyboards, but for software, desks, chairs, lighting, and the whole working environment.

In addition employees will have the right to eye tests before starting work on any kind of display screen, the right to footrests, and the right to work breaks or changes of tasks to cut down the risk of physical problems caused by long periods working without a break on screens and keyboards.

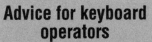

Advice for keyboard operators

- Always have your screen and keyboard separate.
- Keyboards should be just below elbow height when seated comfortably.
- Adjustable height desks (not yet common in Britain) are better than fixed desks.
- Avoid pressure from your chair on the back of the thighs. Use a footrest if necessary.
- Always have a chair that is adjustable.
- Avoid reflections on your screen. Lights throwing light upwards on to the ceiling are best. If possible turn off neon lights.
- Take regular breaks from work.

Information on safety at work

If you want further information on basic guidelines for avoiding safety problems in the workplace, you can contact the Health and Safety Executive on 071 221 0870 or the Trades Union Congress on 071 636 4030. The TUC has 10 regional offices and the HSE has 20 local offices, who may also be able to help you.

The Ergonomics Society is at Loughborough University, Tel: 0509 234 4904, and has lists of experts on the design of office equipment and work routines.

The RSI Association, Christ Church, Reford Way, Uxbridge, Middlesex UB8 1SZ, has an information pack available if you send £1 plus a large self-addressed envelope with a 35p stamp.

Equality at work

Since 1970, the Equal Pay Act has made it unlawful to pay different wages to men and women doing the same or broadly similar work. In addition, since 1984, anyone doing work of equal value to that of a colleague of the opposite sex, but paid less, can make a claim for equal pay.

Equal value is a complex issue, but, in simple terms, it means you can claim equal pay if you can show that your job pays less than others in the same organization, but makes equal demands on you in terms of effort, responsibility, skills and decision-making.

A famous example of this involved a female cook working in a shipyard canteen who was able to successfully prove in 1988 that, although she was paid less than skilled men working in the shipyard, her work was of equal value to theirs and should be paid equally. After taking her case right through to the House of Lords, she eventually received a payrise of £24 a week and back pay, which together totalled £5,340.

You are also entitled to make a claim under the Equal Pay Act for the same terms of employment as a colleague doing the same or similar work. This means, for instance, that you should have equal opportunities to work overtime, or to claim sick-leave and paid holidays.

Although this law was brought in with the main intention of correcting inequalities in pay for women, it is not for women only. It gives the same right to a man to

YOU & YOUR JOB

claim equal pay with a female colleague, if a man feels he is not being paid equally.

Sex discrimination

You do not need to be in current employment to make a complaint under the Sex Discrimination Acts of 1975 and 1986. You can make a complaint whether you are still working for an organization or not. For instance, if you are made redundant, and only women workers have been made redundant while male workers have been kept on, you may have a case for claiming unlawful sex discrimination. You can also claim sex discrimination if you are made redundant merely because of announcing pregnancy.

You can also complain or go to an industrial tribunal about job interviews or recruitment procedures that may discriminate against one sex. For instance, you might complain if you fail to get a job and you were asked questions about your family life and childcare arrangements that were not asked of male applicants.

Sexual harrassment

The Equal Opportunities Commission estimates that sexual harrassment, both verbal and physical, costs the British economy many millions of pounds a year in lost work time through the stresses and strains it causes. More and more employers are now at last recognizing that threatening or intimidating behaviour by (predominantly) male workers towards females need not be accepted as a 'normal' part of working life.

There is still some way to go as it's only in the last ten years that sexual harrassment has been taken seriously in Britain. At the beginning of 1991, a woman painter and decorator who had worked for Islington Council in London received £15,000 compensation and a further £1,500 towards her legal costs because she had suffered sexual abuse, intimidation and assault from male colleagues, and finally left her job suffering from depression.

This may seem an extreme case, but studies have shown that some men are so hostile towards women workers that they act threateningly towards them, often by telling dirty jokes or making smutty offensive innuendoes, to cause maximum embarassment. This has little to do

---

Further information and advice

Free information on the Equal Pay and Sex Discrimination Acts is available from Jobcentres and other offices of the Employment Service.

The Advisory Conciliation and Arbitration Service, 11/12 St James's Square, London SW1Y 4LA, Tel: 071 214 6000, and the Equal Opportunities Commission, Overseas House, Quay Street, Manchester M3 3HN, Tel: 061 833 9244, can offer advice on problems of sex discrimination and equal pay and may provide help with legal costs. Both these organizations have regional offices they can put you in touch with.

YOU & YOUR JOB

with sexual attraction, but is all about power and 'keeping women in their place'.

There is no typical sufferer – the only common factor is that the victim appears to be vulnerable to this kind of treatment.

If you feel that you or one of your colleagues is being picked on in this way, and it's not possible to sort it out directly with the man or men involved, you can approach your personnel officer or trade union representative in confidence for practical help and advice. If you cannot get help in either of these ways, you can try to get help from colleagues. If things are not resolved via your employer, you can make your complaint about sexual harrassment under the Sex Discrimination Acts of 1975 and 1986, and take your case to an industrial tribunal.

Racial discrimination

It is unlawful for employers to treat people differently because of their ethnic or racial origins, and this can apply to policies on recruitment, pay, staff benefits, training, promotion, working conditions, and the awarding of contracts.

There are three legal definitions of racial discrimination.

Direct discrimination For instance, refusing to recruit or promote people because of their colour or ethnic or racial background.

Indirect discrimination For instance, setting conditions of work that people from particular ethnic groups cannot fulfil or comply with for cultural or religious reasons. This could include the compulsory

Further information and advice

The Equal Opportunities Commission, Overseas House, Quay Street, Manchester M3 3HN, Tel: 061 833 9244, can offer advice on problems of sexual harrassment, and may provide help with legal costs.

wearing of skirts as part of a uniform for women workers, or compulsory wearing of hats for men who wear turbans.

Victimization For instance, sacking or penalizing someone because they have made or supported a complaint of racial discrimination against an employer.

Laws on race relations and discrimination do not apply to jobs undertaken wholly or mainly abroad, or to employment in private houses. In addition, selection on racial grounds is NOT unlawful if there is a genuine link between the job and a particular

Racial equality

The Commission for Racial Equality has its head office in London, and there are five regional offices. These are: Birmingham, Tel: 021 632 4544; Manchester, Tel: 061 831 7782; Leeds, Tel: 0532 434413; Leicester, Tel: 0533 517852; Edinburgh, Tel: 031 226 5186. The head office address is: Commission for Racial Equality, Elliot House, 10-12 Allington Street, London SW1E 5EH, Tel: 071 828 7022.

racial background, for instance recruitment of a waiter or waitress only of Chinese origin for a restaurant serving Chinese food, or selection of an actor or actress for a role requiring someone of a particular colour or racial origin.

How to complain

To make a complaint, it is useful to compare yourself with someone of a different ethnic or racial group at the same level in your organization, to illustrate your case for racial discrimination.

If you feel you are being discriminated against, it is a good idea first to take your complaint to your bosses with help from your trade union, staff association or personnel officer to see if things can be worked out satisfactorily within your organization.

If you do not have access to any of these, it is useful to talk to colleagues who may be willing to back you up and support your complaint.

If the matter is not resolved at work, you can take your complaint to an industrial tribunal, which has the power to award financial compensation for injury to feelings, and also recommend the steps an employer should take to remove the discrimination within a duly specified time limit. The Commission for Racial Equality (CRE) may provide legal and financial help.

Smoking at work

Is smoking at work an issue of personal freedom or a health hazard? Recent surveys have shown that in many workplaces smoking is the main issue worrying both workers and managers. Not surprising then that 80 per cent of large companies in Britain now provide no-smoking areas for employees.

Until the 1980s, only a few companies had formal policies on smoking that were not directly related to safety and the prevention of fire. But this had risen to one in five by the beginning of the1990s.

Your employer may have a complete ban on smoking as part of the terms and conditions of your employment, or may enforce strict rules about smoking only in certain designated rooms or areas.

The trend against smoking at work and in public places like restaurants and trains is backed up by government policies that now recognize that breathing in other people's smoke can increase health risks for everyone. It's called passive smoking, and it can be especially damaging for pregnant women or for people with asthma or other allergic conditions.

Forty thousand people in the UK die each year from lung cancer, and official government estimates now state that several hundred of them result from passive smoking.

Your rights and smoking

If a no-smoking policy is part of an employer's terms when you're offered a job, this means you can be given verbal or written warnings for ignoring the policy, and you may eventually face the sack.

If no-smoking regulations are introduced after you have joined the company, you will have to comply with the new regulations if they have agreement from a majority of employees with clear procedures for enforcement.

But if you are a smoker and you lose your job because you feel you cannot work under the new rules, you may have a case against dismissal if you can prove that you were not properly consulted about such changes.

Getting agreement on a partial or total ban on smoking is often difficult, since smokers and non-smokers have directly conflicting interests, and can argue fiercely over the right to smoke versus the right to breathe clean air.

Introducing no-smoking policies

ASH, the organization campaigning against smoking (full title: Action on Smoking and Health), believe the aim of a smoking policy should be to guarantee the right of non-smokers to breathe smoke-free air, but also where possible to take account of the needs of those who do want to smoke.

Some companies may introduce questionnaires or workplace ballots to assess staff feelings on the smoking issue. The Institute of Personnel Management has a free booklet, 'Smoking Policies at Work', which looks at these and other methods of introducing rules about smoking.

For further information you can send a stamped addressed envelope to The Institute of Personnel Management, IPM House, Camp Road, London SW19 4UX, Tel: 081 946 9100.

Or you can contact ASH, 5-ll Mortimer Street, London W1N 7RH, Tel: 071 637 9843.

They have free information packs for both employers and their employees giving information about the introduction of no-smoking rules at work.

Maternity rights

The British system of maternity rights is very complex, and most people find they need advice, either from their employer or from organizations specializing in this field, on how to find out exactly what they are entitled to.

All pregnant women have the right to paid time off for ante-natal care, such as medical check-ups, and ante-natal classes.

If you become pregnant and you have been employed full-time by the same employer for more than two years, or part-time for between eight and sixteen hours a week for longer than five years, you have the right to maternity leave for a maximum of 40 weeks and statutory maternity pay paid by your employer for 18 weeks.

You also have the right to be transferred to a different job or working area, if your job involves the use of processes potentially dangerous to your unborn baby, such as, for instance, chemicals or X-rays.

You qualify for a lower rate of statutory maternity pay payable for 18 weeks, but not maternity leave, if you have worked for your employer for more than six months but less than two years.

If you do not qualify for any statutory maternity pay, but you have worked and paid more than six months full National Insurance contributions in the previous year, you can claim state maternity allowance. This is payable weekly for 18 weeks and you can claim it from your local office of the Department of Social Security.

If you are dismissed or made redundant because of pregnancy, you can make a claim for sex discrimination or unfair dismissal at an industrial tribunal.

Maternity leave

To qualify for your full rights, you must write to your employer at least three weeks before going on maternity leave, stating that you are claiming maternity leave and maternity pay and that you intend to return to your job.

You have the right to up to 11 weeks leave before the birth of your baby and up to 29 weeks after the birth, plus the right to return to your job.

Pay during maternity leave is 90 per cent of your pay for six weeks plus 12 weeks maternity benefit paid by your employer. Some organizations offer higher payments under their own agreements on working conditions.

New European rules

From the middle of 1994 a new European Community Directive on the Protection of Pregnant Women at Work is expected to come into force. This is expected to give all women at work in the EC the right to 14 weeks maternity leave and to improve the position of women in the UK who are not currently entitled to any maternity leave.

Maternity and career breaks

A career break is not a legal right, but an arrangement offered by some employers who do not wish to lose touch with trained or skilled workers while they are caring for young children or elderly relatives.

It is a long period of unpaid leave after which you are guaranteed either your job back or a job at the same level within your organization. If you take a career break, it can cover a period of up to five years without pay, although it may include compulsory short periods of paid work, such as two to four weeks a year, to keep you

Useful organizations

• The Maternity Alliance, 15 Britannia Street, London WC1X 9JP, Tel: 071 837 1265.

• The Working Mothers Association, 77 Holloway Road, London N7 8JZ, Tel: 071 700 5771.

• The Equal Opportunities Commission, Overseas House, Quay Street, Manchester M3 3HN, Tel: 061 833 9244, advises and takes up cases against employers where women have been sacked because of pregnancy.

Free leaflets giving information on maternity rights are available from Jobcentres, Employment Service Offices and Citizens' Advice Bureaux, and it is essential to get advice as soon as possible as you may lose your rights if you do not claim correctly or in time.

in touch with developments at your workplace.

Women starting a family can usually take more than one career break provided they do not exceed the maximum time agreed for this type of unpaid leave. Career breaks are open to both men and women.

Working part time

Part-time work is now sometimes called flexible working. This covers work that is mornings or evenings only, or weekend work, or a job that fits into the six-hour school day, between 9am and 3pm.

Many people want part-time work because they have responsibilities at home caring for children or elderly relatives. Others want a regular part-time income while they work for better professional qualifications. A few are writing books or have other irregularly paid careers as actors, singers, or musicians.

Your rights as a part-time worker

Part-time workers who work fewer than 16 hours a week have no entitlement to redundancy pay or maternity rights. Also, they cannot claim for unfair dismissal. Overtime only counts towards the number of hours worked if it is obligatory. It is always advisable to seek legal advice about your rights.

Some part-time jobs are low paid and without any job security. Some companies regard part-timers as cannon fodder who are always the first to be sacked if cutbacks are needed. However some employers, for instance supermarkets and shops, now have a large proportion

of staff on part-time shifts with proper contracts, and regard them as essential to their workforce.

Whatever type of part-time work you do it is very important that you are paid pro rata. This means your hours are paid at the full-time rate everyone else is getting, and not a special low rate for part-timers (which unfortunately is still common practice). In other words you get the proper rate for the job.

You should get paid holidays pro rata as well. This means that, for example, if the holiday entitlement for full timers is four weeks (20 working days) paid holiday, and you work half the hours they do, you should get 10 days paid holidays.

You can get further information on part-time work from your local Jobcentre and other offices of the Employment Service.

Job-sharing

Several thousand people now share their job with someone else, and surveys have shown that most are happy to do so. Job-sharing has now spread to a wide variety of jobs, including secretaries, shop assistants, hotel receptionists, teachers, probation officers, clerical workers, nurses, doctors, pharmacists, local council officers, librarians, civil servants, and university lecturers.

The advantage of job-sharing over many other forms of part-time work is that it more often gives you a proper contract of employment, and higher pay. This is because if you're going to job-share, it makes sense to share a salary of a reasonable size, so each person gets something worthwhile for their efforts.

Job-sharing is popular with professional women with young children because it means they don't have to fall behind in career terms. They can maintain their pay grades and skills, as well as pension rights and other company benefits, while bringing up their families.

For both men and women who are well organized and can find a job-share partner they can work well with, this can be a very satisfactory type of part-time work. It can also benefit employers who are getting two highly motivated workers for the price of one.

For advice as an employer or an employee on setting up job-share arrangements, drawing up contracts, benefits entitlements and holiday rights etc., you can contact New Ways to Work, 309 Upper St, London N1 2TY, Tel: 071 226 4026.

Temporary work

Temporary work boomed in the 1980s and the number of employment agencies offering temporary posts doubled over the decade. Although this expansion has now fallen back, there's no doubt that temping is here to stay. This is partly because the nature of temporary work has developed. Temps used to be secretaries brought in just to fill up temporary gaps in the workforce. The range of work now offered by temp agencies involves not just other office workers like accounts clerks, computer programmers, receptionists, and word processing operators, but jobs in security,

Job-sharing work patterns

Patterns of job-sharing are very varied. Here are some examples:
- Two-and-a-half days each;
- Three days each with one day overlap;
- Three days each in a six-day week and no overlap;
- One person mornings only, the other afternoons only with a hand-over hour at lunchtime;
- One week on, one week off.

catering, accountancy, and nursing, to name but a few.

Reflecting the changing nature of work in the 1990s, and the new willingness of companies to take on specialist staff for particular projects or assignments, there are even some temporary managers and executives, temping for different organizations at senior levels.

Another change has been in the nature of the employment agencies themselves. The larger national agencies now offer training to their temps, and they offer 'permanent temping'. In other words you work for the agency, go where they send you, and they provide your pay packet on a long-term basis.

Some people temp because they have to, but you may choose to temp if you want wide experience of different workplaces. Some temps use this experience as a way of finding a permanent staff job. It certainly means both they and their new employers know what they're getting as they each have had experience of working together.

Further information

You can find temporary employment agencies listed in Yellow Pages.

For basic information or if you have any problems with temporary work, you can contact the Federation of Recruitment and Employment Services, 36-38 Mortimer Street, London W1N 7RB, Tel: 071 323 4300. They have leaflets on temporary work and a Code of Good Recruitment Practice.

Training and new qualifications

After many years of relying on a system of university training for a few, plus practical qualifications or industrial apprenticeships for others, while many workers had no formal training at all, the Government is now attempting to encourage increased practical and vocational training throughout British businesses.

Locally based TECs – Training and Enterprise Councils – are being set up to take over what used to be national training plans, and in addition, the qualifications available are being reorganized.

Practical qualifications called BTECs – Business and Technology Education Council – are now available in most schools and Further Education Colleges at levels equivalent to GCSE and to A-levels.

New practical qualifications called NVQs have also appeared in the last few years. These are qualifications for all kinds of skills, pulling together a wide range of existing tests and practical examinations, and grading according to the the skill levels involved. The aim is to cover 80 per cent of the working population in five levels of skills, so that NVQ grades one to five will soon be recognized and understood by everyone, just as GCSEs and A-levels already are.

The idea is that some existing qualifications, for instance those awarded by the RSA or City And Guilds or professional bodies, will be replaced by NVQs involving on-the-job training. Some course work is also involved, but the main aim is to provide qualifications based on competencies and skills, not examinations.

If you are working in hotel and catering, management, business administration, agriculture, horticulture, the travel industry, publishing, or hairdressing, to give some examples, you will already be able to take NVQs.

Useful addresses

The National Council for Vocational Qualifications, 22 Euston Road, London NW1 2BZ, Tel: 071 387 9898.
Business and Technology Education Council, Central House, Upper Woburn Place, London WC1H 0HH, Tel: 071 413 8400.
The Institute of Personnel Management, IPM House, Camp Road, London SW19 4UX, Tel: 081 946 9100, publishes information and books on training, retraining and qualifications.

Changing jobs

You may choose to change your job at a time that suits you, either inside or outside your existing employment, or you may find change thrust upon you when you are either made redundant or you can see redundancy coming. Whatever the reasons for changing your job, the same basic advice applies as when you first start looking for a career: be positive, be prepared, and sell yourself.

Don't underestimate your own abilities, and apply for jobs that are beneath you. There are few things less irritating than being told you are 'overqualified' for a post. It makes you feel like a fool despite the implied praise of your abilities.

Make sure your skills are easily transferable. In today's rapidly changing world, it's no use your working in a cul-de-sac job where you learn dead-end skills.

If you never think about your work until it's too late, and you're facing the cold doorway into unemployment, you're not keeping your career fit and healthy. It's not just a question of changing employers. If you stay too long in the same job at the same level, neither present nor potential employers will think of you as adaptable and capable of doing anything else. They key to success is to think on your feet and remain flexible and confident.

Pensions

The state pension scheme and most private pension schemes used to be based on the simple rules that men retired at 65 and women at 60. Some contracts of employment had earlier compulsory retirement ages.

This has changed since 1987, when it became unlawful under the Sex Discrimination laws for employment contracts to have different compulsory retirement ages for men and women.

However, since then neither the British Government nor the pensions industry has managed to agree on a single standard retirement age for for both men and women. So the state pension scheme still has the old fixed ages of 60 for women and 65 for men, despite continuing discussions about setting the same age for both sexes across the EC.

Private schemes can have any age from 55 to 65 as the age when payments start. Some have compulsory retirement ages and some allow you to choose when to retire. But you should remember that under private schemes, if you retire earlier, your income is likely to be that much lower because your money has been invested for a shorter time.

You can get information and leaflets giving general guidance on state pensions from your local Benefit Agency office (that's the new name for Department of Social Security offices).

There are two state schemes for pensions, as described below.

The flat rate scheme

This is the basic original state pension scheme, which began in the late 1940s and requires 39 years of full contributions for women and 44 years for men, to receive the full weekly payment. People who have not contributed for the full period get a proportion of the full payment, which may not go far.

Women who have paid the married women's reduced contribution rate are not entitled to this pension. However a husband of pensionable age can claim his own pension and an additional payment for a non-working wife without her own state pension.

Self-employed people can qualify for the state retirement pension by paying National Insurance contributions at the standard self-employed rate.

The State earnings-related scheme

This scheme, which is known as SERPS for short, was set up in 1978 to provide an extra state pension to top up the flat-rate pension to an amount that relates to what you earned while you were employed. Since 1988, the Government has allowed people to opt out of SERPS and take their contributions to a private pension scheme.

The new policy came in because, with increasing numbers of older people in the population, the politicians decided that SERPS in its original form would be too expensive to operate. So, to cut these costs, the benefits of the SERPS scheme will be reduced for anyone retiring from April 2000 onwards. Younger employees have more incentive to opt out of SERPS, while older people should look carefully at their retirement plans, and not rush to abandon SERPS, unless they are sure they will retire after the turn of the century.

Private pensions

For people who are self-employed or whose employers do not operate pension schemes, there is a wide variety of private pension schemes available from banks, building societies, and insurance companies.

All contributions to private pension schemes get tax relief up to certain limits and this gives pensions an advantage over other forms of savings for retirement.

For free information about private pensions you can contact:
• The Occupational Pensions Advisory Service, 11 Belgrave Road, SW1V 1RB, Tel: 071 233 8080;
• The National Association of Pension Funds, 12 Grosvenor Gardens, London SW1W 0EB, Tel: 071 730 0585;
• The Association of British Insurers, 51 Gresham Street, London EC2V 7HQ, Tel: 071 600 3333.

Company pensions schemes

Most people who are in full-time employment join a company pension scheme, and some of these schemes are open to regular part-

---

Pension disputes

If you have a dispute over a pension claim, and you have not been able to resolve it with your pension fund, you can take your case to The Occupational Pensions Advisory Service, 11 Belgrave Road, SW1V 1RB, Tel: 071 233 8080. You can also get advice on pensions from your local Citizens' Advice Bureau.

time workers as well.

These are known as occupational pension schemes and the main advantage over a private pension (see above) is that, if you join a company scheme, your employer has to make contributions for you on top of your own payments. In addition there is usually automatic cover for dependants on your death. The disadvantage of these schemes is that if you change jobs and move to another company, you will have to make special arrangements to transfer your pension, whereas a private pension is yours whatever jobs you take on.

The good news is that company pensions are now easier to transfer than ever before. People used to lose money on these pension schemes because they were, at best, transferred at a fraction of their real value or, at worst, left behind as frozen assets when changing jobs, and were only reclaimable on retirement.

Now, if you have spent two pensionable years with an employer, you have the right to transfer all your contributions to another scheme, but you may not take the money out and spend it.

Redundancy

Being made redundant means your career is changed whether you like it or not, and the first and most difficult hurdle for anyone made redundant is their own feeling of rejection. But remember it isn't you personally that is redundant – it's your job. The key is to think of the problem not in personal but in practical terms.

Income support

Some pensioners receive income support to top up their state retirement pension. For information about state payments to pensioners you can go to your local Benefits Agency office or Citizens' Advice Bureau and get leaflets explaining your rights.

Of course, if you do have to face being suddenly pushed out of your job with no immediate prospect of another, this type of advice may look to you to be as daunting as trying to jump Becher's Brook without a horse.

But, in fact, your own attitude determines how you cope with being unexpectedly out of work, and how much confidence you can generate in yourself and in potential employers when you go along to their interviews. You can get advice from you local Jobcentre on other jobs, training and retraining if you are unemployed. If you want to set up your own business see the section further on in this chapter.

Your redundancy rights

To qualify for redundancy pay, you need to have worked for more than two years, for 16 hours a week or more, for the same company or organization. If you are a part-time worker you need to have worked for more than five years for between eight and 16 hours a week, generally for the same employer.

Anyone aged 16 to 18 is NOT entitled to redundancy pay, and

work before the age of 18 does not count as part of any entitlement.

Redundancy payments do not apply to people who are self-employed, or to some people on fixed-term contracts. You also do not qualify if your work ends on or after your 65th birthday, or if you work for an organization with a retiring age of less than 65, and you have reached that age.

Your employer must give you a written statement showing the amount of your redundancy payment and how this was calculated. If you don't get the payment that you believe you are entitled to, you can take your claim to an industrial tribunal.

How much can you get?

If your company hasn't actually gone bust (which usually means you won't get anything), minimum payments are based on standard government minimum redundancy pay rates.

These rates have maximum payout limits and it can be a shock to many people on average wages or salaries of more than £250.00 a week, when they find that the payments are based on weekly pay of slightly less than this figure. The maximum length of service that can be claimed for is 20 years.

There are other restrictions relating to age and the length of employment. For older workers, the good news is that the rate goes up to one-and-a-half weeks pay per year of service after the age of 41. For younger workers the bad news is that people between the ages of 18 and 22 get only half a week's pay per year of service.

All redundancy payments are tax free and separate from notice payments or any pay in lieu of notice (which ARE subject to tax). Many firms have more generous redundancy arrangements than the government minimum. For instance, they may offer one month's pay per year of service, instead of one week, and also pay at the employee's actual rate of pay, not the legal minimum.

If you're interested in using your redundancy money to help you set up your own business, remember that a large lump sum could make you a target for conmen. So don't part with any of your hard-won cash without checking thoroughly on your partners, and the type of deal they are offering.

Setting up your own business

Becoming self-employed as a sole trader or setting up a small business employing a few other people can be a shock to the system if you've only ever worked for large organizations. Suddenly you have to know something about every area of your business, from tax and VAT, to stock control, bad debts, and sales and marketing, to name just a few areas of expertise.

Before you plunge into the pool and start swimming or gasping for air, it's a very good idea to draw up a business plan. You can get basic advice on how to do this from the major high street banks, or detailed guidance from some of the large number of business books published in recent years for those setting up small businesses.

A business plan may sound daunting at first, but it involves putting down some facts and figures on paper about your business or business proposal in an organized manner. It doesn't have to be the size of a book – a couple of pages will do to start with, but it is worth the effort. A recent survey by Barclays Bank showed that people who start with a business plan are twice as likely to survive as those who just jump off the diving board without one.

If you really get mystified by figures, fix an appointment with your accountant and sort things out with him or her. If you haven't got an accountant, you would be well advised to get one.

What is a business plan?

All the high street banks offer various kinds of small business starter packs. Barclays' Small Business Pack is very helpful because it has a business plan form with questions covering all the major areas. National Westminster claim to be the largest supporter of small business startups with one in three of all new businesses, and four thousand Small Business Advisers throughout the country.

But whether or not you're going to ask a bank for help, the main points to cover in a business plan are fairly obvious.

Security is vital. Whether you borrow from the banks or not, you could be putting your home at risk if you get into serious debt, as it may be your only asset for paying off creditors. Yes, small businesses can be risky. However, if you don't have a business plan of any kind you are taking much more of a risk. And many people who have drawn up plans for the first time have found them so helpful in clarifiying their ideas and objectives that they use and update them frequently.

Enterprise allowance scheme

The Government's Enterprise Allowance Scheme, which is now operated by the Training and Enterprise Councils (TECs), also requires applicants to include a business plan as part of their proposal.

The Enterprise Allowance Scheme is open to anyone unemployed for more than six weeks who has an idea for a new business. Payments now vary from £20.00 to £90.00 a week, and the payment period can be anything from six months to three years. Women wanting to set up on their own, even if they have never claimed benefits while working as mothers and housewives, are able to apply for the EAS.

Franchising

Franchising is a way of buying a ready-made business package, and being your own boss without the risks of starting from scratch with an untried business idea. Many well-known high street names are franchises, from fast food to fashion to photocopying. There is also a large number of smaller companies as diverse as domestic cleaning agencies or personal colour analysts.

If you buy a franchise you will become a franchisee, and you have the right to use the name, business style and marketing techniques developed by the franchisor. It's a system of business developed in North America that has increased in Britain in the last decade.

If you're interested in franchising, you can get a great deal of useful information from the two Franchise Exhibitions held every year in London and Birmingham. If you decide to take on a franchise, it is important to find an accountant and a solicitor who know about franchising, as this is a specialized legal area. Also, the major banks have advisors who specialize in franchising, and National Westminster has a department in the City of London dealing only with franchisors and franchisees.

Apply to The British Franchise Association, Thames View, Newtown Road, Henley on Thames, Oxon. RG9 1HG, Tel: 0491 578049, for a new franchisee

Main points of a business plan

General description of your proposed business.
- The name and type of business and a brief summary of your business idea.
- State the legal identity, i.e. sole trade or partnership or limited company.
- Estimate the number of employees you will need both when starting up and after a year's trading.
- List your major competitors and explain how your business differs from theirs and why you think there is a gap in the market for your business.
- Outline your own relevant experience and qualifications.

Finance to get started
- Estimate how much you need to borrow from a bank. State for how long you will need it, how you will pay it back and over what period.
- State how you wish to spend your loan.

Your market
- Estimate your sales for each month of the first year, and the total for the second year.
- Outline how you will reach customers. e.g. advertising, direct sales, mail shots, cold calling etc.

Projected turnover
- Give estimates of your projected costs and overheads during the first year plus projected sales figures and projected profits for the first year.
- Estimate when you expect your business to be in profit.

Your existing finance
- Add up all your existing monthly payments.
- Give details of all the capital you require and how it will be repaid.
- List what security will be available if your business fails, e.g. your home.

information pack (£17.50) or new franchisor pack (£30.50), both including postage and packing.

Working from home

More and more people are finding that they can use their skills to work at home at their own convenience with the aid of today's technology. But there are snags as well as advantages to working at home, and it's important to take a professional approach from the start. You need an office or workroom of your own that is not used by your family or other people living in your house, but don't rush into buying expensive equipment until you're sure it's worth the outlay.

You may find after the first year that one service you had thought would be a big earner has not brought in as much as another. So it can be a mistake to rush into a bank loan for new equipment.

You can start in a spare bedroom or front room, and this is usually easier and cheaper than a garage, which may cost thousands of pounds to convert and equip.

If you're considering setting up a secretarial service, you will probably need a separate phone line for a fax machine and your business calls and also an answering machine explaining your hours of business to customers. It can be a false economy to stick to one phone line that is answered by your children when they come home from school.

You also need to decide if you are going to collect and deliver

Useful addresses for starting up in business
• Your local tax office will have leaflets on tax for the self-employed, or you can visit or phone the Inland Revenue Public Inquiry Room, Somerset House, The Strand, London WC2, Tel: 071 438 6420/6425.
• For information on Value Added Tax, contact your local Customs and Excise office, or the Customs and Excise VAT Central Unit, Alexander House, 21 Victoria Avenue, Southend on Sea SS99 1AA, Tel: 0702 601601.
• For information on the Enterprise Allowance Scheme and how to contact your local TEC you can ring the Department of Employment's Public Inquiry Unit on 071 273 6969.

work. Do you need a car ? Will you word process manuscripts or do you intend to specialize in letters, reports and other office tasks ?

Whatever type of business you want to run from home, forward planning and research will help you work out the basic financial realities. You can look at your local paper to see if anyone else is offering a similar service, and find out what their charges are. Then you can draw up a plan for your first three months, which you can review and add to later.

FAMILY PROBLEMS

This section gives advice on how to face some of the problems that family life may bring. Are you struggling to cope with a child with special needs, or a difficult teenager? Are you one of millions suffering from the effects of stress? Or do you need help to survive bereavement or separation? What follows is intended to give comfort, courage and the confidence to seek out your own solution.

Caring for a special child

It comes as a devastating shock to discover that the baby you have been looking forward to has been born less than perfect. The reaction of most parents to the question: 'Would you like a boy or a girl?' is: 'We don't mind, as long as it's healthy.' When you discover that your child is handicapped, you have to face the fact that your future has been turned upside down. It seems impossible to accept that your child may have a progressive terminal illness or disabilities that mean she will need constant supervision and care.

Your reaction to the news may be so extreme that you think you're going mad. You may also be so frightened of the baby that you want to disown her or wish she was dead. Don't feel worried or guilty at such a reaction: it's perfectly natural. Do remember that other parents have been in your situation before and coped. You are not alone, and you will be able to manage as others have done.

Coping with your own feelings

It will take time to adjust to your new situation, and you will need to spend a lot of time talking over your feelings with your partner. Women show their feelings more easily and are able to cry when they feel depressed. If your man was brought up not to reveal his emotions, or even admit to himself they exist, you may have a difficult time at first communicating. Your tears could frighten him into spending less time with you, when what you need more than anything is to be together and share your distress. Be patient and keep talking to him. Keep helping him. It will be a great release for you both when you can cry together.

Anger

Apart from distress and depression, you probably feel angry. 'Why did this have to happen to us?' There may or may not be a reason, but it's no use apportioning blame. The facts are as they are, and it does not help to look back, or keep wishing 'if only'. However, your anger needs to be released. You could find yourself getting very bad tempered and shouting at people. Explosions are inevitable, but you can also channel your anger into vigorous activity, such as running or digging or cleaning or kneading bread. Sometimes you will need to shut yourself away and scream and shout to relieve the tension. Make sure the family understands your need for doing this.

Jealousy

You are bound to feel jealous of the other mothers whose children have been born without disabilities. Jealousy always stems from a feeling of inferiority, and in your case, you feel inferior because you believe you have failed. You must realize that no one is to blame. As your child develops her personality and you come to love her for it, you will start to concentrate on her many positive attributes rather than her disadvantages. Your child is unique and she is yours: think of the good things about her rather than what is wrong with her.

Coping with other people's reactions

Disablity and the difficulties it brings are outside the scope of many people's experience, and they will not know how to react to you and your 'different' baby. People tend to be embarrassed in the face of something they don't understand. Friends and

neighbours may show their embarrassment by offering unwelcome or misplaced comments and advice, or they may avoid you. Try not to be hurt. If you feel up to it, give a simple explanation of your baby's problem. Information dispels fear, and if you also mention the ways in which your baby is making progress, people will be able to enquire in a more positive way in the future.

Perhaps some of your friends will be unable to come to terms with your special baby. But you will be able to make new friends who do understand your situation. Contact A Family is an organization that puts parents of sick and handicapped children in touch with other families with similar problems. Write to them at 16 Strutton Ground, London SW1P 2HP, or telephone 071 222 2695.

Getting help

The people who continue to be close to you, your friends and family, and other children if you have them, will all need to know as much as possible about the condition of your special baby so that they can help you with the job of looking after her. Some disabled children need constant attention, and you will need to take a break from the sheer hard work that caring imposes.

Find out from your doctor if there is a local group of a charity or society for parents of children like yours. They may be able to help with advice about grants or funds as well as offer emotional support. And make sure you get all the information from your GP, from hospital specialists and social workers that you require. Taking a list of questions to the appointment often saves making a repeat visit. Finally, visit your local library and bookshop. The more informed you are, the better you will be able to cope and the more confident and settled you will feel.

You and your child

Because of the amount of time you spend with your disabled child, you are bound to develop a special bond. Try not to spoil her in preference to your other children, or they will resent the attention you give her. Talking to the children about her disability is an important part of sharing. You also need to be able to talk to her about it. Keep your explanations simple, adding more information as the children ask for it and are able to understand it. Don't hide the truth from them, as they will only find out from some other source, which will cause them to lose trust in you.

As your child grows, encourage her to make friends with both disabled and able children. Allow her choice where you can, so that she has some sense of the power of her own individuality, even if you have to do most things for her. Allow her privacy too, in which to think her own thoughts. Above all, be open and honest about your feelings: sharing will make you both stronger.

Time for yourselves

Caring for a disabled child is hard work, physically and emotionally. There may come a time when you

feel you can't cope any longer and you have to consider residential care or placing your child with another family in a better position to look after her. Or it may be that certain adjustments can be made at home and to your lifestyle to make your life easier.

• You could consider moving house to be nearer your child's special school, or your partner could change his job, so that he can take a greater share in the care of the child.

• You need time for yourself, in which to develop your own interests or take a part-time job that will get you out of the house.

• And you need to share time together alone, in which you can do something you both enjoy and find entirely absorbing. Get a baby sitter or your parents to look after the children while you go out.

An adolescent in the family

Adolescence is a difficult time for both children and their parents. During their teens, young people have to come to terms with changes in their bodies that take them towards sexual maturity, and changes in their relationship with society. They are moving from dependence to independence. Learning self-reliance is seldom a smooth or easy process, and often involves patches of extreme rebellion and bad behaviour during the period of adjustment.

As your child moves into her teens, you may wonder who this monster is, who has come to share your home in place of the sweet daughter you once knew. There may be many changes in her character and behaviour, such as obsessive interest in hygiene and appearance, or complete neglect; and she may take up habits that are unsociable, unhealthy, dangerous, or even illegal.

It is all too easy for parents to feel they cannot cope with contrary or rebellious behaviour, and in a frantic effort to 'normalize' the situation, to try to control the wayward teenager with threats or bribes. The parent who resorts to these tactics is desperate, and doomed not to succeed. Bullying and coaxing may work sometimes in the short term, but in the long term they will lose you your teenager's respect, and only widen the gulf between you.

Reassessing your relationship

When your teenager begins to rebel, it is a sign that she is outgrowing the space you have allowed her as a child. It is time for you to begin, very gradually, to let go, and to support her in her efforts to become her own person.

Instead of blaming yourself that your daughter has got 'out of control', and trying harder to keep her in line, take your cue from her and stand back, like she is doing, to reassess your relationship. You may feel anger at her disobedience, frustration because she has become so slovenly, shame because she is so brash, sadness because you are losing her, and resentment because you feel she is letting you down. But she is not a child any longer, and you are going to have to give

up responsibility for her appearance and behaviour. The sooner she becomes aware that you respect her individuality, the less need she will have to rebel against you just to push you away.

It is important to remember that it is impossible to make another person be or behave as you want them to be or behave: all you can do is to treat them with the consideration and understanding that you would wish to receive yourself. When your child reaches adolescence it is time for you both to try to step outside the set roles of parent and child, discard the prejudices you may have built up, and talk to one another as two people who need and want to get along together.

There is no set path that the readjustment of your relationship can successfully take, and there are bound to be pitfalls along the way, but basically your aim is to give your child more freedom in the same measure that she is able to take more responsibility. This means, for example, that you allow her to stay out later with her friends, provided that she can satisfy you she is safe in good company and can be relied upon to come home at the agreed time.

There should always be give and take in your arrangements: your teenager may be obsessed with her rights, but you have rights too, and you need her consideration and cooperation.

Sex education

Sex education should begin at an early age, both formally in school, and informally at home. Children

FAMILY PROBLEMS

How to get on with your teenager

• Talk to each other: the key to good relations is communicate, negotiate, compromise.

• Respect each other's privacy: don't enquire minutely as if you are checking up all the time; don't pry into her possessions; let her tidy her bedroom and change her bed herself.

• Don't nag or mock.

• Always be clear about your own rights (for example, as regards loud music, friends in the house, help with the housework).

• Be honest about your feelings and encourage her to be honest about hers.

• Be angry if you feel angry, but don't blame or punish.

• Don't smother her – you can't be physically as close as you were when she was a child.

• Give your teenager time and space in which to be herself.

• Support her and make sure she knows you love her.

home secure in love. If a child learns to give and receive love and affection and sees his parents behaving in a loving way towards each other, he is less likely to be inhibited when he comes to form his own adult relationships in the future.

The best way to talk to your children about sex is openly and honestly. If you are embarrassed about the subject, your teenager will not feel free to talk to you about his worries or fears, or to ask you questions. If you do feel shy, talk it over with your partner: familiarity in using the language of sex with him or her will make explaining it to your child more natural. If you still feel awkward about it, tell your child so, and tell him why. He will respect you for your frankness much more than for avoiding the issue altogether,

Teenage sex

Whether you like it or not, teenagers in Britain today are having sexual relationships and they need to be informed about all aspects of sex in order to protect themselves and their partners, both emotionally and physically. Make sure your teenager knows about:

• Contraception
• Sexually transmitted diseases (especially AIDS)
• The dangers of promiscuity
• Pregnancy
• Abortion
• The double standard
• Homosexuality

learn much that confuses them in the playground, and it is up to parents and teachers to give correct information as it is needed.

The best start any child can ever have on the road to a successful sexual relationship is to live in a especially if you also give him a couple of books on sex for adolescents. Get a reading list of books on sex for adolescents from your local Family Planning Association or doctor.

Drugs

Curiosity to experiment is natural in young people, so you should talk to them about the health risks involved in taking drugs, smoking and drinking. You'll be in a stronger position if you can teach by example. Young people often come under tremendous pressure from their peers to take drugs, and they will need your support and strength to give them the confidence to say no.

If your teenager has a secret drug habit, you may notice erratic moods and behaviour, a change in sleeping habits, fluctuating appetite and loss of interest. Look out for marks on his body. He may start to lie and steal. Soreness around mouth and nose, coughing and a chemical smell are signs of solvent abuse. If your child does take drugs, you will need to call in professional help.

You can phone Freephone Drug Problems by dialling 100 and asking the operator for this free service. A recorded message will give you telephone contact numbers for counties in England. For Wales ring 0222 383313; for Scotland, 041 221 1175; for Northern Ireland, 0232 229808.

A 24-hour helpline is available for parents who are worried about their child taking or possibly taking drugs. The number to call is 071 603 8654.

Anorexia

Anorexia nervosa is a condition that affects more teenage girls than other members of the population. Anorexia means 'loss of appetite', which is misleading, as a characteristic of the disease is that the sufferer becomes obsessed with her appetite and with food. Though she may be slim to start with, she becomes convinced that her body is gross, and by skipping meals, taking laxatives, or forcing herself to throw up after she has eaten, she manages to lose weight to a dangerous degree.

Anorexia can be a sign that a teenage girl cannot come to terms with growing up and developing sexually. By starving herself, she aims to 'keep control' of her body. In one way, the anorexic succeeds: she may become so extremely undernourished that her periods stop. But in reality, of course, the disease, and not the sufferer, is in control.

The anorectic needs above all to learn to love and value herself, and she needs support and understanding at home.

Signs of anorexia

- **Overestimating one's own weight**
- **Obsessive dieting/calorie counting/weighing**
- **Obsessive thinking about food**
- **Inordinate amount of exercise, even when tired or run down**
- **Feeling of isolation/inability to confide**
- **Making oneself sick/taking laxatives**
- **Periods stop**

If you need help, contact the Eating Disorders Association, 0603 621414, or 0494 21431.

Coping with stress

Lots of us work better under the pressure of a deadline, and everyone enjoys the thrill of a rush of adrenalin, but when stress builds up over a long period it can cause severe and even fatal illness. This section of the book tells you how to watch out for signs that stress is getting on top of you, and gives a selection of relaxation techniques to help you cope.

What causes stress?
Almost every one of us suffers from stress of one kind or another, and even events that are looked forward to, such as marriage, going on holiday, the birth of a baby, or Christmas are fraught with possibilities for anxiety. Problems at home and at work can be exacerbated by environmental factors such as noise pollution, bad air, overcrowding and traffic. So life is never stress-free, and everyone can benefit from learning to cope with stress.

What are the symptoms of stress?
The warning signals to look out for are pain and fatigue – they mean you are overdoing it and need to rest, physically and mentally. However, people under stress are typically too distracted to notice their own symptoms, and sometimes it takes a partner or a friend to point out that you are becoming overwrought.

Have you noticed any of the following in your partner?
- inability to relax
- intolerance and irritability
- forgetfulness
- lassitude
- bouts of crying
- lack of staying power

Do you suffer from any of the following?
- chest pain
- headache
- frequent diarrhoea
- skin rash
- indigestion
- insomnia
- palpitations
- exhaustion

These are all symptoms of stress and should not be ignored.

Drug treatments for stress
Stress is the cause of more illnesses in our society than viruses and bacteria. Vaccines and antibiotics have been developed to control clinical diseases, but drugs cannot successfully treat stress, which comes after all from an overloaded lifestyle. However, in the 1960s a group of drugs called benzodiazepines was developed, which seemed to doctors to provide an instant remedy for their stressed patients. Their popularity grew rapidly, and now each year doctors in the UK write around 30 million prescriptions for drugs such

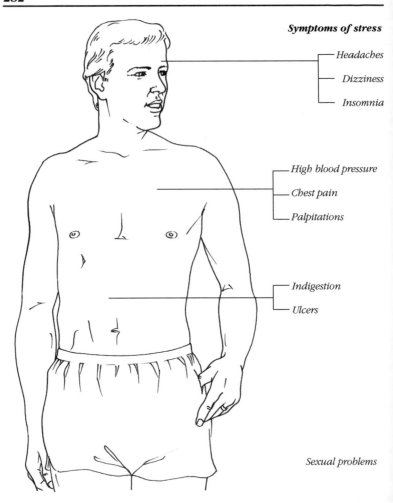

Symptoms of stress

— Headaches

— Dizziness

— Insomnia

— High blood pressure

— Chest pain

— Palpitations

— Indigestion

— Ulcers

Sexual problems

as Valium, Librium, Ativan and Mogadon, and around 3 million Britons – 6 per cent of the population – take them every day.

The trouble with benzodiazepines is that they are addictive. In addition, they also produce side effects that can sometimes be severe, and include anxiety, depression and sleeplessness – the very conditions they are prescribed to cure. Coming off addictive drugs causes unpleasant withdrawal symptoms, such as shaking, panic attacks, giddiness and insomnia. Worst of all, once your system is drug-free again, you are faced with your original problems. Drugs can't solve problems caused by lifestyle or emotions, they can only repress the symptoms of your problems.

How can you relieve stress?

The first and most obvious answer

is to resolve or remove the cause of the stress. You will be only too well aware of what is bothering you: can you make up your differences, cut down on overtime, hand over the running of a local pressure group, take a holiday?

Some problems just can't be removed. Can you distance yourself from the problem periodically to recharge your batteries? Can you spend your leisure time more productively, so that you come back to work refreshed?

People under stress often neglect to feed themselves properly, skipping meals or snatching hurried snacks. You should think carefully about nutrition and exercise, because a fit body and an alert mind will make you stand up better under pressure.

If you can, set aside some private time every day in which you do absolutely nothing. Just sit in a chair alone in a room and let your mind go completely blank. Or give yourself half an hour undisturbed before you get up in the morning. Don't feel guilty that you're wasting time. If you can forget about everything, your mind will soon start to freewheel and daydream. This is a fluid unstructured activity very different to thought, in which you can have some of your most creative ideas: solutions to problems you may have been worrying over for weeks can suddenly spring fully formed and obvious to the top of your mind.

Finally, you can learn relaxed bearing, deep breathing and muscle relaxation, all of which will help you centre yourself in moments of crisis and can be used

continually and unobserved to combat stress of all kinds.

Relaxed bearing

The way we use our bodies expresses how we feel about ourselves and the world around us. Tense muscles reflect inner anxiety and project an image of someone who overreacts, aggressively or defensively. The warning signs are obvious in the images below: which of them apply to yourself?

Good posture, whether sitting or standing, is neither bolt upright,

The body language of stress

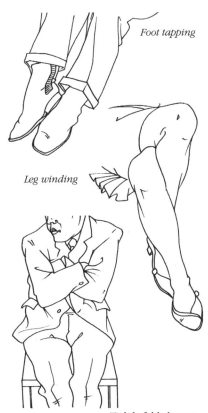

Foot tapping

Leg winding

Tightly folded arms

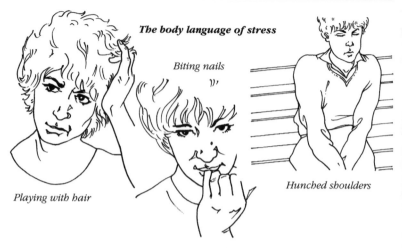

The body language of stress

Biting nails

Playing with hair

Hunched shoulders

Clenching and grinding teeth

Wringing hands

Clenched fist, gripping thumb

military fashion, nor slouching. It is a matter of balance. Stand in front of a mirror and stretch and relax your spine, all the way up from your bottom to your head until you feel a position that doesn't put strain on any part of you. Repeat the exercise, sitting. Put both feet on the floor in a position that's comfortable to you. Rest your hands lightly in your lap.

Sitting or standing, pay particular attention to your head and neck. Your head weighs 5-6kg/12-14lb. If you habitually hold it off-centre, the strain of supporting this heavy weight at an awkward angle is bound to give you problems, and can be one of the causes of migraine. If you no longer realize that you're holding your head on one side, get your partner to help you by pointing it out whenever you fall into bad posture.

You may also need to correct the distortion imposed upon your bearing by your occupation. If you spend all day bent over, like hairdressers and dentists do, then you will need to practise gentle back-stretching exercises as often as you can to stop your body adopting a permanent stoop. If you constantly exercise or put strain on one side of your body, whether by playing tennis or carrying heavy shopping bags, then the working shoulder may become lower, unless you do stretching exercises to compensate.

Controlled breathing, muscle tension and relaxation

It's easy to see the connection between breathing and muscle tension and relaxation if you perform this simple exercise: clench your muscles more and more tightly, then relax. You will notice that you breathed in when you clenched your muscles, and out when you relaxed them. All calming exercises are based on this simple principle.

When you are tense, your muscles contract and your breathing is shallow. Deep breathing will allow your muscles to relax, dispelling tension.

Whenever you find yourself in a tricky situation, getting frightened, or tense, or het up, breathe in and out slowly and deeply, two or three times, concentrating on filling your lungs with air and letting it out gradually. This is a technique practised by actors, singers and public speakers to calm their nerves before a performance. Use it to stop yourself crying or losing your temper if it would be inappropriate or embarrassing to do so. In a situation of prolonged frustration, where events are outside your control – such as a

traffic jam – combine deep breathing with clenching and releasing your muscles. Are you sitting hunched forward, teeth clenched, knuckles white on the wheel? Sit back in your seat, with your spine well supported, and don't let your muscles get tied in knots.

Deep breathing and muscle relaxation can also help you over unpleasant experiences like receiving injections (breathe out as the needle goes in: if you tense up it will hurt more).

Stretching and breathing exercises

The exercises on the following pages are 12 asanas – yoga postures – traditionally performed at dawn as a greeting to the sun.

Use them as a warm-up to other more strenuous exercise or perform the sequence on its own to stretch the muscles and bring flexibility to the spine.

If you can't get into the positions shown, don't force yourself, but extend your reach gradually, imagining the shapes on the page even if you can't achieve them.

The important thing is to move slowly and gracefully, never jerkily, so that you end by feeling relaxed and full of energy, not exhausted and strained.

Follow the breathing instructions to help you move correctly.

1. Stand with your back straight and feet together. Press your palms together in the prayer position. Feel balanced. Exhale.

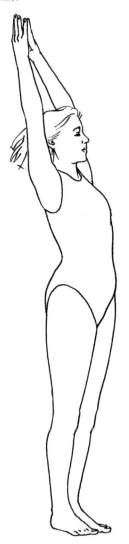

2. Inhale and stretch up your arms, arching your back from the waist and pressing your hips forward. Keep your legs straight and let your neck relax.

3. Exhale and bring your body forward and down so that your hands touch the floor. In time you should be able to press your palms flat alongside your feet.

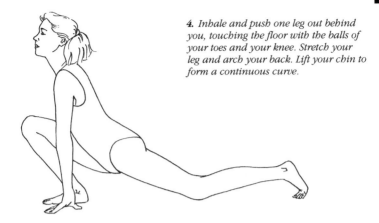

4. *Inhale and push one leg out behind you, touching the floor with the balls of your toes and your knee. Stretch your leg and arch your back. Lift your chin to form a continuous curve.*

5. *Holding your breath, stretch the second leg back to join the first. Raise yourself up on hands and feet. Keep your body in a straight line, looking down between your hands.*

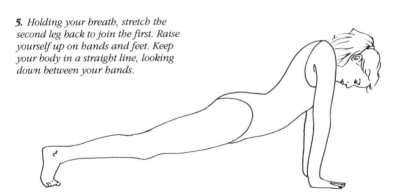

6. *Exhale, lowering yourself to the ground – first the knees, then the chest, then the forehead. Keep your toes curled and your hips raised.*

7. *Inhale, lowering your hips to the ground and raising your torso. Point your toes and completely arch your back.*

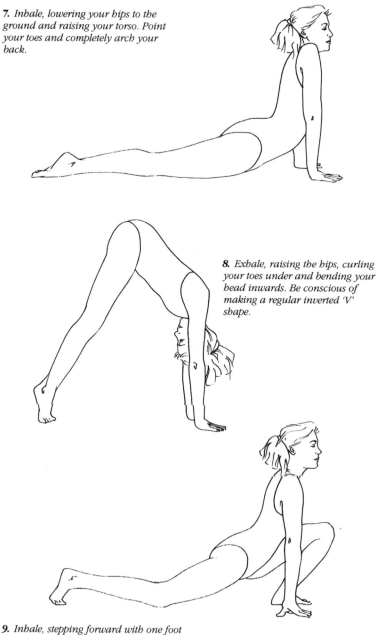

8. *Exhale, raising the hips, curling your toes under and bending your head inwards. Be conscious of making a regular inverted 'V' shape.*

9. *Inhale, stepping forward with one foot between your palms. This position is the mirror of that held in step 4.*

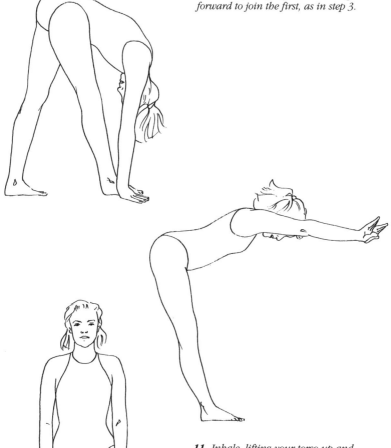

10. Exhale, bringing the second leg forward to join the first, as in step 3.

11. Inhale, lifting your torso up and stretching your arms forward, then back over your head. Arch your back, relax your neck and push your hips forward as in step 2.

12. Exhale, returning to an upright position. Let your arms fall gently by your sides.

Bereavement

Grief is the price we pay for loving. Bereavement is a time of dreadful loneliness and bitter struggle. Even friends and acquaintances avoid you, because death fills them with fear and an awkward sense of powerlessness. So at the time of greatest need, you may be left alone.

The stages of grief

It can help to know that, though your experience is unique in its intensity, the process of grief and mourning does by and large follow a certain course, and that others have shared – and eventually survived – the frightening symptoms you are now feeling.

The purpose of this section of the book is to look at the stages of grief. It is impossible to say how long grieving will last. Nor do the stages of grief necessarily follow neatly one after the other. Allowing yourself to mourn for as long as it takes may be the most painful experience life has to offer, but suffering can be ultimately strengthening and enriching, even though you may not believe it at present.

Shock

No amount of preparation can make ready for the finality of death. Even after a long illness, when someone dies, the first reaction of the one left behind is shock. You may suffer profound shock if the death is unexpected.

In a state of shock, you feel nothing at all, both mind and body are paralysed. You may sit motionless, unable to speak or react. Death has completely shattered your world. Nothing is the same as it was, and it won't ever be as you knew it again. It is just too much to take in. The personality experiences a sort of short circuit. It's as though all your systems must be shut down for a while. This state may last hours, or days. Perhaps you feel capable, cold and heartless. People may say: 'She's taking it very well,' but in fact you're operating on automatic, and you have no sensation at all.

Alarm

Then suddenly, reality begins to break through. You have bursts of realization that your world has been turned upside down and all your points of reference torn from you. You feel disorientated, terrified. Fear and alarm make your heart pound and your lungs work hard. Blood races to your muscles as you tense them to defend yourself against the pain. Emotional pain causes physical pain: if muscle tension is prolonged, waste accumulates in the muscles, prolonging the pain further. Your body may start to ache all over: headache, back ache and neck ache are commonly caused by stress.

Because blood is diverted to the muscles from inner organs like the gut, your digestion no longer functions properly. You may experience loss of appetite, nausea, diarrhoea, belching and heartburn. You may lose weight. Because you are tense all the time, you will be irritable and unable to sleep. You will burst into tears at the slightest provocation. You won't be able to concentrate on anything.

The doctor may offer you sleeping pills and tranquillizers, but these just postpone the mourning process, they don't help you through it. The only thing that will heal the pain is time, and time is very difficult to get through at the moment.

Self-help

- Keep your routine simple.
- Let others help you make arrangements for the funeral, but don't let them take over – it's important that you should be as involved as you want to be. The ritual of the funeral is a necessary public expression of grief.
- Let others get your shopping for you, cook and clean for you.
- Take long hot baths, go to bed with a hot water bottle or the electric blanket.
- Listen to music.
- For other ways of coping with stress, see earlier in this section.

Searching

You will find yourself searching for your mate. You may be constantly looking out of the window, expecting to see him, or going to the door. As you walk into a room, you look over to where you would expect him to be. You wander around the house aimlessly, your eyes scan the people in the streets and shops for a sign of him. Your ears prick up uselessly at familiar sounds. Allow yourself to perform therapeutic tasks, like sorting through drawers and clearing out cupboards. It's a necessary part of saying goodbye.

Anger

Many bereaved people are not prepared to feel anger at the one they have lost, and when it strikes, they feel guilty. Try not to suppress your anger. It may seem irrational, but it is perfectly natural to blame the person who has died for leaving you in this mess and ruining your life. The best way to deal with anger is to examine its roots. Take yourself on long walks to unravel it and come to terms with it. Look upon anger as the first positive sign of your own recovery. Once you are through the anger, you will be able to start making plans for yourself.

In some cases, there may be anger at the way your partner treated you in life. This kind of unresolved argument can be dangerous if left to fester: it can turn to smouldering bitterness and resentment. You should try to confide in a friend who will allow you to talk out the problems of the relationship you have lost.

Friends can be a great support during this stage of grieving, and by carefully managing your friends, you can exercise some control over the situation. For instance, if you have several 'complaints' against the person you have lost, you could choose a friend who has a similar problem with her husband to act as a 'specialist consultant' in that area. Confide in people judiciously to get the response you want: if your partner had a drink problem, talk to a friend whose husband is an alcoholic rather than to one whose husband is a Methodist teetotaller.

Guilt

Often there is a sense of guilt, that 'I could have done more'. The feeling that 'he wouldn't have died if I had behaved as he wanted' is common but completely irrational, and explained by the fact that death is such a powerful blow, way beyond the normal range of our experience, that we have not the means to cope with it logically. It reduces us to a more primitive state, in which any small neglect assumes massive significance.

Don't let this kind of thing get out of proportion: talk about it to a friend, who will help you put it into its proper perspective. If the person you have lost was difficult to live with, you may be feeling guilt for another reason: because you are relieved he has gone. Don't let the idea that you have to mourn because it's expected of you get in the way of your true feelings. If death has freed you from a bad relationship, it will take time to adjust to the fact that you are now free to start building your own life.

Allow yourself to gather strength, and don't imagine that your partner died because you may have occasionally wished him dead. Such thoughts occur to most of us at some stage: they are useful fantasies that allow us to let off steam, and not to be taken literally.

A feeling of uselessness: depression

If your partner has died, you may be left feeling that you are powerless to care for yourself,

helpless and useless. Everything that your partner did for you, you will now have to do alone: to begin with, you may not feel up to it. Without your partner there to give structure to your day, you may not even know what time to eat or go to bed any more, as nothing seems to have any point.

The feeling of not being able to act independently shows how well integrated two lives can become: every action with reference to the other person. As you learn to act only for yourself, you may be surprised to find your own rhythm and preferences begin to show an individuality that you suppressed to fit your life with your partner's. Lonely and painful as it is, this period of getting to know yourself will be ultimately rewarding as you discover the strength to become self-sufficient.

This is a time of dislocation, when your thoughts are scattered and turn inwards. You tend to be awkward and accident-prone, with low concentration and low immunity. Try not to neglect yourself. Look at your hair and complexion: do you need more fresh fruit and vegetables in your diet?

Hallucinations

It is quite common and not at all unhealthy to experience strong feelings of the presence and voice of the person you have lost. Perhaps you find yourself talking to him. If you do have this experience, you will probably find it very comforting, and want to encourage it. If you have been used to sharing a bed, it will seem very empty without him: some people put cushions and pillows under the blankets on the empty side, or take their partner's dressing gown to bed with them. Don't deny yourself any arrangement that gives you comfort.

Acceptance and recovery

Acceptance of death does not mean forgetting, as your memories of the person you have lost will always remain part of your life. When you are bereaved, you have no choice but to let the sensations of loss fill your mind to the exclusion of all else. They completely take over your life. Recovery is to do with owning the pain to the point where you can begin to gradually admit other thoughts and feelings and allow them space beside it. It is the emergence of your self from the swamp of loss.

If you stay with the bad feelings, hold on to them and learn to ride them, you will find you slowly

begin to absorb them. You will become richer, wiser, deeper. As you stretch your capacity to feel your grief, your capacity to feel joy and love will also ultimately be increased.

Separation and divorce

When you and your partner separate, whether you loved him or hated him, or both, the overwhelming sensation is one of loss. You lose everything that you shared: your whole way of life, your sense of identity and belonging as one of a pair. Separation feels at first like amputation; in fact it's more like a journey. All periods of transition are difficult and painful, and this one is more so because of the fact that you may feel a failure in the eyes of society.

It's important to remember that a relationship does not have to be lifelong for it to be a success. Yours may have been a success to begin with, and it may have been a success for many years. Separation and divorce do not mean failure – people fail only when they remain in unhappy relationships for the sake of the status quo. The chances are that you have been growing apart for some time, whether you have acknowledged it or not, and the decision to separate is a brave and realistic one – an acceptance and acknowledgment that the time has come to embark on a new phase of your life.

In Britain today one in three marriages ends in divorce. You can look at this in one of two ways.

Useful information

Your hospital, doctor and solicitor will all be able to advise you of the practical arrangements that need to be made after a death. There are also several books on the subject, one being the *Which?* guide, *What to do when someone dies.*

Cruse is an organization set up to offer help and counselling to all bereaved people. To find a branch near you, contact Cruse, 126 Sheen Road, Richmond, Surrey TW9 1UR; Tel: 081 940 4818.

You can focus on the negative aspects: the undoubted distress caused by the breakup of home and family; but you can also look at it positively. People are no longer prepared to live with unhappiness for the sake of appearances. We are growing up, facing our feelings, taking control of our lives, changing things to allow for a better future. Separation does cause suffering, but it can also be the starting point from which you grow towards a new and more fulfilling life.

Facing your feelings

Your feelings are bound to be in turmoil, with both positive and negative elements directed towards yourself and your partner. The best person to try to work them through with is your partner, but once that is no longer possible, talk to a friend you can trust rather than bottle them up. Only by working your feelings out over a long period of time will you gain peace of mind and the equilibrium on which you can base a new relationship.

Guilt

Both of you will feel guilt, even if the split has been instigated by only one of you. You can blame yourself for leaving, and you can blame yourself for not having done enough to make your partner want to stay.

Relationships end because of incompatibility, and this is no one's fault. However, during the discovery and expression of incompatibility, you will both inevitably have done and said harmful and hurtful things. Regrets are natural, but you owe it to yourself to realize that you acted the way you did because it felt appropriate to do so at the time, and you could not have acted otherwise. If you were put in the same situation now, you would probably have no choice but to repeat your behaviour.

Try to examine what lies behind your feelings of guilt with some kind of rationality. Explaining your feelings to a friend can often help you come to terms with the way you behaved and accept yourself as a mixture of strengths and weaknesses.

Grief

Separation and divorce are in many ways more difficult to deal with than the death of a spouse. If someone dies, the dead person is remembered with affection, and the survivor is treated with respect. The status of both goes up. But when you separate, your status in the eyes of the world goes down.

People think in terms of 'failure' and 'blame'. They take sides. Even those on your 'side' will be wary of you, as a newly single person whose life has been disrupted appears as a threat to other people's domestic security.

When your partner dies, his passing out of your life is acknowledged by a public ritual, the funeral, at which you are supported by everyone who knew you both: friends, relations, colleagues, neighbours. When you separate, you lose the support and understanding of half your friends and relations, and though you still need to say goodbye to the past with sadness and dignity, you have no focus for your grief, because your partner is still alive. Worse still, you may imagine him having a wonderful time without you, and being oblivious or scornful of your suffering.

Read the section in this book on bereavement, as much of it will apply to you.

Anger

Anger is a terrifying emotion, a primitive white-hot force capable of blasting everything in its path. Parents are frightened of its raw power in their offspring, which is why many of us were brought up to suppress and deny our anger. Girls, particularly, are told that anger is unseemly and unfeminine. As a result, it comes more naturally to lots of women to weep and wheedle rather than to blow up because they have been trained to push anger so far down inside themselves that they have forgotten how to use it.

When anger finally breaks through it's a tremendous relief. At last you can own your fury and present it to the other person in such a way that there is absolutely no room for misunderstanding. Even if it's too late to express it directly to your partner, don't be ashamed of your anger, let it rip. Let off steam in front of a friend, or go somewhere private where you can scream and shout undisturbed. Anger is a sign that your spirit is alive and kicking, a positive sign that no matter how much you are suffering, you will recover from your loss.

Jealousy

Jealousy occurs in a relationship when you see yourself as being an outsider. Instead of your attention being centred on your own life, it is focussed on that of the other two. You feel excluded. You no longer have any life of your own because you are obsessed with imaginings of what they say and do together. When you are with your partner, you spend all your time questioning and worrying him about his other relationship, and blaming him for your unhappiness. You live vicariously, through the other woman, and almost cease to exist in your own right.

Jealous people believe they are powerless victims of the emotions of others. As a child, you may have been jealous of your parents' togetherness and felt shut out, small and ineffectual. You are feeling the same thing now, but you are no longer a child, you are an adult, equal with other adults, and with the power to form equal relationships.

If your partner has left you for another woman, it is important that you stop thinking of them as the centre of the universe, and start taking responsibility for yourself. One way of getting an instant and refreshing change of perspective is to go away for a while. If you can afford it, go for a short holiday abroad, perhaps with a girlfriend. A break will make you realize that new horizons do exist for you, that there are places uncontaminated by your partner and his lover, and people to whom they mean nothing. Break out of the crippling narrowness of your jealous thoughts, and allow new horizons to open possibilities in your mind.

When you understand how you have demeaned and belittled yourself by being jealous, you will be angry. Remember that as an adult with love to give, you don't have to share a man with another woman. You deserve better than that: an equal and honest caring relationship. Let go of them and concentrate on getting strong. The power to change your own life lies with no one else but you.

If you have children

• Don't underestimate your children. Even if they're quite young and you believe you have only argued while they were asleep, they will probably understand more about your unhappiness than you realize.

• It's important to tell them as much of the truth as they are capable of understanding. Don't pretend that their father is coming back if you know he isn't. The news will hurt them far more if they hear it from friends or neighbours, and they'll lose trust in you.

• Don't run each other down in front of the children. It will confuse and alienate them. Remember they will want to keep loving both of you.

• Talk to them about your grief and encourage them to talk to you. This will be a sad and bewildering time for them: talking will help all of you to understand and eventually resolve your feelings.

• Reassure them that you love them, but don't let responsibility for their wellbeing force you into a reconciliation that you know will be bad for you. Unhappiness is catching, and what's bad for you will be bad for them too.

LATER LIFE

Getting old is something that will affect us all one day, and for many, the prospect isn't pleasant. Some people assume that retirement age is the time for giving up both work and most physical exertion, but for most people nowadays, there are up to 20 years of potentially productive life left to be enjoyed. Retirement can be the high spot of a long and productive life, and it is during late middle age when you should start planning how you will spend it. Sudden cessation of a career can leave a blank in a person's life that is just as stressful as holding down a responsible job.

Life in retirement

You may be able to find an undemanding part-time job, or might prefer to concentrate on hobbies, DIY or leisure interests. Whatever your previous career or jobs, you will have accumulated much valuable information and insight through the years, and there are always opportunities to put these to good use, especially with voluntary work.

Retired people are thrown into close contact with their partners for 24 hours a day, and this can put a strain on their relationship. For others, it means that they can enjoy the company of their partner, without the worry of work. For most elderly people, increasing age eventually means the need to face the loss of a partner or close friends, and this increases the sense of mortality. Many elderly people fear the approach of the end of their life, while others face this with equanimity. It is a mistake to assume that the loss of a partner must mean a lonely existence for the remaining years. Finding a new partner or companions may never substitute for the original relationship, and neither should it. Instead, such new relationships can open up different approaches to life, and provide renewed interests.

Changing patterns of health

Many 'new' health problems seem to be affecting the elderly. Years ago, 60 was a good age, but now average life spans are steadily increasing, so more old people develop disease as their bodies start to 'run down'.

Avoiding hypothermia

Hypothermia is caused by a drop in body temperature. Old people do not control their body temperatures as accurately as younger people; neither are they so aware of cold. Consequently, many old people do not keep their homes warm enough to keep healthy. This is partly because they do not feel cold, and also because many people on a restricted income simply do not have enough money for heating their home adequately.

The results are that their body temperatures drop to dangerous levels. They may become dazed and sleepy, eventually falling unconscious, and unless they are warmed up quickly, they can die. In addition, prolonged hypothermia can increase the risk of potentially fatal infections such as pneumonia and bronchitis.

It is important that homes are kept warm, even if this means giving up some small luxuries to pay for heating bills. Warm clothes and bedding also help, and the traditional British attitude towards 'bracing cold air' in the bedroom must definitely be avoided. If they find it difficult to sleep in a warm room, make sure they have plenty of warm bedding. Gifts of warm clothes to elderly relatives are a tactful way to help them avoid hypothermia.

Anxiety and depression

Elderly people often suffer from emotional problems because they feel they are losing control of their lives and lack self-esteem. They may experience tiredness, insomnia, loss of appetite, difficulties in making decisions and many other symptoms.

Failing sight and hearing

Senses deteriorate as we get older, but sight and hearing problems can usually be corrected. They should never be neglected and thought of as being inevitable. Regular check-ups are important, especially to diagnose eye problems that can be treated in the early stages.

Foot problems

Most elderly people have problems with their feet, due partly to wear and tear, and also to their inability to care for their feet properly. A chiropodist can provide routine care, and it is important to wear comfortable shoes to prevent further damage developing. Foot care is especially important in diabetics.

Incontinence

Incontinence of bladder and bowel affects many old people. It can be caused by a variety of reasons, one of which is a failure of the body to signal that the bladder is full. In men, urinary incontinence is often associated with prostate problems. It is dangerous to cut down on fluid intake in an attempt to prevent incontinence.

Bronchitis

Along with other lung disease, bronchitis is common in the elderly, especially in life-long smokers. It can be treated with antibiotics, but sometimes attacks can lead to pneumonia.

Poor balance
Old people suffering from poor balance often become inactive because they are afraid of falling. This in turn makes them weaker, and their bones become brittle. Using a walking frame allows continued mobility.

Constipation
This is often a matter of great concern for old people, but is seldom a real medical problem. Failure to pass faeces regularly is usually due to a diet with insufficient fibre. Laxatives are not the answer, and can be dangerous if used regularly.

Solar keratoses
These scaly skin patches often affect people who spend a lot of time out of doors, and they show that the skin has been damaged by the sun. They need to be checked by the doctor to make sure that they are not progressing to skin cancer. Keep them out of the sun as much as possible.

Arthritis
Osteoarthritis is a condition affecting the joints that is sometimes thought to be a part of natural ageing, when the joints 'wear out'. It affects the joints that carry most of the weight of the body, or have to work hardest, such as knees and hips, as well as wrists, fingers, shoulders and elbows. The joint surfaces become worn and roughened. The rubbery cartilage protecting the ends of the bones hardens and flakes away, and the whole of the joint may eventually be destroyed.

By the time they retire, nearly everyone has some signs of osteoarthritis. Because osteoarthritis is the result of wear in the joints, being overweight will only accelerate the damage.

Rheumatoid arthritis also affects the joints. It happens when the body's immune system mistakenly attacks the joint. It affects the whole body to some extent, and people with rheumatoid arthritis usually feel quite ill, as well as having painful joints.

There are all sorts of health recommendations for controlling both forms of arthritis. Some of them, such as keeping the joints warm, or swimming therapy to maintain mobility, are sensible and effective. Others, such as special diets and food supplements available from health shops are no substitute for proper medical advice.

Osteoporosis
Osteoporosis is a disease in which bone crumbles or becomes soft. The body continually breaks down old bone and replaces it with new material. These two opposing processes are normally held in balance under the control of body hormones, so the amount of bone in the body remains constant.

The amount of these hormones decreases as we get older, and in women especially, their levels drop very sharply around the time of the menopause. This means that the rate of breakdown of bone exceeds the rate at which it is replaced, so the bones become spongy and weak. Calcium is an essential part of bone, and diets deficient in calcium can also eventually cause osteoporosis. Lack of exercise also causes loss of bone, but even in old age, steady exercise can actually thicken up and strengthen the walls of the hollow bones in the legs and arms.

The heart and circulation

Many of the most common and serious diseases of old age are associated with the heart and circulation. They are the largest single cause of death in developed countries, but are usually preventable.

High blood pressure

Blood is pumped under pressure to force it through the circulation. The system is designed to withstand the normal pressure, but if this rises, it can cause damage to the blood vessels, the heart itself, and several of the essential organs through which the blood is pumped. Blood pressure rises steadily with age, and what would be considered high blood pressure or hypertension in a young adult is normal for an elderly person.

Uncontrolled hypertension is dangerous, although for most people there are no symptoms. It increases the risk of heart attacks, kidney failure, and stroke.

Untreated hypertension shortens life, which is why insurance companies are always very interested in your blood pressure when you take out a life insurance. But very large studies have shown that effective treatment, which needs to be lifelong, adds years to life expectancy.

Health recommendations for people with hypertension are the same as those for any other disease of the heart and circulation:

- Eat a better diet, low in saturated fats.

- Cut down on salt (this is especially important once hypertension has been diagnosed).

- Take plenty of exercise.

- Stop smoking NOW!

- Avoid stress.

- Keep your weight under control.

- Keep taking the prescribed drugs exactly as the doctor recommends. This may be difficult, because they may make you feel bad, even though you felt fine before. But they could extend your life.

- Hypertension doesn't get better, so be prepared to take the treatment for the rest of your life.

Hardening of the arteries

Fatty substances from the diet can accumulate in the blood, and the excess unused material may then be deposited on the walls of arteries, in patches that interfere with the smooth flow of blood.

Most middle-aged people have deposits of this material in their arteries. As it builds up, however, it damages the walls of the arteries, hardening them and narrowing their bore so that the flow of blood is restricted. This causes pain in the parts that are starved of blood, and can damage the organs.

Most people only find that they have hardening of the arteries when a routine blood test reveals that they have an abnormally high blood cholesterol level. Smoking encourages the growth rate of fatty deposits, which is yet another good reason to give it up. Exercise may help to reverse the process. Surgery may be used to replace some of the damaged blood vessels.

Thrombosis

The build-up of rough patches in the walls of blood vessels causes uneven blood flow, which can cause the blood to clot. Blood clotting narrows the blood vessel, restricting blood flow, and causing thrombosis. If a clot becomes detached, it is carried in the bloodstream until it becomes stuck in a narrower vessel, blocking it completely and damaging the affected organ.

Varicose veins

Varicose veins are swollen and twisted veins in the leg, just beneath the skin, which look unpleasant and are usually painful. The deep veins in the legs contain one-way valves, and if these become faulty, blood can pool in the legs, swelling and increasing the pressure in the veins and stretching their thin walls.

Varicose veins become tender and often itch badly. In the elderly, varicose ulcers may develop as parts of the skin are starved of blood.

Support stockings, elasticated

bandaging, and resting with the legs supported above the level of your abdomen all help to relieve varicose veins. Surgical treatment may be used to block or remove the damaged veins.

Coronary heart disease

The coronary arteries supply blood to the heart muscles. They are quite small, and easily become blocked. Diseases of the coronary arteries cause nearly a third of all deaths.

Heart attacks (coronary thrombosis) are caused by total blockage of one of the coronary arteries with thrombus. This causes the death of part of the heart muscle, so the heart can no longer pump properly.

Nearly two thirds of people experiencing a heart attack recover, but their heart no longer works so efficiently. There is an increased risk of subsequent attacks, and after each of these, further parts of the heart muscle will be damaged.

Aspirin taken daily in a low dose has been shown to reduce the threat of heart attacks.

Angina is a very strong crushing pain in the chest, usually during exercise. It is the result of the partial blockage or narrowing of the coronary arteries supplying blood to the heart muscle.

Drugs are usually effective in mild angina. Glyceryl trinitrate tablets can be placed under the tongue during an attack. Quickly absorbed, they stop the pain.

Heart failure is the result of damage to the heart that reduces its pumping efficiency. It may be the result of a heart attack, or of

Among the known risk factors for coronary artery disease are

- Cigarette smoking; this nearly doubles the risk.

- Diets rich in saturated fats.

- Inactive lifestyle.

- A stressful lifestyle.

- Excess weight.

- Older women taking the contraceptive Pill.

- A family history of heart problems.

- An inherited tendency towards high blood cholesterol levels.

- Untreated high blood pressure.

- Very salty diets, especially in people who already have high blood pressure.

- Diabetes.

There are various causes, but within a few minutes of the blood supply being cut off, the affected area of brain tissue is irreparably damaged.

Stroke is a very common cause of death among the elderly, and people who survive strokes have varying degrees of incapacity. Strokes always affect the opposite side of the body from that in which the brain damage has occurred. Temporary paralysis down one side of the body is common, as is loss of speech.

In most people surviving a stroke, paralysis and speech usually improve to some extent. It is important for a stroke sufferer not to give up hope, because improvement can continue over a very long time.

Cancer

Cancer is not a single disease, but a cluster of various types of disease. They all involve uncontrolled growth of a group of body cells, forming a tumour, and the type of cancer depends on the cells affected, and the organs in which they develop. Some tumours are benign, forming a single 'lump', which can be removed surgically. Others are malignant, breaking up and being carried in the blood to produce tumours elsewhere. Eventually these malignant tumours damage organs to such an extent that they cause serious disease and ultimately, death.

Contrary to popular belief, many cancers can be treated successfully, and the survival rates are increasing all the time. Cancer is treated with chemotherapy (drugs), radiation,

defects of the heart valves, causing waterlogging or oedema of the lungs or other parts of the body.

Medical treatment usually involves taking diuretic drugs, which increase the flow of urine from the body, reducing oedema. Weight must be reduced, and salt in the diet reduced to minimize fluid retention.

Stroke is the result of damage to part of the brain due to interruption of the blood supply.

surgery, or a combination of these approaches.

The most important thing to remember about cancer is that medical advice should be sought as soon as anything suspicious is spotted. This greatly increases the success rate of treatment.

Sensible eating

There are various reasons why many older people may eat an unsatisfactory diet. Their sense of taste may be less acute, so food tastes rather less satisfactory than previously, and this can affect their appetite. Many older people wear dentures, making it difficult to chew certain foods.

Another group of older people whose diets may suffer are those living on their own, who often don't feel it worthwhile cooking a proper meal for one person.

It is particularly important to make sure that the diet contains adequate amounts of fresh fruit and vegetables, which are often deficient in the diets of older people. During the winter, it is also important to eat a diet that provides plenty of calories. A high-calorie diet and warm food help an older person to keep warm and healthy.

Safe and comfortable exercise

Keeping active into old age is absolutely essential if good health is to be maintained for as long as possible. If you have always been active, just carry on as usual, and rely on your body to warn you if you are overdoing things. If you have not been very active during middle

Eating tips for the elderly

• Cut down on fat, sugar, and especially salt.

• Eat as many fresh vegetables and fruit as you can.

• Don't live on convenience foods. It's better to cook a good meal and make it last a couple of days, keeping some of it in the fridge.

• Make sure you eat plenty of high-calorie food in the winter, to help keep you warm.

• Drink lots of fluids.

age, start off cautiously, so your strength can build up. Talk to your doctor about planned exercise if you have (or have had) any of the following:
• Chest or lung disease, like tuberculosis, bronchitis or asthma.
• High blood pressure or heart problems.
• Arthritis, stiff joints or a painful back.
• Diabetes.

Exercise need not involve your whole body, and even if you are unable to get about much, you can still carry out exercises to keep your arms, hands and fingers supple.

Proper footwear for exercise is essential, and although many older people do not like the look of them, modern trainers with padded soles are absolutely ideal. This is because the resilient fat pads on the soles of the feet become thinner in old age, and trainers stop the soles from becoming sore.

Getting your sleep

A lot of old people complain of poor sleep, but this is often because they are still trying to have their 'normal' eight hours' sleep.

We need progressively less sleep as we get older, and having naps during the day obviously reduces this need still further.

Retirement homes and sheltered housing

Most old people fear the time when they can no longer face an independent existence, and must rely upon others for their care – or at least, to keep an eye on them and make sure that they are happy and healthy.

Many old people own their own homes, and although these are comfortable and familiar, they may be no longer the best place to live in under changing circumstances. Usually the old family home is too big and expensive to run. Old people often need guidance and gentle persuasion in order to be convinced of the better lifestyle they could have in a smaller, more economic home. In fact, many of the small 'starter homes' intended for the first-time buyer are also ideal for the elderly.

Sheltered housing is a means by which the elderly can retain their full independence and possessions, while having professional help available whenever needed. These developments usually group a number of specially adapted homes

There are several factors that alter your normal sleep patterns as you get older.

Are these factors affecting your sleep?

• Smoking may make you restless and interfere with dropping off to sleep.

• Daytime naps mean that you will sleep less at night.

• Stimulants like coffee, tea and drinking chocolate contain lots of caffeine, which will keep you awake if taken at bedtime.

• A small snack and a malted drink at bedtime will help you to sleep.

• Stress and worry may keep you awake, so delay going to bed until you feel really tired.

• Heavy meals late at night can cause indigestion and keep you awake.

• Adequate exercise will tire you and help you to sleep soundly.

• Waking up very early in the morning is sometimes a symptom of depression. Ask your doctor about it.

• It is easy to overlook the fact that your mattress is wearing out, and this can be so uncomfortable that it disturbs sleep and causes backaches.

together with a live-in warden or supervisor, who keeps an eye on everyone without being too intrusive.

True retirement homes are best avoided until there is no real alternative. The better homes are privately run, and can be extremely expensive, although contributions can be made towards the costs by the local Social Services.

Retirement homes run by the council usually tend to be of the institutional type, and may have the disadvantage of separating the inhabitants from their most treasured possessions.

There are some important considerations to be faced when deciding if elderly people can really look after themselves.
• Are they beginning to neglect themselves?
• Can they manage the shopping, and prepare food properly?
• Can they wash and clean themselves, and manage their laundry?
• Can they afford to heat their home adequately, while still spending enough on a healthy diet?
• Could they summon help in an emergency, such as a fall?
• Are they so lonely that they would benefit from living with other people, either family or at a residential home?

Caring for an elderly relative

Taking on the care of an elderly relative is a great responsibility, and also a very difficult one. Most old people are fiercely independent, and are naturally 'set in their ways'. They usually dread having to depend upon someone else, and face loss of self-esteem.

Consider some of the physical problems faced by the elderly, and their solutions:
• Make sure that lighting levels are adequate, to help with failing sight.
• Heating must be effective, and draughts eliminated as far as possible. Use of paraffin heaters must be strongly discouraged, due to the fire risk if fuel is spilled.
• Stairs can be dangerous, and may cause falls. Make sure that proper handrails are fitted, and that frayed stair carpet is secured.
• Height of furniture is important. With stiff joints, a high chair is easier to get out of, and the same applies to the bed.
• Getting in and out of the bath is always a hazard in the frail or infirm. Handrails should be fitted to the wall above the bath, and a non-slip mat placed in the bath. Low plastic seats can be fitted, which allow an old person to sit down more comfortably in the bath.
• Handrails may need to be fitted by the toilet, to make it easier to sit down and rise.
• Non-slip surfaces are important in the bathroom, toilet and kitchen, where water could be spilled.
• Give consideration to cooking needs. Heavy pans can be difficult to manage, and for arthritic hands, normal kitchen tools such as can openers may be impossible to use. There are many adaptations and special gadgets for people with arthritis, and details of these can be obtained from Social Services departments, and especially from patient aid organizations.

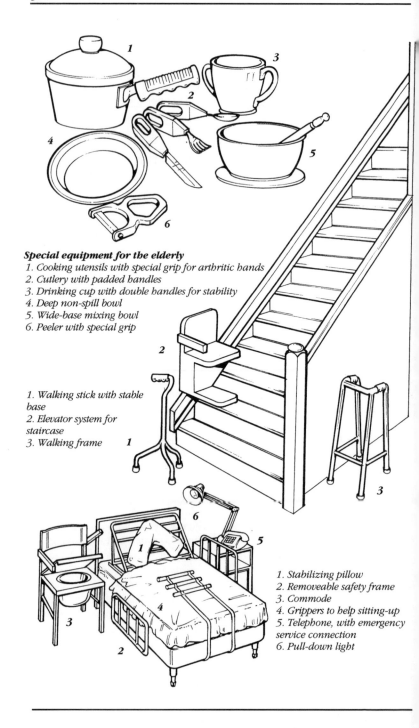

Special equipment for the elderly
1. Cooking utensils with special grip for arthritic hands
2. Cutlery with padded handles
3. Drinking cup with double handles for stability
4. Deep non-spill bowl
5. Wide-base mixing bowl
6. Peeler with special grip

1. Walking stick with stable base
2. Elevator system for staircase
3. Walking frame

1. Stabilizing pillow
2. Removeable safety frame
3. Commode
4. Grippers to help sitting-up
5. Telephone, with emergency service connection
6. Pull-down light

Mental awareness

The brain ages in the same way as the rest of the body, but not necessarily at the same rate. We have all encountered 'a young mind in an old body', and the reverse is also true, when people suffer from senile dementia, and begin to lose their normal faculties.

It is perfectly normal to become forgetful as we get older, and this is due to the steady loss of brain cells. However, constant mental stimulation improves the efficiency of the brain, and can keep people alert into extreme old age.

For this reason, it is important for the elderly to have hobbies and interests in keeping with their abilities. Gardening, knitting or just talking are all ways of keeping the brain active and healthy.

The problem of dementia

Dementia is very common, affecting about 20 per cent of people over 80 years old, but it is not necessarily the end of a useful life, because there are many degrees of dementia. It is not an easy condition to diagnose, but the following may suggest that investigation by the doctor is needed:

- Increasing memory loss
- Childlike dependence on others
- Withdrawal from family life
- Socially unacceptable behaviour
- Self-neglect
- Inability to recognize familiar people or places
- Confused behaviour, such as wandering about in the night.

Alzheimer's disease is an extreme form of dementia which can occur in middle age. Unlike the other forms of dementia, it progresses rapidly and may lead to death in a short time.

Legal and financial aspects of retirement

Retirement, and the period leading up to it, can be a time of uncertainty and mixed feelings. A career may disappear along with a regular structure for your days and a certain sense of identity. New opportunities may present themselves but you may feel uncertain about taking them up. And if you do take them up, how are you going to pay for them?

The importance of budgeting

A household budget should be the foundation stone of your financial plans in retirement. List what you spend under broad headings such as 'household bills', 'car', 'Christmas' and so on. For one-off payments such as for a holiday, divide the total cost by 52 or 12 to give a weekly or monthly figure. For the sake of convenience, it is better to have both your spending and income worked out on the same time basis.

If you have not already retired, make allowance for changes in your circumstances that will come when you give up work. You will no longer pay commuting costs but may find your heating bill rises. Be flexible too about your attitude to the future. In early retirement, you may enjoy the best of health and independence and relish spending your money. But in later years, savings may provide you with the best cushion against the frailty of advancing age.

It is no bad thing to draw up several budgets, each outlining a slightly different set of needs. This is a good way of putting your financial planning in perspective.

While much of your retirement budget will follow the pattern of any previous household budget, there are several areas in which things will be different or need viewing in a new way:

• Your state retirement pension and other entitlements

• Any occupational and personal pensions

• Income and other taxes

• Investments you have made or want to make

• The financial considerations of your home.

You cannot plan for the future without a full understanding of each of these areas. Always seek professional advice if you are at all unclear about anything.

State retirement pension

The age at which you become entitled to a state retirement pension is 60 for women and 65 for men. The rates from April 1992 are £54.15 per week for a single person, £108.30 for a married couple where both partners have led a full working life, and £86.70 for a married couple where the wife has broken her career.

These amounts, which rise each April in line with inflation, are not payable automatically – you must have paid National Insurance contributions for the vast majority of your working life. This explains the difference in payment to the couple who have both worked and the couple where the wife has stopped work, to raise a family for example.

To reach the minimum level of contributions, men must have paid National Insurance for 44 years between the ages of 16 and 65 and women for 39 years between 16 and 60.

If your contributions do not reach these levels, contact your local social security office. You may be able to make up some of the arrears and boost your pension to the figures above.

As well as the basic pension, you may also be entitled to other pension payments from the state:

• **Additional pension:** this part of your pension payment is related to your earnings from April 1978. Basically, the more you earned and paid National Insurance contributions on, the more you will receive in payment although there are deductions for people who contracted out of the state pension scheme.

• **Graduated pension:** this scheme ran from 1961 to 1975. Like additional pension it works on a sliding scale of the more you earned the more you receive. Graduated pension is payable even if you do not qualify for basic state pension.

• **Other payments:** invalidity addition is payable to those who received an invalidity allowance before reaching pensionable age and anyone over 80 is paid an age addition. For many years there has also been a one-off Christmas bonus of £10.

State benefits

The state has a range of benefits which act as a safety net for pensioners living on limited means. Each year, thousands of people fail to make use of these benefits through a mixture of personal pride and lack of knowledge that they exist. The main ones are listed below.

• Income support is designed to bring your income up to a government set minimum. This figure hovers around that of the state retirement pension so you may not receive very much and your entitlement can be reduced because of savings.

• Housing benefit can help with your rent. Like income support, the amount you get may be reduced because of savings.

• Community charge benefit should be claimed by all those who find it hard to pay. As with housing benefit, contact your local council for details.

It can be very difficult to work out your entitlements and how to claim. Details can be found in post offices, local authority-run advice centres, Department of Social Security offices and Citizens' Advice Bureaux. Even if you have doubts about your entitlement, it is always worth applying for a benefit.

Your occupational pension

Depending on the company you worked for, your occupational pension may go a long way to maintaining your lifestyle. There are two types:

• Final salary schemes take a tiny proportion of your last year's salary (1/60th or 1/40th depending on the scheme - check yours) and multiply it by the number of years you have worked for the company.

So, if in your last year of employment you earned £14,000 and had worked for the company for 21 years, your pension on a 1/60th basis would be:

(1/60th x £14,000) x 21 years = £4,899.99 per year.

• Money purchase schemes work by you and your employer paying into a pool that secures you a pension from an insurance company when you retire.

• Check with your employer what your pension rights are.

Your personal pension

These have become very popular as patterns of work have changed and people have sought to use the tax advantages of tying their money up in pensions. There is no contribution from your employer but in other respects these schemes run along the lines of the money purchase scheme above. If you have a personal pension, stay in regular contact with your pensions adviser so that you always know how much you are due.

Taxation

Your liability to tax does not cease when you retire. If you are fairly well off there are some changes and tax plans you should make:

• Income tax allowances are increased once you reach 65. For the 1992/93 tax year the personal

Boosting your pension – AVCs

If, before retiring, you work out that you will not have enough to live on, ask your pensions adviser about making Additional Voluntary Contributions (AVCs). These are simply a way of pumping more money into your scheme so that you have a better income later. The earlier you do this the better, although as you will be locking your money away until retirement, you must plan your finances carefully.

allowance is £4,200 and the married couple's allowance is £2,465. However, these allowances are reduced if your income is more than £14,200 per year. The rate of reduction is £1 for every £2 of income over the £14,200 limit.

• Inheritance tax is payable on the value of a deceased person's estate over £150,000 (1992/93 figure). There are two ways of reducing your heir's liability to pay. The first is to distribute your estate in your will so that your surviving spouse receives an inheritance-tax-free amount and so does everyone else. The second way is to give chunks of your money away before you die. The snag with this method is that to avoid your heirs having to pay inheritance tax, you must live for a further seven years.

Particularly if you own your own home, seek advice about reducing your liability to inheritance tax. If you do not pass on your money wisely, a proportion of it goes straight to the government.

Investments

The key point to remember when planning what to do with your money during retirement is that your income is likely to be drastically reduced. Your pension is unlikely to be enough to bail you out of emergencies – you will need to dip into savings for this. So you must be able to get to a percentage of your money quickly. It is no good if your money is tied up for a fixed period and you do not have access to it.

Elsewhere in this book you will find descriptions of a range of investment opportunities. Many of them tie up money for the medium to long term and these are probably best avoided by many retired people. There are plenty of accounts that pay a steady return and give you full access to your money. An extra one or two per cent a year interest is worthless if you need to get your roof fixed quickly but have all your money locked away.

Now is the time to have a good look at investments you made many years ago, and ask if they are still working for you. Unless you are very wealthy, your aim should be to bring your money closer to you and perhaps simplify your affairs. This can make things a lot easier for someone else should you suddenly die or become incapacitated through illness or debility.

Your home

In retirement your biggest asset may be your home. There are three ways that you can use your home to create income.

• Sell up and move to a smaller place. This is fine if a large family nest is now empty and you can take advantage of a differential in property prices. There are, however, lots of disadvantages not to mention prolonged periods of inactivity in the housing market.

• Home income plans are a way of using your house as security for a loan which you use to buy an annuity (an investment that gives you a regular income). The loan is eventually repaid from the proceeds of the sale of the house. Anything left over goes directly to your estate.

• Home reversion schemes work by you selling your home to a specialist company in return for the right to live in it and an income. The disadvantage with this method of creating income is that if you have signed over all your house, there will be nothing to pass on to your children in your will.

Whatever kind of scheme you use to raise money from your home, even if it is only taking in a lodger, always seek professional advice. You may be short of money in retirement, but you must beware of losing the roof over your head.

Early retirement

If you have a personal or occupational pension that you can call on straight away, you may not suffer unduly through early retirement – you may even decide to take another job at some stage.

If none of these things applies, you should register as unemployed as you cannot get your state pension until you reach 60 for a woman and 65 for a man.

Register straight away even though voluntary early retirement may disqualify you from receiving benefit for the first six months and any pension you do receive may be deducted from it.

INDEX

Page references in *italics* refer to illustrations.